KEEPING TIME

COLLECTING AND CARING FOR CLOCKS

RICHARD GOOD

BRITISH MUSEUM PRESS

Published by British Museum Press
A division of British Museum Publications Ltd
46 Bloomsbury Street, London WC1B 3QQ

Second impression (first in paperback)1993
Revised Edition

A catalogue record for this book is available
from the British Library

ISBN 0–7141–0562–7

Book design by Grahame Dudley
Cover Design by Roger Davies
Set in Goudy Old Style Roman
and Printed in Great Britain
by Bath Press Ltd

FRONTISPIECE
Clocks awaiting attention in one of the
long-established firms in Clerkenwell, now
defunct. All sorts of clocks and clock
movements are to be seen: carriage clocks,
bracket clocks, French and skeleton clocks,
long-case movements and some reproduction
limited edition clocks.

Contents

Acknowledgements

It is both a duty and a pleasure to thank those who have helped in the writing of this book. First I must thank my wife Norma who patiently endured a silent partner for many evenings while the book was in preparation. During this time I was also helped by Beresford Hutchinson, once a colleague of mine, then Curator of Astronomy at the National Maritime Museum and now retired. He was always both willing and able to answer various queries that I put to him. Once the manuscript was completed, Jenny Ashby and my editor, Deborah Wakeling, did much to improve it. I must make it clear, though, that any short-comings of the book are my responsibility.

Eyre Methuen kindly allowed me to reproduce the line drawings which were prepared for me by John E. Wood for Britten's *Watch and Clock Maker's Handbook*. Those of my own clock (pp. 105, 107) were the work of David Penney who specialises in horological illustration.

Finally I must thank in general the British Museum Photographic Service but in particular Tony Milton who was responsible for so many excellent shots.

Foreword

Collecting and caring for clocks can be a most satisfying and interesting occupation. I have known many people who have developed an interest in horology, some very late in life, but have yet to meet anyone who has lost the interest subsequently. There are several reasons for this, probably the least of these being that a clock is useful for telling the time! There is no doubt that clocks have a unique place in the furnishing of a home. A clock with a pendulum seems to have the special ability of bringing a room to life. A long-case clock with its steady and unhurried tick can also somehow soothe the spirit and is redolent of what we think of as a more peaceful age.

The clock is virtually the only mechanical device that is expected to work 24 hours a day, 365 days a year and to go on doing so in some instances for centuries, though it cannot do this without some attention along the way. The enduring usefulness of the clock has led to a very high rate of survival as a type of artefact. The nature of time has not changed nor have its units of measurement. One abortive attempt to metricate it failed and no one has had the temerity to try again since, nor are they likely to now. However foolish mankind may be about his units of measurement or his currency, nobody wants a day other than the one we have. No one wants one that cannot be split conveniently into sixths, quarters, thirds and halves, and those attempts to change this in revolutionary France have merely left us with one more interesting if short-lived variety of clock. The imposition of the metric system of measurement proved difficult even in France and for many years the two systems ran side by side. However, in 1840 the old French inch, and all the other useful things that went with it, were outlawed. Despite this the *ligne*, a twelfth of the old French inch, has remained in use to this day, a measure of the size of a watch.

The survival of so many old clocks means that almost every style is represented: Renaissance, Rococo, Art Deco, all are to be found. This further means that whatever the decorative style of a room, a clock can be found to match it. But a clock has much more to it than its outside appearance, for it also has a mechanism that ranges from the deceptively simple to the self-evidently complex. Many men and women can get a satisfaction from dealing with the mechanical problems of their clock which they are increasingly denied so far as the other items in their homes are concerned. Nowadays an army of specialists is required to deal with the items we use every day. Which of us can repair a television set or washing-machine?

An astonishing variety of people are interested in repairing their own clocks. There is probably no body of men as willing and happy to mix with all and sundry as that of the dedicated collectors and restorers of clocks. Amongst the people I know are doctors, dentists, lawyers, artists, writers, actors, teachers and schoolboys. Many find it a relief from the increasingly difficult and complex problems they encounter in their work to deal with a mechanism that responds to logical treatment, that performs a straightforward function when done, and can be pleasant to look at as well.

The pleasure that can be obtained from clocks does, however, increase with knowledge, and it is the purpose of this book to reveal some of the mysteries of clockwork and to point the way to further reading if study in depth is contemplated.

1 Buying Your Clock

Collecting with a Theme

Some collectors are content to pick up any item that takes their fancy without any particular aim in mind. There is, of course, nothing wrong in this – the chief object in collecting should be pleasure and the best collections in the past were built up by people with no thought of profit in mind. It is not unnatural, though, for a collector to develop a special interest in one particular facet of horology, and he should not resist the resulting temptation to specialise in collecting items that reflect this interest. In this way a considerable knowledge can be gained which will not only assist in choosing worthwhile examples but can also be of use to the rest of the horological world. Articles in the learned journals written by people who have become expert in one particular branch of horology help to fill in the overall pattern of knowledge in depth. There are still many areas where knowledge is woefully incomplete, and it is mainly the work of dedicated specialists that is slowly but surely illuminating these dark corners.

Books on Prices

At any one time there are usually at least one or two books in print giving values of both clocks and watches. Incredibly enough it is not even always made clear in these publications which value is being talked about, for (ignoring valuations for probate) it must be considered that there are at least two different values for any item, the first being what it would be expected to fetch at auction and the second, what one would expect to insure it for. As a very rough rule one would expect the latter figure to be double the former with the differential becoming less as the importance and value increases.

Regardless of complications of this sort, books on prices should be looked upon with suspicion. Some are compiled from sale-room records with no account taken of the condition

YEAR-GOING STRIKING AND REPEAT-
ING TABLE CLOCK BY THOMAS
TOMPION, 1689

The Case is veneered with ebony.
It has two main sections with a dome.
The lower section has a lockable-
hinged glazed front door to reveal
the lower front plate and the pendulum. It stands on four fire-gilt
scroll feet with a mask at the centre
position between the two front feet.
Linking the feet to one another and
to the mask are silver swags. A silver
mask lies behind the glazed panel.
At the sides are fire-gilt handles. The
second tier which frames the dial
has four fire-gilt Doric columns and
silver ornaments. The dome carries
the silver figure of Britannia at its top.
At the front corners of the dome are
the lion at the left and the unicorn
at the right.

At the rear corners of the dome
are the rose on the left and the thistle
on the right. A shield between the
lion and the unicorn bears the private
arms of William III. This rare form
of the arms was only in use for a few
months in 1689. Cast silver panels
are at either side of the upper section
and a removable door at the back
has a cast fire-gilt panel. A hinged
door gives access to the hands; this
door is locked by a catch which is
only accessible when the lower door
is opened.

The Dial plate is gilt and is 5 in
(12.7 cm) square. The chapter ring
and the cherub spandrels are silver.
In the finely matted centre section is
an aperture showing the day of the
week with its deity. This revolves
once in two weeks concentricly with
the blued steel hands; the minute
hand is counterpoised. The silver
cartouche between the dial centre
and 6 o'clock carries the signature
T. Tompion Londini Fecit.

The Mechanism is designed to go and
to strike the hours for a year on one
winding. It also repeats the quarters
and strikes the hour at will. Only the
quarters are operated by the repeat
mechanism; on the completion of
the striking of the quarters the hour
train is let off so that the hours are
struck.

The two barrels, 4 in (10·2cm) in
diameter and 3¾ in (9·5 cm) deep, and
their fusees are housed in the lower

section. The fusees are 'reversed'. The chains are massive, the outer links having five 'leaves'. The gilt and engraved front plate of this part of the mechanism is visible through the glazed door and carries the signature *T. Tompion London Fecit*. Hanging in front of the plate is the pendulum. Mounted on the plate is the elaborate worm-and-sector mechanism which raises and lowers the pendulum for regulation. The pendulum rod carries a decorative piece around the slot for the crutch pin which is also visible through the glass and by its motion shows that the clock is going. The lower part of the clock has five pillars and also carries the second wheels and the rear pivots of the third wheels in either train.

The verge and crown wheel are also housed in the lower part of the mechanism although the rest of the faster-moving mobiles are housed in the top part of the mechanism. The verge has had to be cranked to clear the arbor of the crown wheel. A small plate can be removed so that the faster-running mobiles of the quarter-striking train may be removed without disturbing the rest of the mechanism.

In the upper part of the mechanism are the remainder of the going and striking trains with the verge escapement in a sub-frame. The trains are exceedingly delicate so as to favour the long running of the mechanism. The minute hand is counterpoised for the same purpose. The craftsmanship of the mechanism was and is unsurpassed. The engraving and the casting and chasing work are also of such a high quality as to indicate that all of the decorative aspects of the movement and case were the responsibility of top goldsmiths of the day.

The clock was purchased by the British Museum in 1982. Height 2 ft 4 in (71 cm).

of the item being sold. But this aside, if you want to see just how difficult it is to determine values, look at the record of the finest experts in the world – those who prepare catalogues for major sales – and it will soon be evident. Before the sale catalogue is written, every piece to be in it is looked at carefully and an estimate made as to what it will fetch. The estimate is based on the experience of many years, the compiler having been present at sale after sale, knowing not only the market but what are the trends, who is buying what and even whether or not one of the major institutions is interested. If one then compares the prices realised with these estimates, some shocks will be in store. In defence of the cataloguers I should say, however, that probably overall the picture will not be too bad; what one item fails to fetch can well be made up for when a higher price is realised than was estimated for another item.

RETAIL PRICES

Some are shocked by the mark-up that occurs and think that the difference between the price fetched at auction and that asked by the subsequent retailer is too high. Consider, though, that once the item is purchased it has to be put in order so that it is in a fit state to be sold, it has to be recorded, possibly researched, insured, photographed, and stored or displayed, probably in premises with high rents and rates. Furthermore, if stocked for any length of time, and without working stock a business cannot prosper, it is an investment without a regular interest. Its true value may be eroded by inflation or suffer because of changing fashions, or its purchase may have been funded by a loan or overdraft, the interest on which also has to

CARRIAGE CLOCK BY BARWISE, LON-
DON, c.1840

Gilt case with engraved scenes from
schoolboy life and two riders on top.
2½in (6.4 cm) enamel dial signed *Barwise London* and with mask engraved
with scrolling foliage. Moon hands.
Movement similarly signed and with
chain fusees. Lever escapement
mounted on the back plate. Striking
on a bell.
Height 6 in (15 cm).

be allowed for finally when the item is sold. I am sure that many
a dealer must have wondered at times why he didn't sell up,
invest the money in unit trusts and get a job working for
somebody else. In the past dealers felt somewhat envious of
their customers who were, at least then, buying clocks because
they were going to enjoy having them. There is, however, a sad
trend today towards viewing every purchase as an investment.
Although apparently content that cars, boats, hi-fi equipment,
etc. should suffer depreciation, owners are not usually content
for the value of their clocks even to keep pace with inflation;

LANTERN CLOCK BY VINCENT AND
COMPANY, c. 1870

Probably made in the third quarter
of the nineteenth century this clock
is larger than it might be assumed
to be. It is not a reproduction; no
clock of this design ever existed. The
case is mahogany and the trimmings
brass. The chapter ring with its
Arabic numerals does not really
match the strong Gothic flavour
of the rest. The movement is French
and bears the name Vincent and Cie;
it strikes on a bell attached to the
back plate, the bell above being purely decorative!
Height 2 ft 0½ in (62 cm).

they must do better than this. The result shows in a certain timidity, an unwillingness to pay a fair price for the unusual, since it is not so easy to study form and establish what similar items have fetched in the recent past.

Clocks made by the clockmakers of today are, with one or two exceptions, not bought by serious collectors at all. Whatever cries of delight greet their appearance and their inventiveness, regardless of the interest they arouse, they are mostly purchased by the initiated at a price that means the maker has sacrificed the higher earnings he might have made had he been restoring clocks instead of making them. The reason for this is the same as that already mentioned for not buying the more unusual antique clocks. Modern clocks have no form, nobody can say that this is the usual price for such an object, or that it will appreciate nicely in value over the next five years.

How and Where to Buy

Having dismissed lists of prices as being of little use, the next and natural question is how to set about buying the clock decided upon. Before attempting to make this decision, it is obviously desirable to have a rough idea as to what the cost will be. It is of little use agonising for weeks over what sort of clock to buy only to discover that it is in a price range far beyond what one can afford.

A helpful book for inexperienced collectors is *Antiques and Their Values – Clocks and Watches* compiled by Tony Curtis, which shows 108 bracket clocks, 90 carriage clocks, 60 clock sets (garnitures), 224 long-case clocks, 36 lantern clocks, 270 mantel clocks, 18 skeleton clocks and 72 wall clocks. The book was published in 1981 but this is not of any great importance since the figures can only be the roughest of guides. To give one example, a silver-cased carriage clock is shown on p.29 that bears the name of Nicole Nielsen and which fetched £48,000 at auction. No clue is given as to why it fetched this exceptionally high price – probably the highest price for a carriage clock ever. The reason is that it had a revolving escapement (it was a minute tourbillion) and a perpetual calendar, but neither of these facts was mentioned. The prices quoted were those attained at auctions in various countries and are in both pounds sterling and dollars. The conversion to dollars is quoted as being that at the rate of exchange appertaining at the time of the sale. This takes some believing, however, since a quick check failed to reveal any rate of conversion other than $2.25 to the pound. Such inconsistencies between what is said and what is found are again disconcerting.

Probably the safest way to proceed after the all-important

TURRET CLOCK MOVEMENT,
SIXTEENTH CENTURY

A very clear shot of the crown wheel
and verge of an early verge
escapement. The movement of iron
has striking and alarm work (striking
train on the left, alarm crown wheel
and pulley top right). On top of the
verge is the foliot; the notches on the
top edge of the arms locate the
carriers of the regulating weights.
Supporting the foliot and verge is
a cord whose top end is supported
by the curved arm to the left of the
cord.

decision of what clock to buy has been made; is to contact a
specialist dealer. To assist in this respect a list of such experts is
to be found in Appendix D. Antique shops also, of course,
stock clocks, some giving over quite a proportion of their space
to a type of object that obviously appeals to them. Finding just
what one wants in a non-specialist shop is obviously going to be
more a matter of chance than if one goes to a specialist, but it
can happen, especially if one is looking for a fairly standard
type of clock. If you are felt to be a genuine customer, most
dealers will go out of their way to help to satisfy a requirement;
after all, that is what they are in business for. It is not fair,
though, to use them as a cheap source of education, for this is
not their function.

LYRE CLOCK BY D. D. KINABLE, PARIS
(1794–1830), *c.* 1800

The lyre-shaped support and oval
base are of alabaster with ormulu
embellishments of leafy forms, swags
and a sunburst and mask at the top.
Also the outline decorated with beading matched by the beading attached
to the pendulum that surrounds the
movement and dial. The enamel dial
with the signs of the zodiac around
the outside, within these the months,
then the minute circle and the Roman
hour numerals. Within the chapter
ring the date of the month. Above
VI is inscribed *Kinable a Paris*. The
gold hands show the time, the shorter
blued hand the date and the longer
the month.

The movement strikes the hours
and the halves and has an anchor
escapement. The pendulum is on
a knife-edge suspension hidden
behind the mask. The spurious grid-
iron pendulum has two 'bobs', the
'working' bob at the back of the
movement and the decorative ring
that surrounds the dial. These rings
are usually decorated with pastes;
this one is an exception.
Height 1 ft 4 in (40.6 cm).

If you are tempted to buy a clock but feel in need of a second opinion, ask if you can call in an expert to vet the clock. The reaction to this request may be a refusal and this is the right of the dealer, just as it is up to you whether you buy or not. Make sure, however, that the expert you call upon really is an expert. The dealer will be upset and possibily contemptuous if the man you call upon is incompetent. Some experts – restorers, for instance – will only be willing to comment on the condition of the piece, others will also be willing to discuss the price asked. None of this should be done in the hearing of the man who is trying to sell the piece or the result may be acrimonious. Your expert will also expect to be paid for his services even if he is a friend. No one should ask a man to give away the painfully acquired knowledge that results from a lifetime of study.

If you buy on the strength of your own judgement, make sure that the bill describes the clock fully. In the event that the clock turns out to be inaccurately described, then you will be protected under the Trades Descriptions Act. You would in any case not expect to experience trouble with a dealer who is important enough to treasure his reputation. The position with

EMPIRE-STYLE TIMEPIECE BY VULLIAMY WITH PLAQUES BY WEDGWOOD, *c.* 1820.

The movement is obviously French; the position of the winding arbor shows that it has a going barrel. At the XII is the arbor for regulation. Turning this arbor shortens or lengthens the silk suspension, thus altering the effective length of the pendulum. The sphinxes show the influence of the Egyptian style following Napoleon's campaign in Egypt.
Height 10 in (25.4 cm).

an auction house is somewhat different, for the rule is 'Buyer beware' and disclaimers are to be found in every catalogue. It is now being argued that those who charge the buyer a premium are in fact charging for their expertise and therefore have a duty to protect the buyers' interests. These questions have yet to be satisfactorily resolved. There is in fact a certain code when it comes to catalogue entries, unwritten and not always strictly adhered to. If a piece is described, say, as 'by George Graham', then the auction house thinks it really is. If it is described as 'signed George Graham' then there is doubt. If it is said that it is 'signed George Graham and dated about 1870', then it means it is by another man with the same name as the famous maker or that it is a fake. Never be afraid to ask the resident expert at the auction house if you are in any doubt. Such people are jealous of their reputations and if approached in the right way will usually be extremely helpful.

Having made up your mind to bid for a lot ask at about what time it will be coming up, then get there at least half an hour before this time. Decide before you go what is your absolute limit and only go beyond this if you feel that you are near to success. Even if yours is the highest bid, you may fail to secure the lot, for it may not have reached the reserve set upon it by the owner or the auction house. You may also be bidding against someone who is not in the room. A bid may have been left with the auctioneer, something that you can do if you wish, or someone may be bidding by phone. The auction house may be bidding on their own account, a practice somewhat frowned upon, but which happens nevertheless.

Although bidding often starts slowly, with the auctioneer coming down to a price at which people will start things off, it will then proceed speedily. The price at which things start will probably have little significance and bear little relation to the finished price. If you see a piece apparently about to go at what seems a bargain price, you may be tempted to start bidding at a very late stage of the proceedings. Make sure that you are both seen and heard under these circumstances. The auctioneer has considerable powers and, if he mistakenly knocks the lot down to someone else, all the protestations in the world that you had just come into the bidding will most probably be ignored. I have seen established dealers come a cropper in these circumstances. However, if you obtain the article, you may eventually be disappointed. There might be a good reason why it was not worth any more than you paid for it. This is not always the case, however; it is possible to get a bargain and one of the great attractions of the auction room is the element of chance that exists because of the many factors involved – the most uncertain being human nature itself. It must be confessed, though, that usually prices simply reflect the state of the market

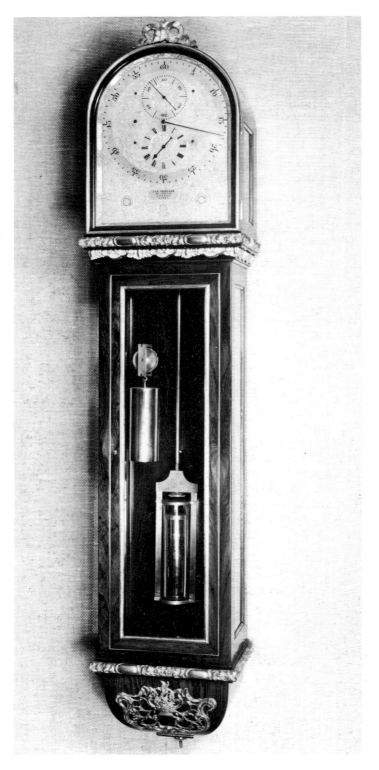

WALL REGULATOR BY CHARLES
FRODSHAM, LONDON, NO. 983, c. 1860

Rosewood case ormulu mounted,
the hood with arched top and glazed
sides. Rectangular dial with arched
top gilded and engraved all over. The
dial set out in regulator style with
subsidiary hours and seconds.
Beneath the minute ring a cartouche
with the inscription *Chas. Frodsham,
84, Strand, London No 983.*

The weight-driven movement,
which is on a substantial cast-iron
bracket, has wheels with six crossings
and jewelled pallets to the dead-beat
escapement. The escape-wheel rear
pivot and the pallet pivots are
jewelled. Mercurial pendulum with
steel jar and beat regulation supported by the cast-iron bracket.
Height 4 ft 6 in (137 cm).

at the time – allowing always that in the main the prices are trade, not retail prices.

Another source of supply is the markets. Well known in London are those at Portobello Road, Bermondsey, Petticoat Lane and Camden Passage. Addresses of these markets will be found in Appendix D. Here knowledge is all-important for, although the stallholders are always more knowledgeable than one would expect, they are nevertheless not as expert as those in the higher echelons of the trade. It is therefore always possible to find a bargain. In the markets it is liable to be the more expensive items that are good value – junk is often more expensive than it would be at auction.

Once you begin to build up a collection and get to know others who are doing the same thing, yet another source of supply appears – your fellow collectors. Often they will only exchange items with perhaps a cash adjustment, an understandable attitude. This means that the items you may have collected in the past and that perhaps no longer fit the collection you are building up, or perhaps are no longer good enough for you, can be disposed of without any loss or with a greater effective gain than you can make by a simple sale.

For serious collectors the first step is to join one or more of the following bodies; THE ANTIQUARIAN HOROLOGICAL SOCIETY in England or its American branch; THE NATIONAL ASSOCIATION OF WATCH AND CLOCK COLLECTORS in America; THE ASSOCIATION FRANÇAISE DES AMATEURS D'HORLOGERIE ANCIENNE in Paris; THE FREUNDE ALTE UHREN in Germany; THE BRITISH HOROLOGICAL INSTITUTE, membership of which gives access to its very fine library in Upton, Nottinghamshire. All of these bodies have their own publications and, by joining, collectors get to know one another, and learn the names of dealers and those providing specialist services. In addition, many of the societies arrange visits to museums under favoured circumstances and even to private collections not normally accessible to the public at all. The full addresses of these societies will be found in Appendix E.

Major Factors affecting Value

There are some general rules about value which can be summarised as follows:

1. Not everything that is old is valuable, but in general the older something is the more costly it will be.

2. Provenance is very important. If a clock is signed by a top-flight maker, is dated and can be proved to have originally belonged to an important royal family, and its complete

subsequent history is known, then the difference in value between it and exactly the same type of clock that is anonymous and has turned up without any history at auction will be so great as to be almost unbelievable. People don't just collect objects – they also collect the romance connected with the object.

3. The higher the quality the greater the price – comparing like with like of course, but the quality of the outside may be of overwhelming importance if the clock can be considered to be a furnishing item.

4. The more original and the better the condition the greater the value.

5. The more elaborate or complex piece is usually priced more highly.

6. Longer going time increases the value considerably.

7. Artistic merit. The ugly has to have a lot going for it before it is accepted, but to a degree this depends upon 8.

8. Fashion – furnishing fashions have a big effect on value and clocks that match the latest fashion will for a time at least fetch higher prices than they would normally.

9. Practicality. A 9-ft (3-m)-tall clock will be of practical use to very few people so that the price will be depressed accordingly. This will not apply to one of Edward Cockey's magnificent astronomical clocks or some other equally desirable piece.

Looking at the above criteria one would imagine that a truly valuable clock might be one made by Thomas Tompion that can be closely dated, made for a king, in a superbly decorated case and running and striking for a year. One such as this was in fact recently purchased by the British Museum for £500,000 – a record price for a clock.

Provenance

Here we come to a very difficult area and one in which it is wise not to expect too much. The truth is that there are few pieces which are documented in any meaningful way and those that are should be viewed with a jaundiced eye. There may be records of a clock being handed down from generation to generation throughout the centuries and accompanying these a clock which is assumed to be that mentioned in the records. But

WEIGHT-DRIVEN LANTERN CLOCK
BY WILLIAM SELWOOD, LONDON,
c. 1620

This clock still has its original
balance; most lantern clocks were
converted once the pendulum had
been invented. Many are now being
changed back and no type of clock
must be looked at more carefully
than the lantern before being
purchased. This clock is virtually
unique as it still has its original
copper sheathed weight for the going
train with room at the top for loose
lead pellets to be added or taken away
as required to alter the rate of going.
   The general design follows that
of the Gothic clock with a square
pillar frame, going train in front,
striking train behind, with the bell
in the canopy. The frets above the
clock are of an early heraldic type;
on the fret at the front is the
inscription *William Selwood at ye
marmade [Mermaid] in Lothbury*.
The chapter ring has no minute
marks, as one would expect at this
time. William Selwood was a free
brother of the Clockmakers
Company in 1633 and died in 1653.
Only a few lantern clocks by him are
known.
Height 1 ft 3½ in (39.4 cm).

are they the same clock? There are also traditions of clocks being given by some well-known person to a faithful servant, but did these personages really have so many clocks that they were constantly giving them away?

Some clocks are numbered and in rare cases – Vulliamy being one such – work books survive. Unfortunately, as yet clocks by Vulliamy are not sufficiently valuable to prompt anyone to publish a book giving full details. One famous maker left a full record of what he made, namely A. L. Breguet, and the firm can still be contacted for details about any particular item.

Unfortunately provenance is more important than it might at first appear if valuable clocks are involved, for not only can it add lustre and interest to a clock, it can also be a guarantee that it is genuine, both as a whole and in all its parts. One important aspect of provenance seldom mentioned is the genuineness of any documents that prove it. The clock may be a perfectly sound piece but the documents suspect. It is best where large sums of money are involved to take the documents to an appropriate national museum to have them looked over.

Fakes

Outright fakes are not common in the clock world. To successfully copy a valuable type of old clock would be such a costly undertaking that only in special cases would it be worth while. Also those capable of such work are seldom the type who would do it. In the past names were altered or added to chapter rings and dials but not in such a way as to fool those who are knowledgeable today. Lesser workmen would put the name of a famous maker on a piece in the hope of obtaining a better price; this was often done abroad. One of the reasons the Worshipful Company of Clockmakers came into being in 1631 was to stop this sort of thing and to encourage high standards among the London makers. One of the results of this is the fact that nearly all English clocks and watches bear a name, a circumstance that aids considerably in tracing a piece. The ways in which this can be done are set out on p.27.

The collector can most commonly be deceived by the following ways of tampering with a clock:

1. 'Marriages' where a case and movement did not originally belong together.

2. Marriages between a movement and a dial.

3. Conversion of a 30-hour long-case movement to a lantern clock.

4. Artificial ageing of honest reproductions of recent manufacture.

5. Movements so copiously restored that they can no longer be considered as genuine pieces.

6. Genuine old movements with reproduction cases artificially aged or made of old wood, possibly, although not necessarily, to deceive.

One advantage of collecting late clocks is that they are less likely to have been damaged by repairers and restorers and

RACK CLOCK BY RICHARD AND
TIMOTHY GOOD, SEAFORD, 1980

Mahogany base, columns and broken arch top. Polished brass bun feet. The clock is driven by its own weight and to this end has a heavy brass case. To add further to the weight the back movement plate has a semi-circular lead weight mounted upon it. The clock is guided in its downward path by the two brass rods; the left-hand one of these has the rack teeth on its inside edge which drive the first pinion in the gear train. There is no glass over the dial and the clock is set to time by pushing around the spade minute hand. The movement has a horizontally mounted lever platform escapement with eleven jewels and a temperature-compensated balance and spring. Height 1 ft 6½ in (47 cm).

certainly unlikely to be faked in any way. During the lifetime of older clocks they were mostly regarded as items of utility and also of furnishing value. Accordingly they were often improved mechanically and even modified externally to fit in with changing circumstances in the home. Complicated work no longer required by owners was often removed or rendered inoperative if dealing with them made the repair more expensive to any significant extent. At an even lower level many repairers were doubtless told to spend the minimum amount of time on even the fundamental repairs needed to make the clock go. The results were horrendous, repairs involving soft soldering, 'punching up', bending and general bodging. Of course, even Victorian clocks can have suffered, if only because for so long they were lumped together and dismissed as unworthy of serious attention, a circumstance that happily no longer prevails today.

Tracking down your Clock

Most people like to have some details about the makers whose names are on their clocks and watches. Often not much information is available, but this is not always the case. Various works of reference are available and these are listed in the suggestions for Further Reading (p.218). The most important is G. H. Baillie's *Watchmakers and Clockmakers of the World* which will often also give the locations of examples of a maker's work. Another is Britten's 9th edition of *Old Clocks and Watches and their Makers* which is especially strong on London makers and sometimes gives more information on an individual maker than Baillie.

There are specialist books on Ireland, Scotland and Wales, and Loomes has produced a vol. II to supplement Baillie which includes makers not covered by Baillie during his chosen period or after his cut-off point (about 1850). It must be confessed however that Loomes's list is more perfunctory, giving much less information about makers than Baillie or Britten. There are also a considerable number of books covering counties or even towns. These often give a lot of detail that could not possibly be included in more general books.

The British Museum tries to keep every book of this type that is published and even has files of articles published during the years in the various professional magazines covering makers and their work. Furthermore this information is at the disposal of the public, and a query by telephone or letter to the Clock Room of the Department of Medieval and Later Antiquities will be answered as fully as possible.

The reader is also referred to Chapter 4, which lists over seventy different type of clocks.

VISITING MUSEUMS IN GREAT BRITAIN

One way of finding out more about clocks is to visit museums which exhibit clocks and watches. A detailed list of these will be found in Appendix C, which also gives information about museums in Europe and the USA. The smaller museums often try to collect the work of local makers and will have researched them thoroughly. With this in mind, and so that the work of any maker represented anywhere in Britain can be located, a card index has been created in the Students' Room in the British Museum. No claim for the completeness or accuracy of this list is made but it is, nevertheless, the only source known to the author. Many National Trust properties contain clocks and a list of these is in preparation, but it is not known when it will be published.

If a visit to a museum is planned, it is wise to check beforehand not only that it will be open but also that the particular gallery you wish to visit is also open. Because of staff shortages many museums have to close galleries on a rota basis. This is usually because there are not enough security staff to go round. The problem will be exacerbated at peak holiday periods – just when the maximum number of visitors can be expected.

If you become interested in the methods of manufacture and repair of clocks, there are several museums, notable among them the new one at Prescot in Lancashire, which have workshop and tool displays.

2 The Installation and Care of Your Clock

Moving Long-Case Clocks

Once you have purchased a long-case clock, or should you be moving house, you will almost certainly need to know how to accomplish this safely. If possible, the clock should be allowed to run right down before it is moved. Various parts of a clock are fragile and easily damaged and those that you are likely to have a problem with when moving a clock are the following: 1. the pendulum suspension spring; 2. the crutch; 3. the hands; 4. the pendulum.

If the pendulum is still on the clock, start by removing the hood, which in all but a few early clocks slides forwards. It may be locked with a spoon or latch, which can only be got at through the main door. Once the door is open the hand must be put up, and, once the nature of the catch has been discovered, it can be operated so as to free the hood. The hood should be put down on the floor with its glazed front against the wall. If the door does not stay closed, it should be bound shut with an old tie. If string is used, this should have pads under it where it passes round corners, otherwise it can leave a nasty mark in the wood.

Open the trunk door and stand on a chair or a pair of steps so that you can get a good view of the back of the movement, and stand on the side opposite the trunk door hinges. Holding the suspension spring at the top above the back-cock in the right hand, take the weight of the pendulum just below where it passes through the crutch with the left hand. Then raise the pendulum slightly until you can pull the suspension spring free of the back-cock, when the pendulum can be lowered carefully through the crutch, this time holding the rod through the open door. This part of the operation can be more safely accomplished with a second pair of hands but can be done alone. At this stage the weights should still be on the clock; if not, the movement may fall off the seat-board supports, for it is often not fixed in any way at all. Therefore take the weights off with a hand holding the movement, again an operation much more

Left
JOHANNES TEGELBERGH, A LATE-
SEVENTEENTH CENTURY ALARM
TIMEPIECE

The dial with a skeleton gilt-metal
chapter ring against a mole-coloured
velvet ground, with an alarm disc
and signed in pierced gilt-metal
Johannes Tegelbergh . . . . Hague. The
movement with verge escapement
with cycloidal checks for the
pendulum suspension, baluster
pillars. The alarm mechanism is
mounted separately in the top right-
hand side of the case. The case with
broken pediment cornice, the sides
of the doors faced with spiral
pilasters, painted black and with
gilt mouldings. Johannes Tegelbergh
is known to have been working in
1670.
Height 1 ft 2½ in (36.8 cm).

Above
SPRING-DRIVEN BRACKET CLOCK
BY THOMAS TOMPION, NO. 243,
c. 1700

One of Tompion's run-of-the mill
clocks should be included. It has all
the features you would expect: a
strike/silent subsidiary dial on the
right, regulation dial on the left for
the rise-and-fall mechanism, mock
pendulum aperture beneath the XII,
calendar aperture above the VI. The
signature *Thomas Tompion Londoni*
Fecit in an engraved cartouche
between the subsidiary dials. The
ebony veneered case with domed
top and carrying handle decorated
with appliqué; there is an escutcheon
and a foliate decorated pierced gilt-
metal panel above the dial and on
the top. Shaped bracket feet.
Movement with latched plates,
quarter repeating and a verge
escapement. Back plate profusely
engraved with scrolling, interlaced
strapwork and foliage and inscribed
Thos. Tompion Londini fecit No 243.
Height 1 ft 3 in (38 cm).

easily accomplished if someone is available to help. If the weights are different, mark which is the striking one.

The movement is then removed. It is best put into a stout cardboard box with packing to prevent the crutch from being bent – a frequent occurrence when clocks are moved. The hands should also be checked – if they can catch in anything they can be torn off. The pendulum should be strapped to a lath which is long enough to go from the bob to the top of the suspension spring; the key can also be tied to this lath. The

TABLE CHIMING CLOCK BY BOY, LONDON, c. 1700

Case of tortoiseshell with basket top, flambeau finials and cushion feet. This is one of the clocks *not* to be picked up by the handle. The presence of the verge escapement is disclosed by the false pendulum. The verge escapement is very tolerant of being moved about and with care the clock can be taken from room to room without stopping. Clocks with tortoiseshell cases can present a problem since one is forbidden to import anything of, or containing, tortoiseshell into America whether it is antique or not. The same rule applies to ivory.
Height 1 ft 2 in (35.6 cm).

weights need another box and should be prevented from rolling around – they can do a considerable amount of damage or make the most disconcerting noises as they roll around in a vehicle.

RISKS IN MOVING CLOCKS

Never pick up a wooden clock by its handle, should it have one. Handles have a distressing habit of pulling away from the case. This might be because the retaining nut or nuts have worked free, the result sometimes of vibration suffered on a journey, or because the case itself is just waiting to fall to pieces. Instead tip the clock until you can get your hands beneath it, then lift it so that the front of the clock rests against your body. Get an idea of the weight of the clock before you start to move it. Musical clocks can be especially heavy and you don't want your strength giving way at a time when there is nowhere to put the clock down.

SUSPENSION SPRINGS The thin flexible spring on which the pendulum hangs can take many forms, some of which are associated with particular types of clock. All have one thing in common: they are delicate and easily damaged. If bent, they can lead to an unsightly rolling of the bob as it swings. If broken, then they have to be replaced. If the pendulum is hanging on the spring when it breaks, this too can be damaged – sometimes disastrously.

Silk Suspensions Not all clocks have a steel suspension spring. Many early French clocks and other Continental clocks have their pendulums suspended on silk. One end of the silk line is fixed above the pallet pivot point and the other is led to and wrapped around an adjusting screw leaving a loop of silk on which to hang the pendulum. Turning the screw one way or the other makes the loop longer or shorter, thus altering the effective length of the pendulum. Unfortunately, variations in humidity have an effect on the silk which makes it unsuitable for clocks with pretensions to accuracy.

When such a clock is met with, taking the pedulum off the silk loop without taking any precautions can result in the turns of silk around the screw unwrapping and thus the regulation of the clock has to be started all over again. The best thing to do is to put an elastic band through the loop and take it to some point on the clock which will keep it under tension.

PENDULUMS

Mercurial Pendulums Pendulums with bobs containing mercury need to be handled with special care. Firstly such pendulums are unexpectedly heavy for their size and because of this can easily be dropped. Even if the mercury jar is steel, such an

accident can ruin the pendulum, but if the jar is glass, which it usually is, the results can be catastrophic. Mercury is very difficult to collect up after spillage, can get into every nook and cranny, and will form an amalgam with gold and silver items such as rings if it comes into contact with them. For an article on this problem, see *Timecraft* (June 1984). Apart from the time and trouble involved in obtaining new mercury, it will also be found to be extremely expensive. Thus it is necessary to remove the mercury jar from the stirrup that supports and contains it. It should then for preference be put in a stout wooden box with plenty of packing under and around it and should be kept upright.

It is not necessary to go to all this trouble with the small double-tube mercury pendulums found in French four-glass clocks, for the tubes are sealed and spillage cannot occur. Obviously these pendulums are fragile and require special care in handling.

Wood-rod Pendulums are also quite easy to break. Many of this type have a heavy bob, and if the pendulum is picked up near

SKELETON CLOCK BY EDWARD FUNNELL OF BRIGHTON, *c.*1850

A most unusual clock by one of the great provincial makers of the nineteenth century. The clock is perhaps more French in style than English. A black marble base supports the plinths on which the clock plates stand. Beneath the marble base is a further cast brass base with foliage bracket feet. At the top of the clock is the large seconds dial. Within the seconds ring of this dial is the chronometer-type escapement and the constant force device or train remontoire. Since the chronometer escapement is single beat and the clock has a half-second beating pendulum, the seconds hand will move forward in second jumps. Beneath the seconds dial is the dial showing hours and minutes. The hands are of blued steel. The grid-iron pendulum has a bob containing a thermometer. Edward Funnell is known to have been at 91 Trafalgar St in 1856 and 1859 and in East St, Brighton, from 1862 to 1878. Height 1 ft 6½ in (47 cm).

'CHINESE CHIPPENDALE' CHIMING
LONG-CASE CLOCK BY THOMAS
TURNER, LONDON, THIRD QUARTER
OF NINETEENTH CENTURY

Case finely carved with a scale
mounted pediment surmounted
by figures of Oriental musicians.
Outset moulded columns flanking
the blind-fret carved hood door
above a serpentine moulded canopy
and outset columns flanking the
glazed waist door and glazed sides.
The lower part with carved panels
and terms on a foliate moulded plinth
with massive hairy claw feet. 14 in
(35.6 cm) break-arch brass dial with
lunar work in the arch with calendar
and seconds subsidiary dial and four
tunes/eight tunes and chime/silent
selector all within the chapter ring
and signed *Turner – London*. Massive
movement with anchor escapement,
chiming on nine rod gongs,
pendulum, three brass-cased weights.
Height 9 ft 10 in (300 cm).

the middle of the rod it can snap like a carrot. Always pick up a pendulum with two hands, one for the bob and one for the rod, grasping this at about its mid-point.

DRIVING WEIGHTS Since weights have to be removed from clocks when they are transported, there is always the possibility that they may be mixed up and that the weights that turn up with the clock at a later date will not be the correct ones. This will not always matter, but sometimes it will. Clocks that run for a month need heavier weights than the normal 8-day clock and a high-quality clock lighter weights than an ordinary one. Below is a chart giving an idea of what sort of weight one would expect to go with a particular type of clock. Naturally this can only be a rough guide.

Clock Type	WT	
	LBS	KILOS
Vienna Regulator	3	1.4
8-day Long-Case Going	8–12	3.6–5.4
Striking	12	5.4
Month Long-Case Going	18	8.2
Year Clock (But a Vienna Regulator Year Clock exists with an 8-lb (3.6-kg) weight!)	40–60	18.1–27.2
Long-Case Chiming Weight, 8-Day	25	11.3
Regulator 8-Day	2–6	0.9–2.7

Weights also vary in shape and certain clocks tend to have weights of special shape connected with them. Dutch clocks often have a pear-shaped weight, cuckoo clocks an elongated pine cone, Act of Parliament clocks a square section weight and so on.

Weights may be of lead or cast iron, they may be sheathed in brass, or of solid brass and they may have integral pulleys sunk into them; they may be short and fat or long and thin. Their length may be important when it comes to achieving the correct length of run of the clock since the available drop in the case is

reduced by the length of the weight plus its pulley. Thus a short fat weight with the pulley sunk into it may give an extra day's run, which in some special clocks may be vital. Higher-quality weights tend to be brass-clad, especially if visible because the door is glazed or in clocks that stand on brackets.

Temperature and Humidity

The owner of a clock can do a lot to keep it in good condition. Nowadays more precautions need to be taken than was necessary in the past, for there is little doubt that one of the main enemies of the wooden clock case is central heating. The reason for this is that no air has to be pulled in from outside to keep a radiator working, as is required for an open fire. This means that a relative humidity as low as 30 degrees is easily achievable. This is too low for wooden clock cases, although fine for the clock mechanisms. In fact the person who is a real worrier should probably collect carriage and skeleton clocks! (Except, see 'glass domes' for skeleton clocks.) Even more dangerous than a low humidity are sudden changes in both humidity and temperature.

In England, unless they were exceptional pieces, clock cases were not made with elaborate joints; butt joints were nearly always used and veneers were present on only one side of pieces that would have been better covered on both. Unsuitable cuts of wood were often used for economy's sake. John Harrison, however, used only radial-cut oak for his movements, wheels, cases and dials, and nothing that he made has distorted or split since the day he made it.

Before this century probably more trouble was caused by damp than dryness, and many a long-case clock has had its plinth replaced because it has rotted away. Polishing of cases gives a measure of protection. Doors especially should be polished on both sides with a good wax polish. If you have control of humidity, set it at about 55 degrees; this should suit both you and your clock cases without being dangerous for the mechanism. Avoid sudden changes and don't put clocks with wooden cases above or in front of radiators nor on a mantel-piece, if you can feel it noticeably warm to the touch. Japanese clocks with wooden cases seem to be in a class of their own and often fall to pieces at the slightest provocation. If parts need to be glued again, they should be glued with a water-solvent glue so that the process can be reversed if necesary.

Clocks with cases of metal merely need to be kept dry, since rust is the main enemy. No clock should be kept too near an open window for, when the wind is in the right direction, rain can be blown on to the clock, possibly with disastrous results if the case is wood. Clocks need a stable surface to rest on and can

MOVEMENT OF GRANDE-SONNERIE BRACKET CLOCK BY THOMAS TAYLOR, LONDON, *c.* 1680–85

The three-train movement has gut fusees and count-wheel quarter striking. Note the small count wheel on the left for the quarters and the large count wheel on the right for the hours. Since the hour is struck at every quarter, each hour has to be repeated four times on the hour count wheel. The back plate is engraved with representations of tulips. The bob pendulum is locked behind its catch piece for safe transport. Note the turn buttons on the edge of the dial. These lock into slots in the case to keep the movement in position.

Thomas Taylor was apprenticed in 1678, was free of the Clockmakers Company in 1685 and Master of the Clockmakers Company from 1710 to 1723. He worked in Holborn.

LONG-CASE EQUATION CLOCK MOVEMENT BY JULIAN LE ROI, PARIS, 1736

This clock is most unusual in that it shows and strikes true solar time, in other words the time shown by the gilt hands would agree with the time shown on a sundial. Other features disclosed by the view of the dial are that the clock is centre seconds (i.e. the seconds hand is concentric with the hour and minute hands) and that the short blue hand shows mean solar time minutes (since the maximum difference between true and mean solar time never exceeds $\frac{1}{4}$ hour, no mean solar-time hour hand is required). Between the two 30s on the dial is an aperture through which an annual dial shows. This shows the month and the date of the month and the equation of time for a month and for the day in question. Obviously the clock is not set correctly since six minutes are indicated by the difference between the hands and ten minutes shown by the dial. The striking and going sides are driven by weights on Huyghens's endless cords. As this means the clock is pull-wound, no unsightly winding holes mar the elegant enamel dial.

easily stop if put on to flimsy pieces of furniture. They can also make such pieces of furniture top-heavy, with the consequential risk of being knocked over.

Clocks with Glass Domes

Clocks with glass domes are a major problem. Many of these domes are quite irreplaceable today, so the consequences of a breakage are serious. Some clocks are so delicate and vulnerable that they demand protection and, if their dome is broken or missing, the answer may be a new base and dome – for this is a possibility. Alternatively a framed rectangular cover can be made. The only proviso here is that the original base should not only be kept but also marked, so that it can be related to its clock when the man who originally arranged the exchange is no longer around. There are good reasons for this – one day any type of dome may again become available or one may turn up by chance that fits the original base. Either way the options should be left open. Although I like to see clocks kept going, if this means lifting a precious dome once a week to wind the

This shot shows the view beneath the dial, the full annual dial being visible as is the pinion that drives it. Beneath this dial and fixed to it is the kidney cam that gives the true solar-time hands their correct motion.

This clock has a grid-iron seconds pendulum with a large bob and an elegant case (these features not shown).

Diameter of dial 10½ in (26.7 cm).

clock, perhaps it is best to leave it as a clock just to be admired as a visual object. Alternatively it might be wound only when a horological visitor is due, a better idea since dust can help to cause rusting more quickly when it all falls on the top side of a stationary arbor.

Fixing Precision Clocks and Setting them up

To give of their best, precision long-case clocks must be fixed to a solid wall. All of the efforts spent to produce a fine movement will be wasted if the case is free to rock about, which is especially likely if the clock stands on carpet. Many regulators are wall-mounted anyway, so that all one has to do is to fix through the battens that should be on the back of the case. If the wall is not flat, fix with three screws only, leaving the fourth, if required, untightened, so as not to stress the case, or else use packing behind the case where the fourth screw comes, so as to take up the gap.

There is, of course, little point in setting up the clock again if it is obviously dirty and in need of attention. It is unfortunately

SKELETON TIMEPIECE BY HAYCOCK
OF ASHBOURNE, c. 1880

To emphasise the size of this clock,
by its side is the well-known French
Exhibition timepiece which is
6½ in (16.5 cm) high. The Haycock
clock looks smaller than it is because
of its simple style. Note the
decorative piece that covers the
setting-up square on the barrel arbor
designed to prevent this square being
mistaken for the winding square.
Dead-beat escapement with plain
pendulum.

Haycock's was founded by the
two brothers John and Thomas. John
retired, leaving Thomas with his
two sons, Thomas, junior, and
William, to carry on the business.
Premises were established at Clifton
Lane (now Station Street) and there
was manufactured every kind of
clock including turret clocks. They
also did iron founding and general
brasswork. Some of the original
frame patterns used by Haycock's
and which were exclusive to them
survive to this day, as does the firm.
Thomas Haycock, senior, died in

1868. William left his brother to
carry on the business which
continued until the death of Thomas,
junior, in 1906. The other brother
William had started another business
under his own name, the one which
survives today, and with his son,
Henry, built a new works at
Southcliffe Northeys, Ashbourne.
William died in 1904. The
production of clocks ceased in 1956,
since when the factory has
concentrated on instruments, gearing
and precision parts.

true that most clocks will go on running long after the time that they desperately needed attention and thus the fact that they are going indicates little about their condition. The subject of overhauling clocks is dealt with elsewhere, so we will assume that the clock is in good condition and that it is not in the 'run-down' condition, run-down in the sense that the weights were as far down in the case as they could go before dismantling was started.

The first thing to do then is to reel the rest of the line off the barrels. To do this each click or ratchet has to be disengaged from its ratchet wheel and the line pulled until it is all off the barrel. If the line is left on the barrel, it can get out of position and jam between the sides of the barrel and the plate. If this happens, it can be very difficult to remove, sometimes even requiring that the clock be completely dismantled. Next, thread the pulleys and lines between the seat-board supports, then put the movement on them. If it was previously screwed on or nailed down, refix in its previous position. If not, get someone to hold the clock whilst you hang the weights on their pulleys. To do this, pull the lines out of the open trunk door and holding the line in place around the pulley put on the weight or weights. Then get someone to wind the clock whilst you yourself guide each weight in through the open door – all of the time keeping the line taut. Next put the pendulum on reversing the procedure detailed on page 29.

Winding Your Clock

At first sight it would appear that there is nothing less complicated than winding a clock but there are nevertheless some tips that are worth passing on. To wind a clock, of course, we need a key and this is where the first opportunity for error occurs since the key needs to be the right one for the clock. Keys are often numbered and will be found to go from 0 to 19. 0 is the smallest and a 19 is for, say, a large musical clock. The average mantel clock needs about a number 8 key but there is no hard and fast rule. If the key is too small it will not go far enough on to the square and may slip. Too large a key will spoil the square on the arbor and again may even slip around if very much too big. It is best to have a key for each clock and keep this with it. If you send the key (or keys) with the clock when it goes for repair put labels on with your name to assist the repairer. If he has to redress the winding squares he may have to supply you with a new smaller key but should still return your original key which may, if it is old, have a value of its own.

A word here about crank keys, which personally I do not like. Although using a crank key shortens the time required for winding, it puts a one-sided strain on the bearings which results

A REGULATOR, MONTH-GOING WITH GRASSHOPPER ESCAPEMENT BY JUSTIN VULLIAMY, LATE EIGHTEENTH CENTURY

A finely figured walnut case with bulges in the trunk sides to clear the pendulum bob. These bulges are required because of the large swing of the pendulum as a result of using the grasshopper escapement. The dial with flat arched top, matted centre and silvered chapter ring. The seconds dial below the twelve and the regulation dial in the arch. On a cartouche *Vulliamy London*. The month-going movement has a grasshopper escapement with ivory pallets, based on John Harrison's but in Vulliamy's own particular style. The grid-iron pendulum is unusually mounted on the case back board despite the presence of the rise and fall mechanism whose arm is also mounted on the back board. The rise and fall pinion is integral with the arbor that passes through the mechanism and has the regulating hand mounted on it.

Height 6 ft 11 in (210.8 cm).

in more rapid wear. This is not so serious with weight-driven or fusee clocks, where the arbors rotate during the going of the clock anyway, but it is not so good for clocks with going barrels where the arbor is normally stationary during the going of the clock and moves only during winding. It is especially important that crank keys fit properly, otherwise the key can rub in the hole in the dial as it flops from one side to the other. I have seen really nasty burrs raised in this way.

Keys sometimes need to be of a relatively small diameter compared with the square size or they will not go through the hole in the dial. As a result they may split and should be discarded or repaired immediately this is noticed; repaired if they are nice old keys. All keys of this type should be of steel, not brass.

Clocks should be wound gently, especially as the fully wound condition grows near: not too gently, however; you should always be quite sure that the fully wound condition has been achieved. In the case of weight-driven clocks, the weights should be observed during winding and winding stopped once they are sufficiently high. They should not be wound until one can wind no longer except when the clock is provided with stopwork. This may be found to be the case with many regulators and more rarely with other clocks. All fusee clocks have stopwork but have their own difficulty. Simply because the fusee is there one cannot feel that the mainspring is getting near to its fully wound condition. The numbers of turns of winding varies enormously and winding can sometimes seem to go on for ever. Impatience can result in over-vigorous winding and, although obviously the stopwork in the clock should be robust enough to take even somewhat unreasonable strains, there is little point in taking chances.

Winding ordinary going barrel clocks is a more straight-forward operation. One can feel that the mainspring is approaching the fully wound condition and it is, despite myths to the contrary, virtually impossible to overwind even a watch, let alone a clock. However, if the going barrel has geared or Geneva stopwork, there is again a danger of breakage if winding is done with a heavy hand.

It is then especially important to go cautiously with a clock that is new to you. Try to find out what the situation is with regard to stopwork or ask a competent clockmaker what special precautions might need to be taken when winding and whether or not the key is correct for the clock. A word of warning, however: a clockmaker may, when it comes to winding, be almost unaware of what he does. When you have wound thousands of different clocks and had one or two unfortunate experiences, the correct approach to winding

AN ASTRONOMICAL CLOCK BY
SAMUEL WATSON, LONDON, c. 1695

Believed to have belonged to Sir Isaac Newton; the 14-in (35.6 cm) silver dial with cherub spandrels, and a border of scrolling leaves, with rotating concentric dials and fixed chapter ring and central dial. The outer circle rotating annually with a needle indicating the sun, and showing the day, month, principal stars at the zenith, the position of the sun at the ecliptic, and the times of sunrise (at the tip of the needle) and sunset (by an inverted vee at the foot of the dial). The single hand showing the quarters, and the minutes marked in two-minute divisions. The dial within the chapter ring gives the relative angle of the moon and sun and thereby the tides and the eclipses. The central fixed silver disc shows the times of the setting and rising of the moon. The back plate finely engraved with scrolling branches and a plain leaf border. Asymmetrically-set winding squares give an indirect wind to the going train; the clock has rack striking. The astronomical train operated by two pinions carried by the arbor bearing the hand, one with 14 leaves (driving the calendar dial), the other

with 12 leaves (driving the nodal dial). Contained in a domed ebony case, surmounted by three finials, representing the elements and seasons, on a waisted plinth.

Perhaps the first clock made in England on the heliocentric principle. In 1687 van Ceulen of Amsterdam had made a planetarium for Huyghens on this principle which is now in the Leyden Museum. The heliocentric principle of Copernicus was later proved by Sir Isaac Newton whose *Principia* was published during the years 1686 to 1688. This clock is thought to have belonged to Sir Isaac Newton, together with a similar example in the Museum of the Clockmakers Company. Little is known of Samuel Watson's life, but in 1686 he was sheriff of Coventry and appears in the rate books for the parish of St Martin's in the Fields, London, in 1692 where he is recorded until 1712. He was mathematician-in-ordinary to Charles II, for whom he made a clock ordered in 1683 and now in the possesssion of HM the Queen at Windsor Castle. This was considered one of the wonders of the world.
Height 3 ft 2 in (96.5 cm).
Width 1 ft 7 in (48 cm).
Depth 1 ft 1 in (33 cm).

WALL CLOCK, FRIESLAND, ANON.,
c. 1850

The elements of a rack-striking
mechanism could not be more clearly
displayed than they are here, for it
is all mounted on the back of this
posted frame movement. Bottom
left is the snail which controls the
number of blows struck. The rack
tail is in contact with the snail, the
clock being ready to strike. The rack
stands vertically in front of the centre
post. The two trains of gears are
vertical, the striking train at the front,
with the going train behind
terminating in the recoil escape
wheel, which is clearly visible. Behind
the bells on the back of the dial plate
is the moon dial with its 59 ratchet-
shaped teeth on its edge.
Height 1 ft (30.5 cm).

becomes an automatic affair, virtually no conscious thought being given to the matter.

Although clickwork seldom fails in clocks, it happens sufficiently often for every clockmaker to be able to tell you a harrowing story of damaged fingers. When the failure occurs with a weight-driven clock it is not usually so bad, but a strong mainspring can injure the hand badly. Make sure then that the clickwork seems to be acting efficiently. The noise as the click falls from one tooth of the wheel to the next should be regular and the action should feel firm. There should not be backward movements of the key that vary in amount according to the position of the key during each turn.

Setting the Hands

Another generally held but incorrect idea is that the hands of a clock must always be set forward. Many later clocks in fact are specifically designed so that the hands can be turned backwards with safety. Unfortunately, even the clockmaker cannot aways tell when he is dealing with a clock of this type until he has taken off the dial. It could be that a clock originally fitted with the necessary safety devices may have had these modified or removed over the years, so one might as well assume that the generally held belief is true and the hands must be set forward only. As to how fast they may be pushed around, this depends upon what type of striking work the clock has.

Striking could be controlled only by a count wheel before the introduction of rack striking in the 1680s. A count wheel has a series of notches which are spaced further and further apart around its circumference. It is the distance between these notches that dictates the number of hours struck, and once striking has commenced, the wheel moves on and will be ready to strike the next hour after the detent falls into the next notch. If the hands are being moved during the striking sequence, then they will get out of synchronism with the hands and, although the clock will still strike at the right time as indicated by the minute hand, the striking may indicate the wrong hour as shown by the hour hand. It is unfortunate that very few clocks are provided with a ready means of correcting this state of affairs, so that the owner needs to be shown what to do and, if not of a practical leaning, may not be able to manage even then. Some clocks with count-wheel striking strike just the hours, some the hours and half-hours, some even the quarters, but whatever the frequency the clock must be allowed to complete each and every strike before you continue to move the hands. If any are missed, the strike will be out.

The same rules apply to chiming clocks and a laborious business it can be following the procedure. There is an alternative, however, since the owner of the clock can often afford to wait until the time of day matches the time shown by the clock, when the clock can be started. In these days when so many wear a watch with an alarm facility, it is easy to use this as a reminder.

Rack striking overcomes these difficulties for the hour hand is mounted on or linked to a cam that controls the number of blows struck and therefore these must always agree with the time shown by the hour hand. Thus the hands may be moved as quickly as desired – the only proviso being that when 12 o'clock is passed the clock should be allowed to complete this strike (the hands being left say at a few minutes past twelve). Many modern chiming clocks have their hour-striking controlled by a rack and the quarters by a count wheel which may or may not be provided with a correction device. If a correction device is incorporated, the hands may be moved rapidly with the normal pause at 12 o'clock. The quarters, if then out, will correct themselves within an hour. For further details on striking clocks, see Chapter 4 and Appendix B.

'Putting in Beat'

A clock is in beat when, as the pendulum is at rest, an equal movement in either direction causes an escape tooth to drop. Obviously this only appertains to double-beat escapement; the term is meaningless when applied to a single-beat escapement. When the clock is in beat, a tick should come at equal distances on either side of the rest position and if the pendulum is moved so as to just unlock the escapement on one side, it will also unlock on the other side. With clocks with no beat-setting arrangement, such as ordinary French clocks, bending the crutch will put the clock in beat. Bend it a little at a time, making sure that each time you are bending it in the right direction so that the ticks sound more even.

All those later French clocks – the majority in fact – that are clamped between the front and back of the case should be able to be put in beat by slackening the screws at the back slightly and then twisting the whole clock in its case. Of course, these screws should then be tightened again or the clock will twist in the case next time it is wound. This will not be an acceptable method of beat-setting if the clock is in beat only when the dial is noticeably out of upright; this will offend many people. But using this method of beat-setting can be a useful exercise in learning about the sound of 'in' and 'out' of beat. As the clock movement is twisted first one way and then the other, the characteristic sounds will be heard and the unmistakable evenness of the 'in beat' sound discovered.

The pendulum cock is often fixed to the backboard in

WEIGHT-DRIVEN LANTERN CLOCK
WITH ALARM BY DANIEL QUARE,
LONDON, WITH VERGE ESCAPEMENT
AND BOB PENDULUM, c. 1680

Note that the dial has no minute
marks, just the quarter hours, all
that is really required by the single
hour hand. The alarm train is very
simple; the crown wheel that operates
the verge that carries the bell hammer
is driven directly by a cord around

a pulley mounted on its arbor. The
fret on the side nearest to the camera
has been removed so as to reveal the
mechanism that it normally obscures,
namely the crown wheel and the
verge that carries the pendulum.
Quare was born in 1649, joined the
Clockmakers Company in 1671,
was Master of the Company in 1708
and died in 1724.
Height 9¼ in (23.5 cm).

regulators. This is to give a more rigid mounting and can make beat-setting more difficult. Obviously with a clock that has little supplementary arc it can take a fairly long time to get the clock sufficiently well in beat. Fortunately, many regulators have a beat-adjusting device. It may be on the cock, so that the position of the suspension spring is altered, or at the crutch bottom as with a Vienna regulator, or even at the top of the crutch.

Because of the problems of setting clocks in beat it is best, if possible, to put them on a surface that is level – as shown by a spirit level, for example. Once they are in beat on this surface, they can be moved to any other level position and will still be in beat.

Suspension Springs

A wide variety of suspension springs are used in clocks and the main types are mentioned below. Methods of attachment vary, so a discussion of each main type will also include details of this aspect.

The suspension spring of the common long-case clock is usually pinned directly into a slit in the top of the pendulum rod. The top of the spring usually, but not always, has 'chops', that is, two brass cheek pieces which prevent it from slipping through the slit in the back-cock. Many types of clock have a pin on the crutch that works in the slot in the pendulum rod. In another arrangement the crutch ends in a fork which embraces the pendulum rod. With both arrangements, if you look for the bright marks left by years of working, it should be possible to determine by measurement the correct length of a missing spring.

Regulator suspension springs are more sophisticated. Firstly there are chops top and bottom of the spring, the bottom chop often being provided with a fixed pin. The pendulum rod then has an end that hooks over this pin and a central slot that fits the

FRENCH WHITE MARBLE AND ORMULU STRIKING MANTEL CLOCK SIGNED ALLEN AND HAYES CALCUTTA WITH PERPETUAL CALENDAR, MOONWORK, AND EQUATION OF TIME, c. 1870

This clock is notable for its double dial. All of the dials are enamel and in the sunken centre of the time of day dial is to be seen the visible Brocot escapement. This is a type of semi dead-beat escapement and the pallets are fitted with D-shaped jewels. The small square showing through the chapter ring just above

the XII shows that it has a Brocot suspension for rating purposes. It is to be doubted if the hands are original; one would expect something more decorative on this clock. The lower dial has an annual calendar ring with the months and the equation of time marked. In the sunken centre at the top the phases of the moon, on the left the day, on the right the date. The word 'patent' refers to the method of achieving the equation of time and the perpetual calendar indications. Height 1 ft 6 in (45.7 cm).

chops. The chops at the top of the spring can be virtually identical to those at the bottom (except when associated with a rise-and-fall mechanism). It is not usual for the spring to fit closely into a slit in the back-cock, which normally has instead a wider slot that fits the chops. The pin is either a fixture in the chops, and rests in vees, or else passes through holes both in the back-cock and in the chops. The top chops can become sizeable blocks clamped together by a bolt and nut, being provided with

TABLE ALARM TIMEPIECE, WITH REPEATING BY PAUL BEAUVAIS, LONDON (WORKING c. 1704–30). EBONISED CASE, c. 1710

Just looking at the clock tells us it is a timepiece (only one winding hole) with a repeating facility (pull cord on the right) and alarm (setting dial at the dial centre). The chapter ring has enamel cartouches. It is to be doubted if the applied piece on the right of the case is correct, since it is a replica of that on the left, which it should not be as no keyhole is required on that side. Movement with pull repeat on two bells, verge escapement and bob pendulum. Height 1 ft 2 in (35.6 cm).

plain cylindrical ends that rest in widely spaced vee grooves. Screws in the back-cock may rest against the bolt ends so that controlled side-to-side movements can be applied to the suspension assembly to put the clock in beat. To improve the control the springs exercise over the pendulum it is often pierced out in the middle or can consist of two elements. This enables the spring to be made wider or thicker (if the width is not increased) without increasing its strength.

Little has been written about the theory underlying suspension springs but choosing the wrong one can have a profound effect on timekeeping. This is for the obvious reason that the suspension spring adds another control to the oscillating system. Instead of the performance of the pendulum being purely dependent on the restoring force of gravity there is also that due to the spring. The amount of impulse required is also affected and this has a secondary effect. To take the argument to absurdity, if the spring were made stiff enough the pendulum could not be impulsed at all.

Mr Kenneth James has recently been at pains to offer proof as to the best spring proportions, but this is of little use except in new work, since what we are discussing here is the correct spring for the clock, one, that is, as near as possible to that used by the original maker.

Suspension springs for French clocks with Brocot regulators are of a special form. The Brocot regulator is discussed under regulation (see p. 55); suffice it to say here that these regulators require a suspension spring that needs to be long and split (a double spring). The bottom chop is furnished with a fixed pin and the top chop is drilled to take a pin and relieved on one side to clear the wheel on the end of the regulating arbor. Because so many French clocks have the crutch and back-cock obscured by the bell, they are often moved without the pendulum being taken off. Although this can be accomplished safely by a skilled man, one of the commonest problems with these clocks is in fact a bent, damaged or completely broken suspension spring. If ordering a new spring to replace it yourself, then make sure it has not got plastic chops – the chops should be brass.

German clocks have a variety of designs of suspension springs. In general they are short and broad.

Regulation

First let it be said that regulation can only do so much for a clock. If a clock left to its own devices will not be consistent to a minute a day, then it is futile to try to regulate it more closely than this. Old clocks, it must never be forgotten, are old and cannot be expected to perform better than they did when they were new, even with the improved oils that we have nowadays.

Some were wrongly conceived in the first place and should be respected as honest attempts that failed to solve the problems. Such clocks should not be tinkered with. The experiments that did not succeed have after all a lot to tell us about the history of horology.

Regulation is one of the things that the owner would like to do but often lacks the confidence to tackle. Like everything else connected with clocks it is not as straightforward as perhaps it ought to be. The method employed varies and many clocks have a pendulum that can be regulated in several different ways.

RISE-AND-FALL MECHANISM

When Thomas Tompion first fitted the suspension spring to a pendulum, he also incorporated another device – the rise-and-fall regulator. He saw that the effective length of the suspension spring and thus the pendulum could be altered if the spring was able to pass through a movable slot that embraced it without gripping it. The spring is at the end of a lever or geared quadrant whose movement is controlled usually from the front of the clock but sometimes from the rear. Such a device cannot be expected to work too well at the time of reversal of its motion, so it is as well to approach the regulation cautiously so that one does not overshoot and have to go back again.

RATING NUT

The provision of a nut (the rating nut) either under, in the middle, or at the top of the bob is the most common provision for regulation. Moving the effective position of the bob is one of the main ways of bringing a clock to time.

The thing to remember here is that the suspension spring must be protected from the twisting that occurs whilst the nut is being turned. Usually the bob is squared on to the rod so that if the bob is held everything is all right. This is not always so, however; some pendulums with wood rods and others with Invar rods may have a rod that is loose in the bob and the rod has to be held whilst the nut is turned. If the bob is tight on the pendulum rod, it may be necessary to push it down so as to keep it in contact with the rating nut if one is turning this down. This must be done with care or the suspension spring may be broken. To help to prevent this, put the other hand under the rating nut and push against some resistance. Although rating nuts may be calibrated, the divisions do not necessarily represent any particular rate-alteration. Assume, however, that one small division represents a second a day, then make the appropriate alteration and observe the result. If the divisions mean something else, then a simple calculation will show what alteration should really have been made.

If a clock has a rise-and-fall mechanism, use the same

approach; assume that the small divisions on the dial mean an alteration in rate of a second a day. Don't expect the same consistency of results, however, for a rise-and-fall device has to pull the suspension spring through a slit in the back-cock which must of necessity not grip the spring. If the spring was gripped, it could be pulled up, but the weight of the pendulum would not be able to return it again. This need for clearance at this vital spot must lead to uncertainties in performance. Older clocks may have a screw extension to the top of the suspension spring and a butterfly nut to pull the spring through a slit in the back-cock. All adjustments that are at the top instead of the bottom of the pendulum have the advantage that adjustments to rate may be made without stopping the clock.

Later clocks may have a rating nut above the pendulum bob; this is a feature common to both French and English clocks, although somewhat differently arranged in either case. The English type is usually associated with bracket-clock pendulums that are not temperature-compensated. A linking piece has one end fixed to the bob centre and a threaded end which passes through a nut located in a slotted piece fixed to the pendulum rod. In many cases the position of the nut makes it more accessible than if it is beneath the bob. The French type is to be found on grid-iron pendulums both in long-case and bracket clocks and looks more like the conventional rating nut merely moved from the bottom to the top of the bob. However, this is not so, since again there is a linking piece which joins it to the centre of the bob. Here the linking piece is usually a triangular-shaped piece of flat steel.

Very fine adjustments in rate may be made to precision clocks by adding or taking away weights from a tray situated about two-thirds of the way up the rod. Adding weight slightly raises the effective centre of gravity of the pendulum assembly and thus makes the clock gain. Since one can use chemical balance weights, finer alterations to rate can be effected than the stability of the timepiece can justify. The other advantage of this system is that rate adjustments can be made without stopping the clock and without the uncertainties attendant upon moving the spring through a slit. It should be mentioned, though, that some rare clocks have a slit that can be clamped on the spring which is released only when the spring has to be moved. Others have an adjustable slit so that it can at least be closed on the spring as much as is practicable and can also cope easily with a change of spring.

Security

Having bought your clock and safely installed it in your home, there arises the question of security. Advertising your

TABLE REGULATOR BY WILLIAM
NICHOLSON, WHITEHAVEN, 1797

Arch-topped case with glazed front,
sides and top, and with flame finial.
Silvered dial inscribed *Wm Nicholson
f. 1797* with shuttered winding hole.

Centre seconds hand. The movement
has a chain fusee and a gravity
escapement. The pendulum is
supported by an A frame with a most
unusual temperature-compensation
device which raises or lowers the
pendulum suspension spring through

chops. The elements of the brass-
and-steel sandwich are supported
by a double-ended wedge device
which, in conjunction with two
sliders controlled by a screw, can
lower or raise the whole pendulum
to effect regulation. Beneath the

pendulum there is a beat scale. The maintaining power, which is of the Harrison type, is mounted not on the fusee but on the centre wheel. Altogether a most unusual clock. The feet are adjustable so as to enable the clock to be levelled.
Height 2 ft 2½ in (67.3 cm).

whereabouts and the fact that you have a collection is one way of inviting a robbery. Thirty years ago collectors habitually revealed themselves in print, but this is no longer a wise thing to do, and has not been for a decade or more. If you are publishing anything at all, an advertisement, for instance, ensure that replies are forwarded to you through the publication involved. Beware too of using the obituary columns; it is a common practice at the more sophisticated levels of crime to scan these columns to pinpoint easy pickings. At this time houses can temporarily stand empty, the contents largely unknown and relatives may even get the blame if things disappear.

Remember that from the point of view of a thief small is good. If you live in an area especially prone to burglaries, then it might be better to collect clocks that are heavy enough to make even the strongest thief think twice before making off with them. Of course, nothing is safe from the 'thief-with-removal-van'; all you can hope for here is that your insurance cover is adequate.

I do not feel that this is the place to discuss burglar alarms, but it might be in order to say that if you can service your own clocks then you are undoubtedly clever enough to install your own alarm system, a thing that can be done for much less than the cost of one of your better clocks. Most burglaries today are of the quick 'in-and-out' variety, and anything that delays or slows down the intruder will tend to put him off. All accessible windows should have locks and outer doors should be double-locked by deadlocks. The thief is denied a quick exit unless he breaks a large pane of glass, then has to leave in an incriminating way. Do not lock small clocks in cabinets, for you are just asking for the piece of furniture to be damaged; although he may not like to smash what is visible from outside, the thief will not hesitate to damage what is within the house.

PHOTOGRAPHING YOUR CLOCK AND INSURANCE

Every clock of any value should be photographed, even if you only have a polaroid camera. If possible, there should also be a shot of the mechanism. On the back of the photograph should be any relevant details, maker's name, any numbers, inscriptions, marks or scratchings. The height should also be noted to give a scale to the photograph. Duplicates of these photographs should be lodged with your insurers with the values and the dates that the valuation were made, should your insurer so require. He will almost certainly require such details for any clock in excess of a certain value, and he should tell you so.

'He who holds the negative holds the copyright' is the legal position with regard to photographs. If your clocks are photographed by a professional and no agreement is made to the contrary, then he, not you, holds the copyright. There are, of course, moral and ethical considerations which should be taken into account but these do not affect the legality of the matter. Unfortunately, clocks are difficult items to photograph, so that if you need high-quality photographs for, say, publication, you need to be good enough to take them yourself and will have to have the necessary lighting equipment.

Remember too that your clocks may be regarded as a collection if you have more than the normal number in your household. You will then find out, in the event of a theft, and only then, if my experience is anything to go by, that the amount that will be paid is limited to a certain proportion of the sum for which you are insured overall. Also, unless you have an all-risks policy, you will not be covered if your clock is taken out of the house. You should check the position especially if it is going away for repair. Do not be lulled into a false sense of security because you have a policy that offers to reimburse you at replacement value. If you have not constantly updated the full amount for which you are covered to allow for replacing everything at the current values, you could be in trouble even on a single item that goes missing.

All of this may sound obvious but it is a shock to find out what you should have known and what ought to have seemed obvious *after* a burglary has taken place. Asking the right questions could have put you in the picture, had you known enough to ask them! Create a master card like the one shown below; you will be amazed at how soon it is possible to forget the most important points about the items in your collection. You may also need the information in the event of making a capital gain that has to be declared. Every expense incurred in connection with the clock can be deducted providing that documentary evidence exists.

TYPE OF CLOCK: ....

MAKER: ....

CASE DETAILS: ....

CASE DIMENSIONS: ....

DATE ACQUIRED: ....

SOURCE: ....

PRICE PAID: ....

VALUED BY (DOCUMENT ATTACHED): ....

INSURED BY: ....

INSURED FOR: ....

POLICY LAST UPDATED: ....

PHOTOGRAPHED (PHOTO ATTACHED AND BY WHOM): ....

CLOCK MARKED (WHERE AND HOW): ....

DIAL AND
              HANDS: ....

MECHANISM DETAILS: ....

REPAIRS AND RESTORATIONS (INVOICE(S) ATTACHED): ....

RELATED WORKS: ....

3 Cases, Dials and Movements

The mechanism of a clock is known by horologists as the movement and is often not visible, although it is sometimes the entire clock, as in skeleton clocks, where the movement is merely mounted on a base and protected by a glass dome. However, most clocks will have a case and virtually all will have a dial. These main parts will now be considered.

The Case

This is often described using terms not familiar to the public. A list of those terms connected with cases and their decorative aspects will be found in Appendix A. Technical features are to be found by recourse to the text with the help of the Index. Many of the terms connected with decorative features of cases come from architecture. Some go back to Egyptian times, and indeed most of the recognised styles, Egyptian, Greek, Roman, Gothic, Renaissance, Baroque, Rococo, Art Nouveau and Art Deco, are represented in clock cases.

WOODS USED IN THE MANUFACTURE OF CLOCK CASES

In the early architectural period oak carcases were veneered with ebony. After this cases were nearly always ebonised using stained pearwood veneer. Ebony was not only a scarce wood, but it also sucks up grit with the sap, a circumstance that can ruin tools whilst it is being worked. Because veneers had to be sawn at this date, they were thick and small in area requiring careful selection and fitting to give a good result. During the last quarter of the seventeenth century olivewood was introduced. It was hard and durable (olive trees take a long time to grow) and could be veneered to produce attractive rings which were like oyster shells in appearance. Thus they were often called oyster pieces. An oyster case is much prized, being very fine and instantly recognisable. Walnut was another favoured veneer from the earliest period of wooden cases; it has to be examined carefully as it is especially vulnerable to woodworm.

LONG-CASE WEIGHT-DRIVEN NIGHT
CLOCK BY EDWARD EAST, c. 1675–80

Marquetry case of high quality with
walnut-veneered sides. The front
has floral pattern made up of various
woods and green-stained bone. The
door is rectangular. The rising hood
has spiral columns and solid side
doors which give access to the lamp

shelf which lies above the level of
the movement. The gilded brass dial
is finely engraved and has a pierced
lunette cut in its upper section
through which a succession of Arabic
hour numerals show. These numerals
are pierced so that a light behind can
show through, and pass pierced
minute marks, these being on the
upper edge of the lunette. Above

these the quarters are pierced out
as Roman numerals: I, II, III. Beneath
the lower edge of the lunette is
engraved the signature *Edwardus
East Londini*. The setting square is
at the dial centre and the winding
square at the bottom of the dial.

Edward East, born in 1602, was
a founder member of the
Clockmakers Company in 1632,

being an assistant to the court. He was Master of the Company both in 1645 and 1652 and died in 1696. He was one of the most celebrated of the early English makers, being clockmaker to both Charles I and Charles II. The movement of this night clock is a fine example of his work and is unique inasmuch as it is the only English long-case night clock with this type of under-dial mechanism. It also is one of only two known to exist.

The weight-driven movement runs for 8 days and has four wheels in the gear train. It has slanting top covers which cap the gabled plates. There are eight ringed pillars, which are latched. The escapement is an early example of the anchor escapement and the pendulum is seconds beating. An ingenious yet simple system operates the succession of the hour numerals. The hour is shown by a changing numeral which appears in a circular aperture and moves from left to right in the semicircular lunette. Between each quarter hour is a small pierced indication representing each $7\frac{1}{2}$

minutes past the quarter. The minutes are indicated around the upper edge of the lunette by 60 small holes. Two groups of four pierced holes arranged in a diamond shape indicate both the commencement of the hour and its end.

How the indications are operated. Behind the main dial is a disc fixed to the movement which revolves once every 2 hours. The disc has two pierced circular apertures with adjacent tear-shaped minute pointers. The aperture on the right shows the hour that is just past and that on the left the hour that is just commencing. Fixed to and beneath this disc is a ten-sided metal wheel around which the chain with its attached metal plates revolves once every 2 hours. The numerals are so arranged that as one hour passes the next numeral appears in correct sequence on the opposite (left-hand) side.

It is not certain that the case and movement belong together, although the case is probably contemporary with the movement. The hood has been reconstructed possibly because the original was burnt, fire being a constant hazard with this variety of clock. The movement of a night clock also sits low compared with the dial and the ledges which support the movement have been cut down considerably to accommodate it. Height 6 ft 10 in (208.3 cm).

Burr-walnut was especially popular because of its scrolled appearance.

Veneer could of course be laid in any direction, its weakness across the grain being unimportant. This made it especially useful for edging, banding, herringboning, etc. This soon resulted in the idea of using different colours of woods to produce patterns (see MARQUETRY in Appendix A). Earliest among these patterns were stars usually of alternate triangles of black ebony and yellow boxwood inlaid in a base of olivewood veneer. Sometimes hollywood and ivory dyed green were used.

Undecorated burr-walnut continued to be used until the mid-eighteenth century, but owing to a change in import laws many new woods became available after this date; mahogany was the chief of these, and has continued in use to this day.

There was also a fashion for carved oak cases in the second half of the nineteenth century. Oak cases were sometimes, in the eighteenth century, veneered with pollarded oak, which has an interesting grain with straight lines of dark dots crossed by light wavy bands. The cheapest clocks of all were in softwood cases painted and grained. These can be found before 1750 and continued to be made in the nineteenth century. From about 1875 there was a vogue for tall carved mahogany cases with glazed door and tubular chimes, often made with great care and craftsmanship.

The woods used in the making of clock cases were those currently being used in furniture-making. Certain woods are particularly associated with certain periods:

JACOBEAN CROMWELLIAN	} oak
CAROLEAN QUEEN ANNE	} ebony, ebonised pearwood, kingwood, walnut, olivewood
GEORGIAN	mahogany, satinwood
VICTORIAN	rosewood

The following list gives further details of some of the woods used in clocks:

AMBOYNA A burr variety of padnak, a timber of the Andaman Islands, sometimes called Andaman redwood.

BOXWOOD A dense close-grained light-coloured hardwood from Turkey and many other parts of Europe and Asia. Particularly good for fine detailed carving.

EBONY Now almost unobtainable and always scarce. A black wood streaked in brown, purple and grey. Grows in India and Sri Lanka.

Coromanda A streaked variety of wood from Sri Lanka.

Kingwood From Brazil, is a deep violet-brown colour, sometimes called violetta.

Laburnum Native to Britain and with an olive-green colour.

Mahogany Spanish, a heavy close-grained wood of a deep brown colour; Cuban, higher in colour and with an attractive wavy grain; and Honduras (often called baywood), a lighter wood reddish brown in colour.

Olivewood A dense hardwood from East Africa. It is a rich yellow-brown colour with darker markings.

Rosewood From Brazil or the East Indies. A heavy dense wood, purplish brown with streaks of dark brown. Honduras rosewood comes from the West Indies.

Satinwood A light yellowish-brown wood with a rippled appearance from India and Sri Lanka.

Tulipwood A wood with many shades of red in it from Thailand.

The Dial

This is, of course, of great importance to a clock. It usually gives the name of the maker or designer or seller of the clock and shows furthermore what some of the complications of the mechanism are likely to be. Dials have been made of iron, brass, enamelled copper, silver and even gold. They have been embellished with engraving, engine-turning, painting and enamelling, and have habitually had pieces applied to ornament them. The style of the dial can reveal a lot about the age of a clock and its country of origin. Such a bewildering variety exists that it has been thought best to let the clocks illustrated tell the story of the dial and to this end it is separately described in most of the captions. The chapter ring is the term used for that part that carries the hour numerals.

The Mechanism

This can be subdivided as follows:

The Motive Power

Early clocks were weight-driven; the mainspring was not applied to clockwork until the middle of the fifteenth century. The mainspring made the portable clock possible but was not only applied to portable clocks. It, and the barrel it is so often associated with, are described in some detail in Appendix B.

The weight is discussed in the section in Chapter 1 on moving clocks (see p. 29).

THE FUSEE was one of the most important inventions in the history of spring-driven mechanisms. Its purpose is to equalise the pull of the mainspring which gives out less and less force as it unwinds. The barrel that contains the spring is connected to the fusee by a line or chain. The fusee is a sort of cone pulley with a groove to guide the line. As the mainspring unwinds, the line reels off the fusee and the part of the fusee on which the line acts increases in diameter. This means the line can exert a greater leverage and, if the fusee is designed correctly, the increase in leverage exactly offsets the lessening force available from the mainspring, so equalising the pull throughout the run.

No one knows when the fusee was first designed or introduced into clockwork, but it seems to have been virtually from the time the mainspring was first introduced into the clock. Certainly what is possibly the earliest spring-driven mechanism to have survived, probably made about 1450 (it is on loan from the Victoria and Albert Museum and on display at the British Museum), contained a fusee. The clock has suffered over the years and a model has been constructed to show how it probably was originally.

THE GEAR TRAIN

This is the collection of gears that connects the motive power to the escapement. Since no clock can display intervals of time smaller than the interval of time between the unlocking of one tooth of the escape wheel and the unlocking of the next tooth, it follows that the controller must have a time of oscillation that is short. Some early clocks have a foliot that takes 6 seconds to complete an oscillation, but few clocks made after the introduction of the pendulum and the balance spring have a period longer than 4 seconds and even these are rare. Any clock that shows seconds must have a controller with a beat rate of a second or less. If a clock is to have a running time of even 30 hours, then it is plain that the gear train must speed the rate of revolution of the first rotating member of the train considerably; usually a minimum of 1:120 but often 1:1,000. This is accomplished using three to four wheels and pinions, pinion being a horological term for a driven gear with a number of teeth less than about 20. Usually one of these gears rotates once an hour, and the minute hand is mounted on it.

One of the greatest changes in horological production took place because of the advances in gear-cutting techniques that took place in Tompion's time. Before the introduction of dividing machines, gears had to be cut by hand and only the finest craftsmen could produce gears that were good enough to give any sort of result at all with the balance without spring and the foliot. The new controllers with their natural rate of oscillation in the shape of the pendulum and the balance and spring, coupled with the easing of the problem of making good gears, made it possible for craftsmen to produce accurate clocks, who would have been quite unable to do so before. This resulted in a relative explosion in production and made the clock available to people other than the very rich.

There are two main forms of gearing used in horology, involute and cycloidal. Cycloidal gearing is that commonly used, but for many centuries it was developed merely empirically and the theory underlying the form of the teeth was not understood until the nineteenth century. It is a common misapprehension that designs aim at a tooth form that gives a rolling motion without rubbing between the teeth of the driving and the driven gear. This, however, is an impossibility if the main requirements of gearing are met. These are as follows:

1. The tooth shape must be easy to produce accurately to form.

2. There must be a constant velocity ratio; that is, if the ratio of the gears is 1:10, then at any time one gear should be revolving exactly ten times faster than the other regardless of which parts of the teeth are in contact. This does not only depend on the tooth shape but on various other factors involving truth, out of uprightness and out of flat of the wheel. However, as far as is possible the tooth shape should be tolerant of these other errors.

3. The tooth shape should be strong but not so sloping that there is a strong radial thrust tending to separate the gears and causing undue forces at the pivots.

4. The action should take place largely after the line of centres so that the teeth in contact are separating rather than approaching one another. This leads to lower frictional losses and less wear.

5. From the point of view of economy one wheel should gear with others of the same pitch no matter what their number of teeth.

6. The pinions should be of a shape that is easy to polish without destroying their correct form.

Strangely enough the gear form that most meets these conditions is the involute, but nevertheless it has not been able to gain favour with clockmakers. The lantern pinion is also a very good type of pinion to use with an epicycloidal wheel but is looked upon with scorn by most clockmakers, owing to a lack

FALLING BALL CLOCK BY JACOB MAYR OF VIENNA, MID-SEVENTEENTH CENTURY

The weight of the clock is its own motive power with this type of clock, as in the rack clock and the inclined-plane clock. The ball hangs on a chain which passes inside the mechanism and is connected to the barrel. The hour is indicated by the angel. When the clock has fallen as far as it can, it is rewound by lifting it. As it is lifted the chain is wound back on to the barrel by an ancillary spring. In recent years reproductions of this type of clock have been made, although nearly all have been suspended on a steel strip instead of a chain. Diameter of ball 4 in (10.2 cm).

of understanding. It is true that the lantern pinion and the involute pinion are more difficult to make properly as an individual item, but there is no obstacle to their accurate production under factory conditions.

THE ESCAPEMENT

The escapement in a clock is that part which turns the rotary motion of the gear train into the two-and-fro motion of the controller. It serves both to count the oscillations and to provide the impulse required to maintain the oscillations of the controller (the pendulum or the balance). For many centuries after the invention of the mechanical timekeeper there was effectively only one escapement, the verge, but the development of the anchor escapement led to hundreds of different types being developed. For the mechanically-minded the variety of escapements is a very important aspect of horology. A rare escapement can add both interest and value to a piece, and it is therefore important that there is some understanding of those that may be met with.

The verge escapement was in use from the thirteenth until the eighteenth century. The invention of the pendulum in the mid-seventeenth century made the development of a superior escapement necessary, but even though this came along in 1670 the verge was still in use until about 1800. Why was this? The reason is that the verge is a tolerant and especially useful escapement in portable clocks. When well-made it enables the clock it is in to go for a fairly long time between overhauls and to be tolerant of the position it is placed in. In fact it is possible to lift and carry a verge clock to another position and put it down again, all without it stopping. It is, however, more expensive to fit into a clock than the next escapement to be invented – the anchor. This is in fact almost a rearranged verge escapement but rearranged very effectively since the pallets can be made from a thick piece of flat steel and it needs no face-cut escape wheel or contrate wheel. Tailor-made for easy production, it has continued to be made from the time of its invention until today (it is still fitted in clocks currently being made in Germany).

The next escapement to be developed was the dead-beat escapement. Designed by Thomas Tompion, it was perfected by George Graham and has been used in the form designed by him ever since. In this form it is actually called the 'Graham' escapement. It is the recoil escapement modified so as to split each pallet face into two distinct parts, locking and impulse. When the tooth tip falls on to the pallets at 'drop', it falls on to a face that is 'circular', i.e. circumferential about the pallet pivot. Because of this the escape wheel is not caused to recoil. During

TABLE REGULATOR BY RICHARD GIBSON, LONDON, c. 1860

Table regulators are not common and this example is particularly unusual because of the landscape in the lower half of the front. A small door gives access to the movement from the top. The centre seconds enamel dial is inscribed *Rich Gibson Fecit London*. The movement has a dead-beat escapement and a mercurial pendulum. A Richard Gibson is known to have been in business in Redcar, Yorks., at 130 High St in 1866; no other maker of this name is recorded. Height 1 ft 2 in (35.6 cm).

BRACKET TIMEPIECE WITH DATE AND
REPEATING WORK BY DANIEL QUARE.
c. 1690

Green and gold lacquered case, the
lacquering having survived
untouched. This is unusual; most
'lacquering' has had to be completely
or partly redone over the centuries.
(See index for detail on lacquering
and japanning, which is discussed
elsewhere in the book.) The
lacquering shows Oriental figures,
buildings and landscapes and has
trellis panels. Verge escapement,
but the controller is not a pendulum
but a balance and spring. The balance
is mounted vertically and can be seen
through a glazed aperture in the back
door. The back plate and balance
bridge are engraved. Both front and
back door are hinged. The dial is not
original nor is the repeating work.
Quare was born in 1649, was made
free of the Clockmakers Company
in 1671 and died in 1724.
Height 13¾ in (35 cm).

the supplementary arc of the pendulum the wheel simply
remains stationary, hence the term 'dead'. When the pendulum
reverses, the locking face of the pallets slides past the wheel
tooth until this reaches the 'locking corner', whereupon
impulse begins, the wheel tooth sliding along the impulse face
and giving the pallets a push in the process. The escapement
avoids the 'recoil' present in both the verge and anchor
escapement. Recoil occurs with these escapements when the
wheel tooth first drops on to the pallet face, for the whole of
this face is an impulse face but is acting at the time of drop in the
reverse direction, thus pushing the escape wheel and the rest of
the gear train backwards. This is wasteful of power and leads to
more rapid wear than would otherwise occur. If a seconds hand
is fitted it can be seen to recoil at each beat, thus revealing the
general type of escapement fitted without one even having to
look at the mechanism. Later an escapement was to be
developed that incorporated the features of both the recoil and
the dead-beat escapement. In this mechanism, known as the
half-dead beat, the impulse plane is divided so that recoil is less
severe than with the conventional anchor escapement but still
present.

The dead-beat escapement was followed by John Harrison's
'grasshopper', known as such because of the 'kicking' action of
the pallets. Harrison looked for a design that would enable the
escapement to work without oil. Oils were very poor at the
time, drying up, going gummy and thick, and causing all sorts of
obstacles to the achievement of precision timekeeping. In the
grasshopper escapement there is virtually no sliding of the
wheel tooth on the pallet faces, although there is recoil.
Harrison also developed special gearing which is efficient even
when being recoiled. Although there is no chance of obtaining
one of Harrison's own clocks, the grasshopper escapement was
used by others, especially Vulliamy, and is still being incorporated into clocks being made today. It is showy in action and
invariably impresses those who see an example.

A variant of the Graham dead-beat escapement made on the
Continent had pins at right-angles to the plane of the escape
wheel which acted as the teeth. The pallets of these escapements
are usually although not invariably on the same side of the
escape wheel and are often designed so as to allow for
adjustments to be made as wear occurs. The pin-wheel
escapement, as it is known, was not favoured by English makers
because they felt it did not offer as good a chance of keeping the
oil where it was meant to be.

The gravity escapement in its various forms is always
interesting in its action but often tends to be noisy and should
therefore be considered carefully before purchasing, if the
clock is intended for use in a living room. It was originally

GRANDMOTHER REGULATOR BY
HENRY BAKER, LONDON, WITH
MAHOGANY CASE, c. 1790

This diminutive clock is only 4 ft
7 in (139.7 cm) in height as the light-
switch position shows. The dial
discloses the fact that it is a regulator
and we would expect it to have a
dead-beat escapement of the Graham
variety and a compensated
pendulum. The pendulum is in fact
of the wood-rod/lead-bob type. The
expansion of wood (dry deal) is a fifth
of that of brass, and ebony and teak
are reputed not to expand at all over
the range of temperatures that are
relevant. Lead on the other hand
expands seven times as much as
wood, so that a lead bob of $\frac{1}{7}$ the
diameter of the length of the rod
supporting it will provide good
compensation. It must be added here,
though, that probably only a few
pendulums of this type were ever
properly matched, which does not
prevent good results under normal
conditions.

The dial is arch top with the
decoration not applied but engraved.
Many restorers would automatically
resilver the dial; in my opinion it is
not yet bad enough to merit this.
Henry Baker was free of the
Clockmakers Company from 1781
to 1790. He worked in Westminster.
Height 4 ft 7 in (139.7 cm).

invented by Thomas Mudge, although no clock bearing his name survives with his escapement. One of the earliest examples recently come to light is in a clock by Henry Ward of Blandford. These clocks are of the late-eighteenth – early-nineteenth-century period. In these two centuries a bewildering variety of escapements was produced, and Mudge's gravity escapement was the first of a new type known as constant force escapements. Such escapements do not transmit the inequalities of force to the controller consequent upon the shortcomings of gear trains or the variation in the motive power itself; instead the force of a subsidiary spring or weight is employed at the escapement so that the impulses to the controller are absolutely uniform. The main weight or spring is merely used to rewind the weight or spring at the escapement.

THE CONTROLLER

As soon as the pendulum had been invented it became evident that its rate changed with temperature. A clock with a brass pendulum rod will lose a quarter of a minute a day in the summer as compared with in winter. The substitution of a steel rod for the brass one will improve this situation and using a wooden rod will improve it yet again, provided the rod is well varnished to make it impervious to the effects of moisture.

However, for the finest clocks pendulums were produced that used the different expansions of two metals to offset one another. The downward expansion of one metal is offset by the upward expansion of another so that the bob is kept a constant distance from its point of suspension. Two radically different pendulums were developed at virtually the same time by George Graham and John Harrison on these lines. Graham's pendulum was of steel and mercury. The downward expansion of the steel is offset by the upward expansion of the mercury which in Graham's example was contained in a glass jar. Harrison's pendulum, known as the grid-iron and which was introduced in about 1729, consisted of five rods of iron and four of brass. In essence, however, there are three rods of iron to two of brass, the arrangement of the greater number merely being for symmetry. Since the ratio of the coefficients of linear expansion of iron to brass is 11:19, the lengths of the rods merely have to be in the inverse proportion to this to achieve equal expansions and thus compensation.

The whole subject of compensated pendulums is a large one and a whole collection could be based on the variations found. It is a specialist study and some idea of the examples met with can be found in the clock examples illustrated by recourse to the Index. Pendulum suspensions are dealt with in the sections on moving, installing and regulating clocks.

4 The Different Types of Clocks

The variety of clocks and watches developed throughout the centuries must be a source of perpetual interest to the collector, and a tremendous amount of enjoyment can be derived from reading about them and visiting exhibitions of them in museums. There follows a list of about seventy types of clock. This will possibly be of help when there is uncertainty about what sort of clock to collect, or indeed just what the choice is. Obviously not all types of clock are mentioned – this would require a book on its own! Further guidance can be obtained from specialist books which will be found mentioned in the list of Further Reading. Specific examples are to be found illustrated in the text and can be traced through the Index.

ACT OF PARLIAMENT CLOCK In 1797 a tax of 5s. (25p or 20 cents) a year was put on clocks. The Act prescribed that 'For and upon every clock or timekeeper, by whatever name the same shall be called, which be used for the purpose of a clock and placed in or upon any dwelling house, or any office or building thereunto belonging, or any other building whatever whether private or publick belonging to any persons, or company of persons, or any body corporate, or politick, or collegiate, or which shall be kept or used by any person or persons in Great Britain, there shall be charged an annual duty of Five Shillings.' The yield from the tax was disappointing and nearly ruined clockmakers. In less than a year demand for clocks had fallen by a half and thousands lost their jobs. In April 1798 the tax was repealed.

During the time the Act was in force the Tavern clock was one of the few that remained on public display for the benefit of customers and as a result became known as the Act of Parliament clock. It was of a recognisable design being a wall clock with a large dial of wood painted black with gilt figures, no glass, and a trunk long enough to allow for a seconds pendulum.

ALARM CLOCK A clock that has in addition to its other

mechanism a device, audible or visible, that can be let off at a predetermined time.

ALMANACK CLOCK Alternative name for calendar clock.

ASTRONOMICAL CLOCK This clock shows the motions of some of the heavenly bodies; it can also be a clock with its chapter ring divided into twenty-four hours to correspond with the astronomical day, and used in conjunction with an instrument for observing the transit time of a star. Ferguson's astronomical clock (*figs 1, 2*) has a dial made up of four pieces: 1. outer ring divided into the twenty-four hours of day and night, each hour divided by twelve, so that each subdivision represents five minutes; 2. age of the moon ring lying in the same plane as the hour ring, divided into 29·5 equal parts, and carrying a star to point out the time on the hour circle; wire A continued from the star supports the sun, S; 3. within the moon dial is one with the months and days of the year on the outer edge; further in, a circle with the signs and degrees of the ecliptic, and further in still the ecliptic, equinoctial and tropics are laid down as well as all the stars of the first, second and third magnitude, according to their right ascension and declination; first magnitude distinguished by eight points, second by six, and third by five; 4. at the centre a fixed plate, E, represents the earth around which the sun moves in 24 hrs, the moon arm in 24 hrs 50·5 min, and

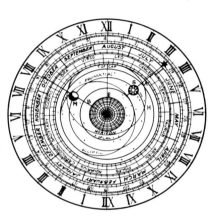

Figure 1

Figure 2

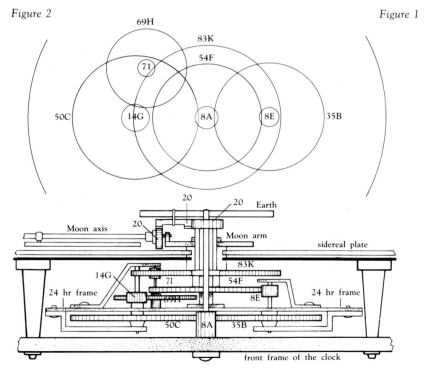

the stars in 23 hr 56 min 4·1 sec. The ellipse H is drawn with a diamond on the glass cover and represents the horizon of the place the clock serves; across this horizon a straight line even with the XIIs represents the meridian. All the stars within the ellipse are above the horizon at that time. The astronomical train (*fig. 2*) is between the front plate of the clock and the dial. The earth, E, is stationary and is supported by a stalk fixed to the front plate. The hollow axis of the frame that turns once in 24 hours works on this stalk; fixed to the stationary stalk is a pinion of eight leaves, A, which gears with a wheel of thirty-five teeth, B, and with a wheel of fifty teeth, C. On top of the axis of B a pinion of eight leaves, E, turns a wheel of fifty-four teeth, F, running on the pipe of the 24-hr frame and carrying the moon round by the wire, B, in *fig. 1*. This wire has a support fitted to the arbor of F. On top of the pipe of the 24-hr frame is a wheel of twenty teeth gearing with a wheel with the same number of teeth but with two sets, one on the edge and the other on the face; it is pivoted to the moon wire support and the face teeth gear with another wheel of twenty teeth that carries the moon wire. On the axis of C is a pinion of fourteen leaves, G, that turns a wheel of sixty-nine teeth, H, on whose axis is a pinion of seven, I, turning a wheel of eighty-three teeth, K. This is pinned to the sidereal plate of the dial. The age of the moon ring is attached by pillars to the 24-hr frame and turns with it; the moon is a round ball half black and half white.

ATMOS CLOCK A clock which is wound by changes in temperature. Early versions of this self-winding clock were wound by the changes that occurred in the atmospheric pressure, hence the name Atmos. In the later versions, wound by temperature changes, it is the movements of an aneroid box that wind a small mainspring. It is claimed that a change of 1°C is sufficient to keep the clock running for two days. The mechanism of the clock is similar to that of a 400-day clock. At one time everyone was seeking the answer to perpetual motion and clocks were made which pretended and sometimes even succeeded in realising this dream. A clock by James Cox now in the Victoria and Albert Museum was one answer to the problem. This used variations in the air pressure to wind the driving weight; it is shown in *fig. 3*.

AUTOMATON CLOCK Any clock with representations of man or beast of which any part moves is called an automaton clock.

BALL-CONTROLLED CLOCK A clock that has balls as its controlling element, such as the Congreve clock. Although Congreve

Figure 3

took out a patent on his ball-controlled clock, there was nothing new about using the rolling of balls down an incline as a time standard. What was different was that Congreve moved the incline so as to reverse the direction of the running of the ball at the end of each cycle.

BALL-DRIVEN CLOCK A clock that has as its motive power, balls. These usually act on the periphery of a wheel.

BINNACLE CLOCK A clock used at sea that shows the nautical watches. The minute hand goes around once every half-hour and the small hand three times a day.

BIRDCAGE CLOCK Singing bird in a cage with a clock housed in the base and its dial either underneath the cage or on the side of its base. When the clock dial is under the cage it must, of course, be hung up for the time to be seen. See p. 218.

BRACKET CLOCK From time to time one meets with a true bracket clock, that is, one that still has its matching bracket. These always command a higher price since they are unusual – most brackets having been separated from their clock and lost over the years. Brackets can be very useful to the collector who runs out of space for standing clocks. However, the illustration (fig. 4) shows what is usually, albeit incorrectly, called a bracket clock, for it is in fact more correctly described as a table clock.

Figure 4

CANDLE CLOCK An early method of time measurement when a candle was marked or notched so that the shortening of the candle was used as a measure of the passage of time. Sometimes pieces of metal were inserted into the candle so that when the wax holding one eventually melted, it fell with a clatter into the holder. Thus one had both a visual and an audible record. Even for moderate results the candle flame had to be shielded from draughts and the shield was sometimes made of horn. A type of alarm clock which had a candle was made in the sixteenth century. At a predetermined hour a spark was struck which lit tinder. This in turn set light to the wick of a candle that was lying horizontally. The candle then sprang upright and cast its light upon the clock.

CARRIAGE CLOCK The great Thomas Tompion was the first to produce what we now recognise as a carriage clock. It is always a portable clock, usually but not always in a metal case and balance-controlled. It can have any type of escapement. It can also have most of the complications associated with other clocks. Made in all sizes from miniature, about 1 in (2·5 cm) high, to giant, their variety is fully explored in Allix's book *Carriage Clocks*.

CARTEL CLOCK A clock that hangs on the wall. It refers to an

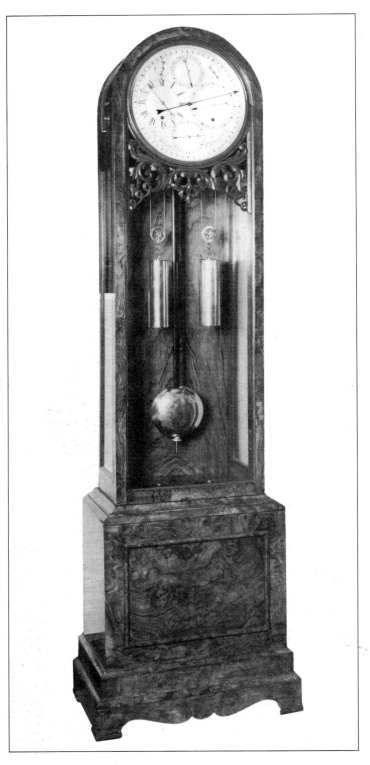

STRIKING LONG-CASE REGULATOR
BY THOMAS MORGAN OF
MANCHESTER, c. 1860

Walnut case, glazed sides and top.
Dial with centre seconds, and
subsidiaries for minutes, hours,
days of the week, date of the month,
months of the year and moon phases.
The illustration opposite (see also
jacket) shows what lies beneath the
dial of this clock when the dial is
removed. The clock also strikes the
hours. It has a wood-rod pendulum
with a brass-faced lead bob. When
a clock like this is cleaned, every part
must be removed for proper cleaning
to be carried out. This clock by
Thomas Morgan of Manchester
must be one of the most complex
of the regulator type of clock.
Height 6 ft 6 in (198 cm).

elongated style of case usually made of ormulu but it can be of wood, deeply carved and highly decorated. Although usually considered as a purely French clock, some English examples were in fact made.

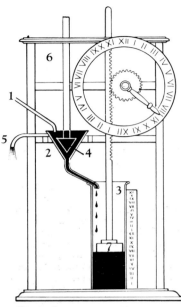

Figure 5

CHIMING CLOCK A clock which chimes on bells, tubes or gongs at the hours and quarters in addition to striking at each hour. See also STRIKING CLOCK, particularly the entry for *Ting-Tang striking*.

CLEPSYDRA A machine which indicates time by the passage of water. One form (*fig. 5*) in use in Egypt about 200 B.C. was quite sophisticated. A supply of water runs through the pipe, 1, into the cone, 2, and from there drops into the cylinder, 3. A conical stopper, 4, regulates the flow, and the superfluous water escapes by the waste pipe, 5. The Egyptians, as did other people of the time, divided the period from sunrise to sunset into twelve equal hours, so that the conical stopper had to be adjusted each day; and marks for every day in the year and for the latitude of the place were cut on the stalk, 6, as a guide to the position of the stopper. A floating piston, 7, terminating in a rack actuates a pinion, to the arbor of which an hour hand is fixed. See also WATER CLOCK.

CLOCK Early clocks did not show the time but gave audible evidence of its passing by striking a bell. Hence the name, which is derived from the Latin for a bell, *clocca*. Today the term is widely used for all timekeepers that are not watches or marine chronometers.

COLUMN CLOCK A clock and pedestal combined. Usually French, but Vulliamy did make some examples.

COMTÉ OR COMTOISE CLOCK A French clock usually made in the town of Morbier. It is the French equivalent of the English long-case clock and has a special form of rack-striking work. See also MORBIER CLOCK.

CONICAL PENDULUM CLOCK. This clock has a pendulum whose bob describes the path of a circle. This type of pendulum is mostly used for the equatorial clocks where continuous motion is required. The pendulum makes one revolution in the same time as an oscillating pendulum, whose length is equal to the vertical height of a conical pendulum, describes two beats. As impulse is increased the conical pendulum describes a larger circle and hence the periodic time is shortened. There is no escapement. Instead the train terminates in a wheel with an attached finger. This touches the pendulum. There is sometimes a further extension to the pendulum which terminates in a paddle. This dips into a vessel containing glycerine or some other damping fluid. As the impulse and the arc described by the pendulum increase, the paddle dips deeper and, damping the motion, returns the pendulum to its normal and desired revolution.

MUSICAL CLOCK BY RIVERS AND SON, LONDON, c. 1800

Break-arch mahogany case with brass inlaid canted corners, ball finials and ogee bracket feet, concave-sided cresting with blind fret. Arch-top dial of silvered brass. Within the main dial is inscribed *Successors to Daniel St Leu Watchmaker to Her Majesty*, in the arch of the dial *Rivers and Son Cornhill London*. Two subsidiary dials, on the left the date and on the right the tune selector. Just above XII the not chime/chime aperture. The triple-fusee movement similarly signed and also numbered 1013, the plates with engraved borders, playing on a carillon of ten bells. Anchor escapement. Rivers and Son were in Cornhill from 1790 to 1812. They succeeded D. St Leu. Height 2 ft (61 cm).

CRUCIFIX CLOCK. A clock in the form of a crucifix. Often with a revolving globe with chapter ring. Usually German.

CUCKOO CLOCK Notwithstanding Orson Welles's famous remark that centuries of peace in Switzerland resulted only in the production of the cuckoo clock, this was in fact invented in

1740 by Anton Ketterer of Schönwald in the Black Forest, Germany. It is usually housed in an elaborately carved case, and pendulum-controlled; on the hour and the half-hour a cuckoo springs out of a little door and calls the appropriate number of times. The call is simulated by two pipes actuated by bellows. Many versions also strike on a conventional wire gong.

CUCKOO QUAIL CLOCK. A cuckoo clock with an extra; the quarters are sounded on another set of pipes imitating the cry of the quail.

DECIMAL CLOCK. The dial is divided into ten hours and each hour is divided again into ten, the minutes are each divided into 100 seconds and the day thus has 100,000 seconds instead of the normal 86,400.

HENRY DE VIC'S CLOCK About 1370 Henry de Vic made for Charles V of France a tower clock, one of the first of which there is reliable record; it had iron frames and wheels and was situated in Paris at the Palais de Justice. Vic is by Château-Salins in Lorraine. The front and side views of de Vic's clock are shown in *fig. 6*. The clock is no longer in existence.

1. verge
2. foliot
3. weights for adjusting the clock
4. pinion for driving hour wheel
5. hour wheel, the arbor of which carries the hand
6. barrel
7. frame
8. ratchet and click

Figure 6

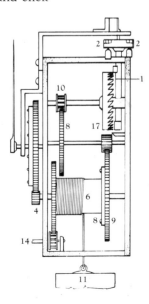

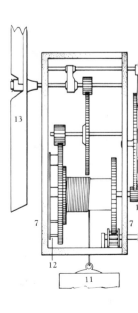

9. great wheel
10. escape pinion
11. weights
12. pins for raising the hammer tail
13. fly
14. pinion for driving count wheel
15. count wheel
16. lever for letting off striking work
17. crown wheel

DIGITAL CLOCK A digital clock shows the time in digits.

EQUATION CLOCK A clock that registers the equation of time.

FOUR-GLASS CLOCK A clock glazed all round like a large carriage clock but pendulum-controlled.

FOUR-HUNDRED-DAY CLOCK As opposed to a year clock this term is specifically used to denote the type of spring-driven clock with a torsion pendulum. It is also known as an anniversary clock. This variety of clock has a sufficiently long history for the early examples to be collectors' items.

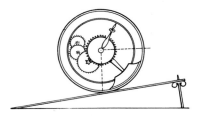

GLOBE CLOCK See WORLD-TIME CLOCK.

GRAND-DAUGHTER CLOCK A smaller version of a grandmother clock, from 3ft 6 in (1m) to 4 ft 6 in (1·4m) high.

Figure 7

GRANDFATHER CLOCK A long-case clock 6ft 6in (2m) high, or more. Associated with the domestic clock that strikes, as opposed to a regulator or to an astronomical clock of the long-case type.

GRANDMOTHER CLOCK A small edition of the grandfather, between 5 ft 6 in (1·7m) and 6 ft 6 in (2m) tall. Grandmother clocks by old masters are rare.

GRANDE SONNERIE Where both the hour and the quarters are struck at every quarter.

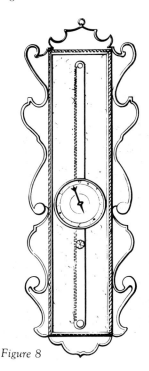

GRAVITY CLOCK A clock where the motive force is the weight of the clock itself. One such is the inclined-plane clock (*fig. 7*). Another is the hanging-ball clock, and a third type runs down a rack and a pinion which transmits power to the gear train (*fig. 8*). Raising the clock is equivalent to rewinding. *Figs 9, 10* show modern versions of the inclined-plane clock. (*Fig. 9* shows a clock designed and made by Richard Good.) Within the inclined-plane clock is a weight which constantly seeks the lowest point. This provides the motive power for the train. When the clock reaches the end of the inclined plane, it has to be replaced at the upper end. Some types run for 30 hours, some for a week. If the clock runs for a week, it is usual to have

Figure 8

Figure 9

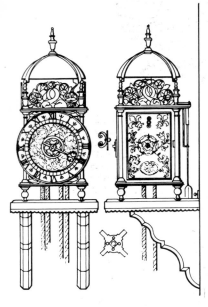

Figure 10

the days of the week marked along the edge of the plane. This type of clock was first made about 1600.

LAMP CLOCK. See OIL CLOCK.

LANTERN CLOCK This was almost the standard domestic weight-driven clock in England in the seventeenth century and the first half of the eighteenth. It is closely related to the Gothic wall clock, enclosed with brass panels and doors (*fig. 11*).

LIGHTHOUSE CLOCK A clock in the form of a lighthouse with the clock underneath the lamp. A glass cylinder rotates to simulate the flashing of the light.

LONG-CASE CLOCK This is one of the most popular types of clock with collectors. It is known as the grandfather clock to the public, but this is a term seldom used between *aficionados*. The most popular height is about 6 ft 6 in (2 m), for a niche can be found for such a clock in almost any home. For equivalent clocks any increase in height above this will be accompanied by a decrease in value. London clocks will in general command more than country clocks, although there are notable exceptions to this rule. Oak-cased clocks are not as well thought of as veneered clocks, although the veneer is usually on an oak carcase. Walnut clock cases are usually early and should be looked at carefully for woodworm; walnut is particularly vulnerable. Mahogany with its rich and pleasant colour is desirable and in particular is tolerant of bad environmental conditions. Marquetry cases are always expensive, are especially vulnerable and costly to restore.

Figure 11

One might be forgiven for thinking that this clock is French but Vulliamy had a successful business which covered all aspects of the clockmaker's art. The quality of his cast work was superb. (A chandelier made by him in the early nineteenth century cost £1,000.) The high position of the winding arbors reveals that the movement has fusees. The arbor in the centre of XII shows the presence of a rise-and-fall mechanism. The drum case is surmounted by a bronze cherub framed by sprays of flowers and leaves and supported on the back of a bronze elephant, his head turned and trunk upraised on a beaded rectangular gilt-metal base.

The dial is of enamel and is 6 in (15.2 cm) in diameter. The pierced gilt hands are in the French style. The back plate is signed *Vulliamy London no 281.* At one time in the collection of the 4th Baron Wrottesley. Height 1 ft 7½ in (49.5 cm).

89

LYRE CLOCK A specifically French clock. The pendulum bob is in the form of a circle of paste stones which surrounds the dial. The pendulum is supported at the top of the lyre-shaped surround to which the drum case of the clock is fixed. The basic material is marble and has ormulu decoration.

MAGIC LANTERN CLOCK A type of NIGHT CLOCK in which an image of the dial and hands is projected on the wall or ceiling. A large version was once made which employed a searchlight to project the time on to the clouds.

MAGNETIC CLOCK A loose term for a clock with a magnetic escapement. This escapement is frictionless. There is no coupling between pallets and escape wheel other than magnetic forces. Invented by C. F. Clifford of Bath.

MARINE CHRONOMETER This is not strictly speaking a clock, but neither of course is it a watch. The mechanism is housed in a brass bowl with a screwed bezel which is glazed. This brass bowl is 'gymballed' in a wooden box; the gymbals allow the bowl to remain horizontal regardless of the attitude of the wooden box, being a sort of universal joint. Gymbals were first invented by Girolamo Cardano (1501–76) to suspend oil lamps at sea.

MORBIER CLOCK A type of clock made towards the end of the eighteenth century in the Morbier district of France. Early examples have a primitive look, with a frame of iron bars like the old LANTERN CLOCK. The verge escapement is inverted, with the teeth pointing down, and is worked with a seconds

LATE VICTORIAN WEIGHT-DRIVEN LONG-CASE CHIMING CLOCK WITH CARVED MAHOGANY CASE, ANON., c. 1900.

Although the dial is perhaps a trifle florid for some tastes this clock is of high quality. It chimes on eight tubular gongs which date it after the last quarter of the nineteenth century. In the photograph can be seen the cast frame that supports these gongs. The frame sits on top of the plates and is retained by two bolts that screw into the top pillars. This frame also supports the hour gong which is on the extreme left of the clock viewed from the front. Two brackets on the movement back plate support the pin barrel and hammer block. The pin barrel is shifted along to change from Westminster chimes to Whittington or St Michael. Clocks that give these three different chimes are unusual.

The pendulum is supported by the double bracket with vees and the crutch provided with a beat-setting arrangement. The pallets are most unusual, being built up from two plates with the acting part, the nibs, sandwiched between them. The temperature-compensated pendulum is the wood-rod/lead-bob combination. The dial is decorated with high-quality pierced and engraved spandrels and is heavily engraved in the centre. The chapter ring has raised Arabic numerals. The case (not shown) is glazed at the sides both on the hood and the trunk, and the plinth is panelled. Ball and claw feet carved mouldings and carving on the break-arch hood put the finishing touches to a high-quality Victorian product. Height 7 ft (213.4 cm).

pendulum or longer. The rack unusually, is straight and vertical, and a further peculiarity is that after the hours have been struck they are repeated two minutes later. The half-hours are also struck. These are known as Comtoise clocks, from France-Comté, in which Morbier is situated; or Comté, literally county clocks. The long violin-shaped cases were often made of white wood and grained by painting. The pendulum, also often violin-shaped, was made of embossed sheet iron and elaborately coloured.

SILVER CARRIAGE CLOCK BY SPINK AND SON LTD, LONDON, HALL-MARKED 1904

Clocks in hall-marked precious metal cases are uncommon – when they occur it gives an opportunity, only too rare, to date the clock exactly. Without this assistance it would have proved difficult to date this clock with any degree of accuracy for it has no recognisable style. Height 10¼ in (26 cm).

MYSTERY CLOCK Mystery clocks have been made for many centuries. The object is always to show the time or to provide motive power in a way that cannot be readily understood. The mystery lady clock is one of the better known of this type. The statue holds in its extended hand a pendulum which oscillates for no apparent reason. The impulses to the pendulum are in fact provided by a tiny and sympathetic movement of the statue – a motion so minute that it cannot readily be discerned. Another mystery clock has hands that revolve for no apparent reason. Here the hands are mounted on glass plates which have gearing on their edges. These edges are hidden in the mounting.

Yet another type has a hand freely pivoted in front of or between plates, or on a support. The hand rotates in 12 or 24 hours and one end indicates the hours. It is not fixed and can be swung, whereupon it will oscillate until it finally comes to rest, still showing the correct time! A weight is carried by the hour wheel of a watch hidden in one end of the hand and as this moves it causes the centre of gravity of the whole hand to shift uniformly. Thus the hand revolves in time with the weight. Two modern clocks based on this ingenious invention have been produced by the author. A further type has a pendulum bob that is itself the movement. The movement has an oscillating weight that, driven by the escapement, impulses the pendulum sympathetically by altering its effective centre of gravity at each swing.

The tortoise clock is another type of mystery clock: a tortoise floats in a dish of water and moves around its edge once in 12 hours thus indicating the hours. This clock would not, of course, be very mysterious to the people of today who would be only too ready to suspect the presence of the magnet beneath the bowl.

NEF CLOCK A clock in the form of a ship.

NIGHT CLOCK A clock which shows the time in the dark. Early night clocks had an oil lamp whose light showed through pierced numerals. Many of these clocks caught fire. Pepys recorded one in the Queen's chamber (24 June 1664): 'After dinner to White Hall and there met with Mr. Pierce and he showed me the Queen's bedchamber where she had ... with her clock at her bedside wherein a lamp burned that tells her the time of the night at any time.'

OIL CLOCK This clock is similar in principle to the CANDLE CLOCK, but the passage of time is shown by the rate of consumption of oil in the lamp (fig. 12).

ORRERY This is a mechanical device for portraying the relative motions of the sun, moon, earth, and possibly other planets. It

Figure 12

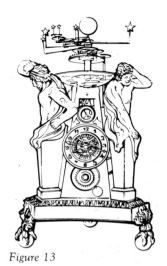

Figure 13

QUARTER-CHIMING BRACKET CLOCK
BY THOMAS GARDNER, LONDON,
c. 1700

An ebonised case with bell top,
caryatids, pine-cone finials, leaf-
scroll feet and break-arch top to the
dial. In the arch a strike/silent dial.
The case also inlaid with gilt-metal
bandings. The dial with maker's
name Thos Gardner on an applied
plaque, above the centre a false
pendulum aperture and below a
calendar aperture. Rococo spandrels.
The three-train fusee movement
chiming on eight bells, the back plate
engraved with foliate scrolls. Despite
the fact that the false bob is still
present, the escapement has been
altered from verge to anchor. With
the clock going, the reduced angle
of swing of the false bob would
disclose the alteration to the
escapement even without looking
inside the clock. Thomas Gardner
was in the Clockmakers Company
from 1689 to 1724.
Height 1 ft 8 in (51 cm).

is operated by hand or by clockwork (e.g. *fig. 13*). The first
orrery is thought to have been by Tompion and Graham, c.
1710, and subsequently seen and copied by John Rowley in
1716; it passed into the possession of Charles, 4th Earl of
Orrery, after whom the instrument was named. Rowley's
orrery was restored in 1937 and is now in the Maritime
Museum at Greenwich.

PICTURE CLOCK A clock in the form of a picture with the dial
part of the detail such as in the tower of a church.

QUARTER CLOCK OR CHIME A clock that strikes or chimes at the
quarter hours. When a clock is said to chime or to be a chiming
clock, it is generally understood that it chimes at the quarters
(see STRIKING CLOCK).

REGULATOR A precision clock with compensated pendulum.

REMONTOIRE CLOCK Even if a clock is weight-driven, and thus
supplied with an almost perfectly uniform power supply, there
will not be a similarly constant supply of power at the
escapement. This is because of the inevitable shortcomings of
the train of gears that lies between the power source and the
escapement. Even gears made as perfectly as can be using the
most sophisticated of modern-day methods cannot by their
very nature give perfectly uniform transmission of power. The
fundamental reason for this lies in the fact that the perfect
transmission can take place only on the line of centres of the
pairs of gears, but the whole topic is really too complex to
tackle here.

The first clock that is known to have contained a remontoire
was designed by Jost Burgi in about 1695. Not many were made
from the first until the time of the development of Mudge's
constant force escapement, when the remontoire was finally to
move to the last wheel of the train and therefore operated at
every beat of the balance. The surviving examples are so few
that any that turn up are almost sure to end up in a museum and
it is only nineteenth-century examples that are likely to become
available to collectors.

You will often read that constant force escapements were a
blind alley, and because of their complexity were ultimately
discarded. Although this may be true for the vast majority of
horological products, in fact the finest and most precise of
timekeepers, those that set the standard, were all ultimately to
contain some type of constant force escapement, that is, until
the advent of the quartz crystal as the new frequency-con-
troller. Quite apart from this, however, watching a constant
force escapement in action can be a fascinating experience and
understanding it a stimulating mental exercise. An elegant and
fine example in the British Museum is one by Edward Funnel of

Brighton. This is typical of the most eagerly sought-after examples of nineteenth-century work which are now beginning to be hard to find.

SEDAN CLOCK A small hanging clock associated with the period of the sedan chair, although there is no evidence that it was ever used in one. It measures about 6 in (15 cm) across and is fitted with 30-hour verge watch movements.

SELF-WINDING CLOCK In 1751 Le Plat of Paris made a clock that was wound by changes in atmospheric pressure; Lepaute published designs for a similar clock in 1755; and in 1765 James Cox made another clock (fig. 14) which was wound in the same way. His was the first to be wholly successful. Changes in temperature were also used to wind clocks, but Cox employed mercury as the moving force which, under the influence of the rise and fall of atmospheric pressure, operated rocking arms which wound up a weight. Whole series of attempts on similar lines were tried in the nineteenth century but they were mostly unsuccessful. However in the first half of the century one remarkable clock was produced, namely the hydrogen clock of Pasquale Andevalt of Trieste. In this, hydrogen gas is generated by the action of diluted sulphuric acid on zinc pellets. These are

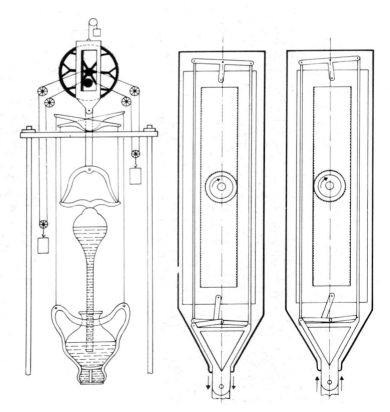

Figure 14

allowed to drop into the acid container at controlled intervals. The gas pressure so generated forces up a rod which carries around a large wheel. On this wheel runs a cord which carries the remontoire weight. The clock is pendulum-controlled; it is to be seen at the Guildhall, London, in the collection of the Worshipful Company of Clockmakers.

TWO ENGLISH DIAL CLOCKS, c.1830, BY BENJAMIN LEWIS VULLIAMY, LONDON

Both of these clocks have a dial 12 in (30.5 cm) in diameter, and the Royal monogram of George IV. That on the left is numbered 1071. The movement also signed as the dial. The escapement half dead-beat.

Height of the plain rectangular drop case 3 ft 1 in (94 cm).

The clock on the right is also marked on the dial *Poor Law Commission*. Height of shorter drop case 2 ft (61 cm).

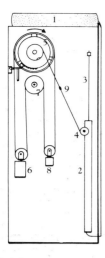

Figure 15

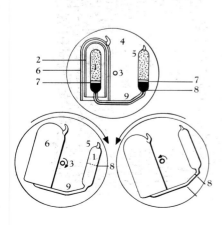

Figure 16

Horstmann's self-winding clock, by Gustave Horstmann of Bath, is wound by the expansion and contraction of a liquid consequent upon changes in temperature (*fig. 15*). A strong metal vessel, 1, is filled with an easily expanding fluid, e.g. benzoline, mineral naphtha, etc. A cylinder, 2, and a piston, 3, are connected to the vessel by a strong tube with a very small bore. As most expanding fluids are incapable of driving a piston because they are too volatile and thin, the cylinder and tube are charged with a thicker and more oily fluid, e.g. glycerine. The vessel containing the expanding fluid is higher than the piston and cylinder to prevent them mixing, as benzoline is lighter than glycerine and therefore rises to the top. It is easy to see that when the temperature rises, the expanding liquid will force the piston upward. The piston will fall on the temperature lowering. The piston terminates in a cross-bar, at each end of which is attached a steel ribbon like a wide watch mainspring. These two bands are brought down over pulleys at 4, fixed on each side of the cylinder, and then carried direct to the winding mechanism, 5, which is all fixed to the back of the case and independent of the movement. The two bands join into one a little before they reach the winding. A large pulley, 5, is fitted on a stud at the back of the case, and is driven by means of a ratchet and click. The pulley, 5, has a flat groove, and is studded with short pins at equal distances apart, over which works a long steel ribbon perforated with oblong holes. This 'chain' passes down through the weight pulley, 6, which also has a flat groove, but no pins, and is carried over the main wheel pulley, 7, which is supplied with pins, the same as the winding pulley. It then passes under the pulley of the counterweight, 8, and is joined to its other end, thus forming an endless chain. As the piston falls, a coiled spring causes the smaller pulley at the top of the case to turn independently of 5; and to coil the band, 9, on to itself, ready for the next rise of temperature.

In 1913 J. E. Reuter, a Paris engineer, again revived the idea of a perpetual clock and produced many experimental models based on the expansion of liquids and gases, which were successful but not suitable for commercial use. At last, in 1926 the first commercial self-winding clock was produced, the Atmos, which has a torsion pendulum of the 400-day clock type and a special lever escapement. The power in this first model is derived from changes in temperature which act on a tube of mercury to upset the equilibrium of a drum (*fig.16*) pivoted about the point, 3. A glass U tube, 9, contains mercury, 8, and a liquefied gas, 7, as well as its saturated vapour, 1. One of the branches of the U tube is shielded by insulating material and an open-ended vacuum flask. This part will respond very slowly to changes in temperature. The other end is left exposed and therefore responds quickly to changes in temperature. This

Left

SWISS GRAND-SONNERIE STRIKING
AND REPEATING CARRIAGE CLOCK
FOR THE TURKISH MARKET BY ROBERT
OF GENEVA, c. 1830

Highly decorated cast and gilded
case with entrelac, berried laurel
and foliate scroll decoration. Doors
at both front and rear and foliate
handle. The enamelled dials set
behind are engine-turned, gilt mask
also with foliate scrolls and musical
and military trophies. The numerals
are of the type often referred to as
Turkish but are in fact Islamic. The
upper dial gives the time of day, the
subsidiary dial on the left is an alarm
dial and that on the right gives the
date of the month. The date-of-the-
month dial differs from normal,
having 30 divisions instead of 31.
The Islamic year is divided into
months alternating between 29 and
30. Manual correction of the date
is thus needed every other month.

Striking and repeating on two bells
in the base. On the back plate is a
three-position lever for grand

sonnerie, petite sonnerie, and silent.
The mechanism with striking and
going train and a platform with lever
escapement.
Height 6¾ in (17 cm).

Centre

AN ENGLISH CHRONOMETER STRIKING
AND REPEATING CARRIAGE CLOCK
BY J. AND A. JUMP, LONDON, NO. 172,
c. 1870

Modified corniche type case of gilded
brass finely engraved all over.
Reeded-and-scroll handle. Engraved
rear panel with winding/setting
shutters. Enamel dial with gilt engine-
turned mask and bevelled surround,
the dial inscribed *J & A Jump no 1A
Old Bond St. London 172*. Chain-fusee
movement similarly inscribed to
dial with spotted platform with
Earnshaw spring detent escapement.
Compensated balance with blued
steel helical balance spring with
terminal curves. The clock strikes
and repeats on a gong mounted on
the back plate and there is a strike/
silent lever.
Height 6½ in (16.5 cm).

Right

FRENCH REPEATING PETITE-SONNERIE
CARRIAGE CLOCK BY MANGAINE
OF PARIS BUT SIGNED *EXAMINED BY
DENT . . . LONDON*, c.1875

Gilt brass gorgé case with leather
travelling case. Enamel dial inscribed
*Examined by Dent 33 Cockspur St
London*. The movement stamped
AM and CV. AM the mark of
Mangaine of Paris, a celebrated Paris
maker of carriage clocks, and CV
the mark of Charles Voisin.
Platform with lever escapement and
compensated balance. Going barrels
and the strike on two gongs on the
back plate. A selection lever in the
base for silent or petite sonnerie
(where ting-tang quarters are struck
but only the hour at the hour).

Even a firm like Dent was not
averse to importing from abroad.
However, the term 'examined by
Dent' means just what it says; nothing
would have left their premises
without their being certain it was
perfect.
Height 6¼ in (16 cm).

Below

NIGHT TIMEPIECE BY J. W. BENSON, LONDON, *c.* 1890

Gilt-bronze case with double-arch top, moulded base and bun feet. Glass dial with fretted mask and chapter ring and a crown above the chapter ring and monogram beneath. Behind the mechanism a space for a lamp. In a leather-covered travelling case with impressed inscription *J. W. Benson.*
Height 7½ in (19 cm).

Opposite

QUARTER-STRIKING SKELETON CLOCK BY JAMES CONDLIFF, LIVERPOOL, *c.* 1860

Scrolled plate design with six pillars screwed at both ends. Glass dial marked I-XII and 13–24. The hands are difficult to see in the illustration but are skeletonised spade – the centre seconds hand also. The intermediate brass base with ball feet carries a plaque inscribed *James Condliff LIVERPOOL.* Twin chain fusees with pierced barrels revealing the mainsprings. Both fusees with maintaining power. Three gongs are in the moulded walnut base which has gadrooned feet. A lever escapement maintains a compensation balance, which has a helical spring. Another clock by Condliff is in the Liverpool City Museum dated 1862.
Height 1 ft 10 in (56 cm).

EPICYCLIC SKELETON CLOCK AFTER
WILLIAM STRUTT OF BELPER,
DERBYSHIRE

Heavy brass scrolling H frame 8 in
(20.3 cm) in height, with pierced
chapter ring on heavy chamfered
oval base with decorated ball feet.
Sun-and-planet (epicyclic) gears
rotating behind the dial. The
epicyclic or sun-and-planet gearing
serves the dual purpose of gearing
up the escape wheel and at the same
time gearing down the hour wheel
in a most ingenious manner without
the need for the usual motion work.

The centre arbor is driven as is
usual by the fusee (fixed to the frame
is the sun wheel) and carries freely
a large ring with both internal and
external teeth. Pinned to the centre
arbor rigidly is an arm which carries
an integral wheel and pinion, this
being counterpoised. The pinion
has 8 leaves and meshes with and rolls
around the central sun wheel of 66
teeth; the wheel on the driving arm,
which has 68 teeth, meshes with the
144 inner teeth on the large ring, the
resultant ratio being 4.9 to 1. The
outer teeth of the ring are 168 in
number and drive the escape pinion
of 6 leaves, the escape wheel having
36 teeth. The pendulum therefore
makes 164.64 vibrations a minute,
having an effective length of 5.2 in
(13.2 cm).

The minute hand is a sliding fit on
the end of the centre arbor. The
gearing down of the hour hand is
done as follows. Behind the central
sun wheel of 66 and concentric with
it is the hour wheel of the same
diameter but with 72 teeth, this being
free to revolve. The pinion on the
driving arm engages both the fixed
sun wheel and the movable hour
wheel such that the hour wheel is
impelled to move forward six
additional teeth at each revolution
of the arm, i.e. every hour. Since six
teeth is $\frac{1}{12}$ of 72, the hour wheel will
thus revolve every 12 hours.

William Strutt lived from 1756
to 1830 and although not a
clockmaker was nevertheless a
prolific inventor who was able to
produce this elegant and ingenious
clock. It is said that only twenty of
these clocks were made in his lifetime
although many others were to be
marketed later by D. Bagshaw of
London. Strutt was elected a Fellow
of the Royal Society in 1818. The
firm of Dent of London recently
made a hundred of these clocks as
a limited edition.

INCLINED-PLANE CLOCK DESIGNED
BY THE AUTHOR AND MADE BY THE
AUTHOR AND HIS SON, 1972

Plane of solid mahogany with
polished and lacquered brass scroll
pieces, ball feet for levelling. The
scrollwork can be completely
dismantled to facilitate refinishing.
The drum clock takes a week to go
from top to bottom of the plane, its
position against the silvered day strip
giving the day of the week. On
Sunday, on reaching the bottom
of the plane, the clock is lifted back
to the top of the plane.

The mechanism is driven by a
heavy semicylindrical weight. As
the weight of the whole clock urges
it down the plane it lifts this weight
until the clock can roll no further.
The weight is connected to the first
gear in the gear train and can rotate

as it urges the gear train forward and
thus provides the motive power to
the platform escapement. However,
as the weight rotates the clock
progresses down the plane so as to
restore the weight to its original
position. All pinions are of hardened,
tempered and polished steel. The
platform with lever escapement and
the balance temperature
compensated.

The dial plate inscribed *R Good
and Son Seaford*, the chapter ring
silvered and engraved. The dial is
fixed direct to the mechanism and
remains upright as the clock
progresses down the plane. This
clock is a hand-made prototype. Fifty
more were made by the author for
Thwaites and Reed Ltd. They were
sold in the USA.
Length of clock 2 ft 4 in (71 cm).
Diameter of case $4\frac{3}{4}$ in (12 cm).

difference in temperature at the two ends of the tube produces
differences in pressure between the ends. This in turn forces the
mercury along the U tube in one direction or the other and
results in a turning force thus tending to rotate the drum which
then winds the small mainspring that powers the clock. A later
Atmos clock still employing torsion pendulum and a lever
escapement has, effectively, an aneroid drum to provide the
power; the drum is filled with ethyl chloride, C_2H_5Cl, which
has a vapour pressure approximately equal to the atmosphere

A TRIPLE TOURBILLON CARRIAGE
TIMEPIECE DESIGNED BY THE AUTHOR
AND MADE BY HIM AND HIS SON, 1979

Figure I

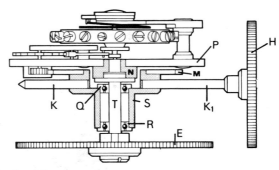

Polished and gilded brass case with
doors back and front. Pillars
engraved with key pattern, large
round glass on top for viewing
tourbillon carriage. Gilded brass
dial plate engraved *No 1 Triple*
Tourbillon R Good and Son Seaford.
Silvered brass chapter ring
incorporating both the main and
the large intersecting seconds dial.
Engraving by Christopher Elton,
Clerkenwell. Blued steel spade hands.

Eight-day movement with all brass
parts gilded. The six main pillars with
polished facets. Going barrel with
twelve days reserve of going and
unbreakable spring. All pivots, apart
from those for the barrel and one
in the carriage, are in ball bearings.
All wheels and pinions separately
mounted on their arbors. Tourbillon
carriage rotating in all three planes,
the first ever to be made. Constant

(continued on p. 107)

Key to Figs I and II

A = Main carriage support bearing
in plate.
B = Train wheel driving complete
assembly.
C = Main plate.
Cl = Main plate.
D = Bearing in small contrate F.
E = Gear rotating arbor T which
carries platform P.
F = Small contrate.
G = Ring support.
H = Centre assembly driving wheel.
J = Large contrate.
K = Support arbor (cone bearing
end).

Kl = Support arbor (plain bearing
end).
L = Main carriage support bearing
in large contrate.
M = Fixed fourth wheel.
N = Platform and arbor linking
piece.
P = Escapement platform.
Q = Top arbor bearing.
R = Bottom arbor bearing.
S = Centre assembly support piece.
T = Platform arbor.
U = Piece carrying arbor bearing.
V = Spacing sleeve.

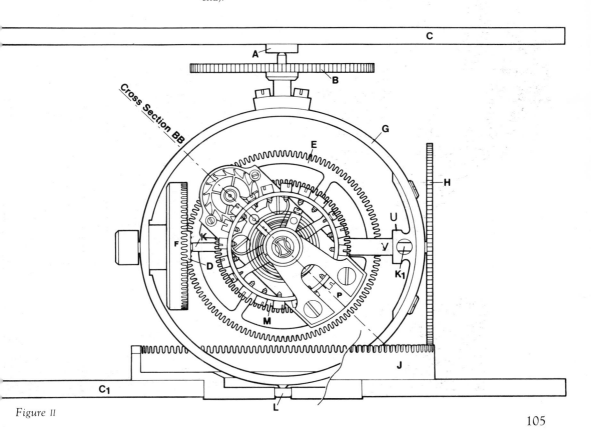

Figure II

force escapement of the Portescap type. The carriage rotates in 40 seconds in one plane and in a minute in each of the other two planes.

This is one of a family of three clocks, the first with tourbillon rotating in two planes, the second, this clock, and the third, another triple tourbillon cased as a marine chronometer. This last clock was commissioned by and made for the Time Museum, Rockford, Illinois, USA.

The triple tourbillon carriage is shown in the photographs. A section of the centre assembly is shown in *fig. I* and a plan of the complete carriage in *fig. II*. The explanation of its action is as follows:

Ring G is integral with the last gear B of the main train and carries all of the carriage parts. It is supported by cone pivots running in ball races at A and L.

As it rotates, gear H is caused to turn since it is in mesh with the fixed large contrate wheel J. Gear H is integral with arbor, KK1. This arbor carries support piece, S, and runs

in a cone race at one end and a ball race at the other. Gear E is mounted on arbor T, which rotates in ball bearings mounted in support piece, S. Arbor T also carries piece N, on which is mounted the platform, P, that carries the escapement and balance.

Rotating the arbor T causes the escape pinion to run around the 'fixed' gear M, which is mounted on support piece S. As gear H is caused to rotate, gear E also rotates because it is in mesh with 'fixed' small contrate F, this being mounted on ring G. This then causes the platform P to rotate and thus the escape pinion.

The escape pinion is not, however, rigidly fixed to the escape wheel because of the constant force device at the escapement, this being of the well-tried and tested type made by Portescap SA, of Switzerland.

There are then three 'fixed' wheels associated with the carriage, J, F and M, which cause a rotation of the platform P in all three panes, each at right angles to the other (*fig. III*).

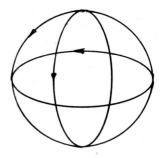

Figure III

when the temperature is 12°C (54°F). The sealed drum also contains a strong spring which tends to push the drum back outwards. A rise in temperature reacts on the bellows of the drum and presses the end inwards; and a fall in temperature presses it outwards. A lighter coiled spring is fixed to the drum at its opposite side, to the back, and a chain is attached by a plate to its free end. This chain operates on the mainspring-winding mechanism and it is the action of the lighter coiled spring expanding in low temperatures that winds the mainspring. A 1°C variation in temperature will wind the clock for 48 hours' going, while the reserve in the mainspring is enough to keep it going for 100 days even if no change in temperature occurs. The lighter coiled spring is just too weak to wind the mainspring fully so there is no danger of overwinding and no need for any slipping attachment. If the point of equilibrium is reached the bellows will move with no result until the clock has run down a little.

SHIP'S CLOCK Although this is known as a ship's clock, it is really a timepiece since it does not strike. It is normally housed in a strong brass case with a thick glass, wound from the front, and has a platform escapement.

SKELETON CLOCK This type of clock can be easily recognised because the mechanism has no case in the accepted sense, being protected instead by a glazed cover or a dome, with the plates that support and contain the wheels, levers, etc. being skeleton-ised to make the parts even more visible.

At the beginning of the sixteenth century many early Gothic iron domestic clocks were of a 'skeleton' nature, but this was mainly due to the scarcity of metals and the methods of construction used. Technically, they have never been known as skeleton clocks, which is a term applied to a later type of timepiece, and skeleton clocks were mainly products of the nineteenth century. However, there had been a number of notable forerunners, which is usual in horology where little appears suddenly on the scene without precedents of some sort. There is one just such example, made about 1780, which must be one of the few skeleton clocks with a verge escapement. It has cylindrical dials of enamel which rotate against a fixed indicator to show the time.

However interesting they may have been, skeleton clocks contributed nothing to the art of good timekeeping. Neverthe-less, they presented an irresistible opportunity for the crafts-man to show off his skill and workmanship, and for the owner with a mechanical turn of mind to enjoy them. From about 1750 French masters such as Pierre Le Roy, Jean André Lepaute, Ferdinand Berthoud and Jean Antoine Lepine produced clocks with movements that could be fully viewed, although they did not fulfil all the requirements that would normally lead them to be described as skeleton in type.

It should be noted that all types of escapement are encoun-tered acting with pendulums or balances. It should also be said that the French makers remained true to their tradition as regards the appearance of their skeleton clocks, for they concentrated on the artistic development of the frames, employing the finest artists and sculptors in their manufacture. This, however, limited their production and later in the nineteenth century the English came to dominate the skeleton-clock field. It was the fashion to make the plates of many models in the form of a well-known church or cathedral, St Paul's, Lichfield and York Minster being especially popular.

A most impressive type of skeleton clock was one built on glass plate which one must confess has maximum visibility for the 'works' of the clock. There is a very large great wheel of 320 teeth with fancy crossings. The barrel is small compared to this wheel. Behind the barrel is the pendulum bob. The pendulum is 11 in (27·9 cm) effective length, the bob weighs $2\frac{3}{4}$ lb (1·25 kg). The escapement is the pin-wheel type of dead-beat escapement with 64 pins although it is only $1\frac{5}{8}$ in (41 mm) in diameter! There are only two wheels and two pinions in the train.

There is another clock of this type in the Musée des Arts et Métiers in Paris (fig. 17).

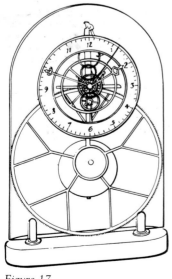

Figure 17

YEAR-GOING TIMEPIECE BY
FERDINAND BERTHOUD, PARIS (1727–
1807), c. 1795

This skeleton-type timepiece is
spring-driven and goes for one year.
It has a pin-wheel escapement
(probably invented about 1741 by
Louis Amant (*maître horloger* in
1725). Above the XII on the dial,
which is surrounded by a bezel
chased with a leaf and rope pattern,
is inscribed *Ferninand Berthoud*. The
movement is inscribed *Pendule allant
un an Executé e par Ferdinand Berthoud.*
The pendulum is a grid-iron.

The great wheel-and-barrel
assembly can be removed without
the need to dismantle the clock. The
barrel has stopwork. The year train
is as follows: great wheel 132; 2nd
wheel 200; pinion 10; 3rd wheel 210;
pinion 8; 4th wheel 75; pinion 10;
pin wheel 60 pins; pinion 10. The
pin-wheel arbor carries the seconds
hand. An unusual feature is that the
drive to the motionwork comes from
the extended fourth wheel pinion.
The movement is mounted on a
marble base.

Height of movement 1 ft 2½ in (37 cm)
Width of movement at base 9½ in
(24 cm)
Thickness of movement 2¼ in
(5.7 cm)

STRIKING CLOCKS There follow details of various types of striking and chiming clocks.

'One-at-the-Hour' The simplest possible type of striking, a variety most often met with in skeleton clocks. At each hour the clock strikes just once, this being accomplished by a cam mounted on some part that rotates once an hour. The cam simply lifts the bell-hammer and allows it to fall and thus to strike the bell. This is often called 'passing-strike'. This type of striking work, of course, needs no separate striking train.

Hour Strike is the form that is most familiar where the hours are struck 1–12, 1–12 each day.

Hour and Half-hour is self-explanatory; the only point that needs to be made is that there are a few clocks which strike the hour normally but where the half-hour is passing-strike!

Dutch Striking, where at the half-hour the next hour to come is struck, on a higher-tone bell than that used at the hour.

Ting-Tang Striking is a simple type of quarter-striking. Two blows are struck at the first quarter, one on a high-tone and one on a low-tone bell, then two double blows at half-past, three double blows at a quarter to and four double blows followed by the hours at the hour. There is a modified type of Ting-Tang where no double blows are struck at the hour, only at the quarter-hours.

Comtoise Striking Here the hour is struck twice, once at the hour and again at about two minutes past.

Quarter-Chiming Chiming in general means the use of a minimum of four bells or gongs. All are familiar with the best-known chiming, that of the Westminster clock, often known as Big Ben (which is really the name of the hour bell).

Grande Sonnerie The hours and quarters are struck at each quarter. Some clocks are normal quarter-striking with Grande sonnerie repeating. Clocks are usually made to repeat by pulling a cord, but carriage clocks have a push piece which may be on the top or the side of the case. Most of the different types of striking can have repeating associated with them. The repeating function is almost invariably powered by its own spring which may be a small mainspring or a leaf spring. Some clocks repeat the quarters using the ancillary spring and then utilise the main train for the hour strike.

SINGING-BIRD CLOCK, PROBABLY BY H. L. JACQUET-DROZ, c. 1780

Although singing-bird mechanisms are still being made today by Rouage in Switzerland, no clocks with singing-bird mechanisms are in production. The bird sings hourly instead of the clock striking. The notes are played on miniature organ pipes. The bird is covered in real feathers, opens and closes its beak realistically whilst singing, and moves its head and body from side to side and also its tail up and down.

The cage bears four enamel plaques and a Berlin porcelain figure is at each corner. The centre seconds movement has a verge escapement. A very similar example to this is in the Collection Maurice Sandoz at the Musée du Château des Monts, Le Locle, Switzerland.
Height 1 ft 8 in (51 cm).
Width 1 ft (30.5 cm).

MINUTE REPEATING CARRIAGE CLOCK BY BREGUET, NEVEAU AND CIE, PARIS, NO. 5100, c. 1850

Why not show all this interesting work that is normally hidden beneath the dial? Breguet's type of repeating work is distinctive with the large circular minute rack fully in evidence. Breguet invented the rod

gong; only bells had been available before this advance. The two rods run down the right-hand side across the bottom and some of the way up the left-hand side of the plates. The A and the R on the discs at the top of the movement stand for *Advance* and *Retard* (French for fast and slow)

and show which way to move the regulator on the platform escapement.

The view below shows the front of the clock. The dial is enamel and bears the inscription *Breguet & Neveau & Companie* and the number 5100. The dial is surrounded by an engraved mask. The case is of gilded bronze.

Height of clock 5⅛ in (13 cm).

Ships Bell The ship's bell strikes nautical time as below:

12.30 a.m.	1 bell	⎫		12.30	1 bell	⎫
1.00	2 bells	⎪		1.00	2 bells	⎪
1.30	3	⎪		1.30	3	⎪
2.00	4	⎬ Middle		2.00	4	⎬ Afternoon
2.30	5	⎪ watch		2.30	5	⎪ watch
3.00	6	⎪		3.00	6	⎪
3.30	7	⎪		3.30	7	⎪
4.00	8	⎭		4.00	8	⎭
4.30	1 bell	⎫		4.30	1 bell	⎫ First
5.00	2 bells	⎪		5.00	2 bells	⎬ dog
5.30	3	⎪		5.30	3	⎭ watch
6.00	4	⎬ Morning		6.00	4	
6.30	5	⎪ watch		6.30	1 bell	⎫
7.00	6	⎪		7.00	2 bells	⎬ Last dog
7.30	7	⎪		7.30	3	⎪ watch
8.00	8	⎭		8.00	8	⎭
8.30	1 bell	⎫		8.30	1 bell	⎫
9.00	2 bells	⎪		9.00	2 bells	⎪
9.30	3	⎪		9.30	3	⎪
10.00	4	⎬ Forenoon	10.00	4		⎬ First
10.30	5	⎪ watch	10.30	5		⎪ watch
11.00	6	⎪		11.00	6	⎪
11.30	7	⎪		11.30	7	⎪
12.00	8	⎭		12.00	8	⎭

Some so-called ship's bell clocks do not strike the out-of-sequence bells in the dog watches, but merely repeat the 1 to 8 bell sequences for each four hours.

Carillons Here the clock plays a tune either at every quarter, each hour or more likely at three-hour intervals.

Musical Boxes are of course often associated with clocks and may or may not be let off by the clock.

Rarities Many oddities are met with. Among them are: 1. clocks that speak the time; 2. clocks that play organs; 3. clocks that play trumpets; 4. clocks with singing birds and so on.

For fuller technical details of striking, see Appendix B.

THREE-PART CLOCK A chiming clock with three separate trains – one for the time, one for the strike and one for the chime. Chiming clocks are also made with two trains. See STRIKING CLOCKS.

TIDE CLOCK This clock often has what is effectively lunar work that displays the times of highest and lowest water each month. The moon revolves around the earth once in every 24 hr 50 min (approximately), which is why the tides are roughly an hour later each day. However local conditions have a profound effect on the tides and it is no use the owner of a tidal clock expecting it necessarily to give accurate results for his port. As is well known, Southampton has four tides a day – this is enough to illustrate my point.

V.A.P. A clock of French manufacture, named after its makers, Valonge à Paris, with either a tic-tac escapement and bob pendulum, or a lever escapement. The lever escapement clock is fitted with the lever and escapement inside the main plates and the balance outside, and not with a platform escapement as might be expected.

Vienna Regulator Made in Austria about the last quarter of the eighteenth century, these were mainly weight-driven wall clocks although there were long-case versions. They were precision clocks mostly with wood rod-lead bob pendulums and could be either timepieces or with striking. In the mid-nineteenth century the firm of Lenzkirch in Germany made replicas of these clocks in large quantities. Although of high quality many of these clocks were made with pendulums shorter than a seconds pendulum yet retaining a seconds hand and a 30-tooth escape wheel. The result was that this seconds hand did not revolve once a minute, a disconcerting circumstance.

Water Clock or Clepsydra The earliest known timekeeping device independent of astronomical observations. Dependent upon the constant flow of water through an orifice, the earliest of which there are records is the Karnak water clock. This was of the sinking-bowl variety. A bowl with a hole in its base is put into a container of water and takes a reasonably uniform time to sink. The clock at Karnak (Egypt) was made in 1570 B.C. and was used to establish the difference in length between the hours of dark and daylight from the solstices to the middle of winter.

World-Time Clock As one side of the earth is in daylight and the other in darkness, it is obvious the time must differ as one travels in any direction other than due north or south. From an astronomical standpoint each 15 degrees travelled around the earth in an east-west direction means a change in time of one hour. Simple world-time clocks merely show this alteration, but it is meaningless as far as the civil time of any particular place is concerned, since this depends upon what time zone it is in, and this is decided more or less arbitrarily. A clock designed by the author shows the globe with the time zones marked on it and the actual civil time at any place (ignoring summer-time complications) can thus be worked out.

5 Restoration and Your Restorer

The whole question of restoration is a very vexed one which leads to constant arguments between the various authorities. The divergence of views is astounding, ranging from those who would like every clock to look as if it has just come from the maker's workshop to those who believe that every object should be virtually cocooned so as to preserve it indefinitely. The latter school think that to keep an important clock going is a heinous crime because of the inevitable wear that must take place.

As in most of these questions there is a middle road that can be followed which avoids the excesses of the extreme factions. The code of practice for museums cannot for instance be the same as that followed by professional restorers. Museums are in general only interested in conservation and do not normally replace missing parts to make a clock perform as was originally intended. The restorer is however working for the owner of the clock who is almost certain to want it put in working order. He may also have fixed ideas as to how this is to be done, some of which will leave a restorer with a conscience wondering whether he should comply with the requests made.

The Dialogue between the Clock Restorer and the Clock Owner

For a while the clock world was in danger of losing the restorers upon whose shoulders lies the responsibility for keeping the clock population hale and hearty. This was partly because clock owners were not aware of the skill and dedication required to deal properly with the conservation and restoration of their property. Nor were the craftsmen very good at the public relations aspect of their work, so that they put up for far too long with unsatisfactory rewards, often taking up work in industry in allied fields rather than being willing to insist on a decent living wage. No clearer evidence is required than that

116

JAPANESE WEIGHT-DRIVEN ALARM
CLOCK, ANON., 1678

Single-handed clock showing equal
hours. The hand revolves once in
24 hours, there being six periods per
12 hours in Japan until 1873. The day
began at the end of twilight and
unequal hours were kept. Since Japan
is at a higher latitude than Great
Britain this meant an even greater
difference between the length of the
day and the night throughout the
year. When European clocks first
entered Japan, they were keeping
equal hours, as in this example;
Europeans gave up keeping unequal
hours once clocks became common.
It was not long, however, before the
Japanese modified the clock to keep
their own unequal hours, refusing
to bow to the dictates of a mere
machine.

The holes in the dial are in the night
hours, one for each half-period.
When the hand contacts a pin placed
in one of these holes the alarm is set
off. This clock is dated on the case
bottom 1678 (or at least the Japanese
equivalent to this date). The case is
damascened.
Height 1 ft 1¾ in (35 cm).

furnished by the virtual disappearance of the specialist services that the craftsman himself regularly needs, such as dial-painters, cutters of gears, enamellers and so on.

Then about fifteen years ago things began to change. Firstly the prices fetched by clocks began to escalate and, as far as the prime pieces are concerned, this trend has not ceased to this day. Recently the British Museum paid half a million pounds for a Tompion year-going clock that both strikes and repeats. Although this is a unique piece, the sum paid for it can be usefully compared with £60,000 paid in 1958 for the major part of the Ilbert Collection. Among the clocks, about 191 in number, were very important examples, including 59 Japanese clocks. In addition there were 39 chronometers and 44 scientific instruments.

As clocks became more valuable so it became both sensible as well as necessary to pay to have them looked after properly. It happened just in time, and the whole of the horological field is now strong again in almost every aspect concerned with clocks (watches are another matter). Money considerations were not, however, the only important factor in the change of climate; education also played an important part – not only education of the craftsmen but also of the owners, who found an increasing awareness through reading books, listening to the radio and watching television. In this respect two other important events occurred that were of significance. One was the setting up of the Horological Students' Room at the British Museum. Because of the importance of the Museum's horological collections and the unique service offered by its Students' Room, an account of both of these is given in Appendix C.

The other landmark was the founding of the Antiquarian Horological Society. Of course, the British Horological Institute had always been around; it was founded in 1858 and has published a journal virtually without a break ever since. By 1952, however, the antiquarian sections felt dissatisfied with the coverage their particular sphere of interest was receiving and broke away from the Institute to form their own society and publish their own journal. This journal is now the most prestigious in the world in its chosen sphere. The Antiquarian Horological Society fulfils three main functions. One is the quarterly publication of its journal, which carries articles that are usually of impeccable scholarship. It also carries the advertisements of dealers, collectors and restorers. The second is the publication of specialist papers, monographs and books, and the third is the mounting of regular lectures on a wide variety of topics.

The British Horological Institute is also beginning to turn its thoughts towards antiquarian and restoration topics – an

WEIGHT-DRIVEN MONASTERY CLOCK WITH ALARUM, ANON, PROBABLY ITALIAN, FIFTEENTH CENTURY

Verge escapement with castellated rim to the balance. The alarm bell beneath the balance. Twenty-four-hour rotating dial with a geared edge driven directly by a two-tooth pinion on the extended barrel arbor. The sun effigy below the dial is the alarm-trip lever. The hooked end on the left holds the winding handle for the alarm barrel (the cord missing on this). The other extended piece is caught by the pin which can be inserted in any of the 48 holes around the edge of the dial.
Height 1 ft 3 in (38 cm).

119

NIGHT CLOCK BY EDWARD EAST, LONDON, THIRD QUARTER OF SEVENTEENTH CENTURY

This was a magnificent clock but has suffered badly, the movement being a nineteenth-century replacement.

Nothing was spared originally to make this clock the finest of its type; the dial is superbly engraved all over and the case covered in the most delicate floral marquetry. Note the blind-fret frieze.
Height 1 ft 11 in (58.4 cm).

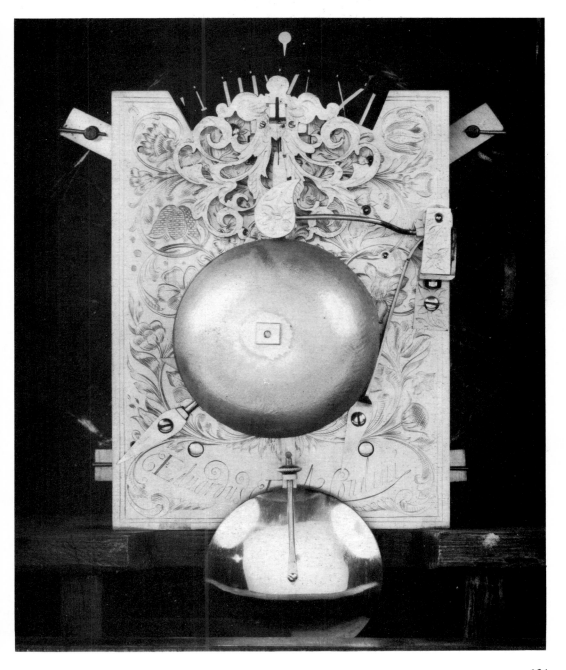

important move if it is to remain viable. Membership of the Institute, both Craft and Fellowship, is still the only universally recognised qualification in the field of horology. Except in some special cases both qualifications mean a mandatory number of years have been spent at the bench.

A few colleges exist (see list in Appendix E), some of which train for the examinations of the British Horological Institute, with one or two concentrating purely on restoration. These educative forces have resulted in an increasing awareness of the importance of treating our horological heritage with intelligent care but have also highlighted areas of doubt and uncertainty. It is to be hoped that this book will go some way to assist in resolving difficulties where they exist.

BENEATH THE DIAL OF A CARRIAGE CLOCK BY A. L. BREGUET, PARIS, NO. 178, SOLD 1804

This clock has a quarter repeating work which is operated by the plunger at the top. The moon dial can be seen in position; it has 118 teeth and thus revolves once every four lunations. The calendar indications are by drums; the date shown would be Saturday, 30 May.

This type of calendar work is particularly associated with Breguet and with A. F. Cole, who made Breguet-style clocks. Note the two-turn stopwork on the right-hand side of the movement just above the small wheel.
Height 4½ in (11.4 cm).

Restoration to Museum Standards

This phrase is often bandied around but is in fact a contradictory statement since museums should not be undertaking restoration but should only be conserving the objects in their care. This does not rule out normal repairs such as bushing, repivoting, supplying new teeth and so on. Without an overwhelming reason, however, missing parts should not be replaced, and if they are it should be made abundantly clear that they have been replaced. The reason for this policy is that objects in museums may and should be studied and, if the information obtained is to be valid, the objects must be left in their original form without the addition of parts which, however skilfully made, might be wrongly conceived. This policy seems straightforward but, of course, nothing is ever simple. What should be done when, say, a clock has been updated in the seventeenth century by the replacement of its balance or foliot by a pendulum? The answer is that this is a valid part of its history and the piece should be left as it is. In any case there is no possibility of putting back the original parts.

If this is the declared policy for museums, how does this affect items privately owned? Is an owner free to do exactly what he likes with his own property and therefore also free to ask a restorer to do whatever he fancies? This problem is so complex that there is no straightforward answer. The reason, of course, is that the issue is one of morality. A government can stop an individual from burying radioactive material in his garden but no one as yet can stop governments dumping the same material in the sea. They have a legal right at the moment, although I suggest no moral right. Similarly one is free to buy a Stradivarius violin and put it straight on the fire. Although a legal act, this would be abhorrent to civilised men, the act of a barbarian.

In the same way one can take a fine clock movement that has lost its case and marry it to a case that has lost its movement. The job may be carried out so skilfully that for ever after they are accepted as correctly matched instead of the marriage that they are. Does it matter if two half-objects have been made into a satisfactory whole? It may or it may not: if the objects really match and do not provide faulty evidence in the future it may be argued that no harm has been done. The problem is that our state of knowledge at the moment may not be sufficient to enable the correctness of the match to be determined – even if the effort is made with all the available academic resources called upon to help.

If one really cares about the past, and much of the interest in antiquarian objects must surely be the result of this caring, then one should not want it messed about and distorted. This is where the restorer comes into the picture, for he at least should be aware of the preceeding arguments and should do his best to put the point of view over if the need arises. In most cases he probably would, too, given the ammunition, for the dedication required to be a good restorer goes with a man who is conscientious. Things being what they are, the restorer is seldom the owner, so a dichotomy of interests does not usually exist.

The Restorer

The combination of qualities that are needed to be able to deal sympathetically with the repair and maintenance of the whole range of clocks met with, is not often found in one person. The reason for this is that it is not sufficient just to make parts that work; they must also be, as far as possible, as the original maker would have made them. If a number of parts are missing (striking work was often completely removed in the past), then the new parts should also be made so as to utilise the existing holes in the plates – again if this is at all possible. The man who can successfully manage these feats must be partly scholar, partly mechanic, and singularly ingenious. Above all he must have experience and this is hard to obtain now that the old system of apprenticeship is no longer with us. It is true that books can help but they can only do so much; in the end the restorer has to fall back on his own resources.

What happens, for instance, if a clock comes in with the name Bloggs on the dial and the restorer is asked to have this removed and the name Thomas Tompion put on instead? Well, here the answer is obvious. The restorer would say 'No'! But supposing the case is not as straightforward as this. Supposing a clock was auctioned which bore the vestiges of a signature, this being read by the auction house, a highly reputable one, as

TOWER CLOCK OF PERSPEX BY C. HOUTHUESEN, SUNBURY-ON-THAMES, 1983

Why shouldn't horology be fun? What a marvellous effect has been produced by the use of a transparent material for plates, wheels, flys, etc. The escapement is the double three-legged gravity. The bearings are ball races.

being that of a famous maker. If, however, it required the eye of faith to interpret the signature so, although it was possible and in fact probable that the clock was by the maker named, what would the restorer do then if asked to have the signature engraved over so that it could be seen clearly? It is a moot point, and it could be argued that no harm could be done as the clock had already been catalogued and the entry could be checked at any time by a potential owner. Nevertheless, it is my opinion that it should not be done. It is always possible that the clock would be even more interesting if the true maker were known and that in the course of time equipment might become available that would enable the original name to be read with certainty. Engraving over the signature might destroy this possibility.

Many people are already aware of the sort of things that do happen. A clock comes up with an obviously wrong dial and no case and reappears some years later as a complete and apparently perfect clock. It is quite possible that the previous owner had the case and dial made without any intention to

SPRING-DRIVEN TABLE CLOCK, ANON.,
POSSIBLY ITALIAN, *c.* 1670

This 30-hour table clock is probably
not in its original case, which would
no doubt have been much more
ornate. The upper part of the case
contains an automaton figure of
Father Time. The head moves slowly
from right to left and then rapidly
returns. Father Time's hand rises
and falls every 108 seconds and at
the instant it falls on to the hour-glass
a bell is struck. The posted-frame
movement has a verge escapement
and has been converted from balance
to pendulum. The striking is of the
Dutch type where the hour to come
is struck at the half hour on a higher
pitched bell.
Height 1 ft 8½ in (52 cm).

deceive, but on his death anything can happen – once again possibly quite innocently if no written records of the clock were kept when it was worked upon. These are the cases where nothing fraudulent was ever intended, although we must face the fact that many restorations are done with the deliberate idea of deceiving the next purchaser. However, speculation is of little use: what really matters is what should or should not be done if one is honest.

REPLACING WORN PARTS AND CONVERSIONS

An old mainspring is a precious thing and may well be signed and dated, making it a very important piece of the clock. Despite this, some restorers tear mainsprings out as a matter of course without bothering to ascertain whether or not they will still do their job. In fact they may well match the fusee better than any replacement spring, so that to take out the original spring becomes an act of vandalism.

This raises an important point about restoring clocks; do not replace any part unless it is absolutely essential. The gut line must have been replaced many times in a mechanism of any age and should be replaced as a matter of course each time the clock is overhauled. Wire lines only came into use this century, but the plastic-covered variety do not look too anachronistic, are stronger, and will not mark the barrel. Broken chains can be repaired provided none of the chain has been lost. At least two sizes of chain are also available again – an average size for marine chronometers and one for bracket clocks. For clocks that are valuable enough, advertise for a chain but be prepared to pay a lot. Chains can even be made by hand if you know the right

MONUMENTAL CLOCK BY HENRY BRIDGES, c. 1735

Only the mechanism of this clock now survives – it is at the British Museum – the case has long gone. One of the most impressive examples of a complicated clock with automata, it was exhibited in 1741 at the Mitre near Charing Cross. Within the pediment was a scene representing the Muses on Parnassus which changed periodically first to a forest scene with Orpheus and wild beasts and then to a sylvan grove with birds.

On the upper dial, which is 1ft 1in (33 cm) in diameter, amid the four smaller dials are indicated the seconds, minutes, hours, sunrise and sunset, equation of time, the age and phases of the moon, and the signs of the Zodiac. On the lower of the two large dials is shown the Copernican system with the sun at the centre and the planets revolving around it. On the panel below was a landscape and the sea with representations of moving persons and vessels and on a second panel men at work in a carpenter's yard. There was also an organ which was set off at intervals. It is recorded that there were over a thousand wheels and pinions in the complete mechanism.

In 1770 the clock was again exhibited, this time by an Edward Davis, who wrote a description of it. Little is known about Bridges, who lived at Waltham Abbey, apparently having been trained as an architect. The print shows him with Sir Isaac Newton.
Height 10 ft (305 cm).
Width at base 6 ft (183 cm).

man, but this is extremely costly. A clock may be too old to possess a chain but have one just the same. Chains did not come into use until about 1650 and at that time many clocks were updated accordingly. Changes made at the time they should have been made are a legitimate part of the clock's history and should be left strictly alone. Early chains tend to have longer links than was subsequently the case and are sometimes curved to fit the circumference of the barrel.

People are only too fond nowadays of restoring clocks to what they think was their original form. If the first anchor escapement was put into a virtually finished verge clock, then doubtless this has already been changed back to a phoney verge. Although many restorers are quite competent at putting back a verge escapement, how many know enough to prevent them throwing away an exceptionally early anchor escapement? If it was pure greed that prompted the conversion, then in a case of this sort the reverse would be achieved to what was desired.

Supposing a clock has been converted from verge to anchor during the nineteenth century, should it be changed back to verge? I think the answer to this is no. The early conversion is a valid part of the history of the clock carried out for good reasons and probably done well. Holes that were stopped up will have to be opened again and further holes stopped up, and for what? Well, usually to make the clock more valuable. If it must be done, then at least there is little likelihood of the fact remaining undiscovered permanently, for during the course of time, however carefully the metals have been matched, the stoppings reveal themselves. If the plates are gilded, this will not be so, and for this reason gilded plates are a special hazard to those who have to authenticate pieces. At the same time it should be made clear that for a short while after the conversion has been carried out, and in any case without getting the clock out of its case and probably removing the dial, it will not be possible to tell that an escapement reconversion has been carried out if the work has been done by a fully skilled man.

The restorer can also help to prevent the temptation to pass off his work as original by making it clear that he keeps proper written and photographic records of what has been done. This should be routine in any case, since one never knows when such records can be useful. Thefts of clocks and watches form the greatest proportion of stolen goods, and the owner can turn to the restorer to aid in identification should the need arise. One craftsman recently had published a lifetime's notes (see Further reading) on striking and repeating work as an aid to others who have problems in this, the most difficult of areas. Additionally one builds up one's own dossier and being able to refer back to a sound specimen of the item one has to deal with can prove invaluable over the years.

Over-restoration

It has already been mentioned that there are some who believe that when a clock has been restored it should look as it did when it came from the maker's workshop. What they are usually referring to is the mechanical part of the clock.

If this argument is carried to its logical conclusion, the case would also be completely stripped and refinished so that it was in a comparable condition. What one would then have would be a clock that would resemble nothing so much as a good modern reproduction. I do not think this is what owners of old clocks ought to want. Neither should they be given back a mechanism whose dial has been restored so as to give it a new appearance, if this can be avoided, for it will not blend well with a case that has all the signs and patina of honourable age. It is fortunately now possible to resilver a chapter ring without cleaning it back to the bare metal. Each time this is done some of the engraving depth has gone. A succession of comprehensive resilverings can result in all the fine engraved detail being completely lost. The rule here, then, is to have the chapter ring resilvered using the gentle method until this is no longer satisfactory and only then to have the dial cleaned off completely. One advantage of the gentle method is that it does not give the dial that startlingly new appearance.

The aim of the exercise should after all be to produce a harmonious whole with a mechanism and dial looking reasonable and matching the case as far as possible. Your restorer, once he understands what you want, should be perfectly well able to achieve this result. Many restorers complain, though, that they are more or less forced, as they put it, to 'tart up the clock', since otherwise many owners feel that the job has not been done properly. It would be as well to have an example handy showing what the owner can expect if he follows the advice of the restorer.

Finding a Restorer

If you already have a good man who does your work, all well and good. If you have not, and you have purchased your clock at one of the major auction houses, then ask their expert whom he would recommend. He will probably not only know of a good craftsman but will also know who is best at doing your particular type of clock. Having contacted the restorer, tell him exactly what you want and then ask him if he agrees with your suggestions. Insist on a quotation even if you are charged for it. Expect that if the job goes ahead you will then not be charged for the quote and say so: this can avoid trouble that may occur because of misunderstandings.

Nobody minds you being businesslike in your relations with them if it is business that is being discussed. I know friends who also do business together and the only reason they remain friends is that the business is discussed as if they were craftsman and client. Ask for a completely itemised account when the job is completed; you should know of everything that has been done. Ask for any parts that have been replaced and keep them in a labelled box – this is an insurance that with any luck will never be needed.

If a clock comes in for a routine overhaul, nobody is as pleased as the man who has the job to do. Such occasions are not in fact as rare as one might think. Many owners who look after their cars intelligently exercise the same approach to their clocks and put them in for service at regular intervals. However, when the clock is accompanied by the statement 'It keeps perfect time', then the clockmaker draws back in horror, for he knows that such a state of affairs – if true – is a chance balancing of errors and changing anything will upset this balance. The heading of 'changing anything' certainly includes cleaning and oiling. The temptation not to touch the clock at all is overwhelming. Who wants to be faced with an irate customer saying, 'What have you done to my clock? You've ruined it!'

Of course, perfect time means different things to different people. Some clocks can gain 10 minutes in the first part of the week, lose 10 minutes in the second half, and thus never need to be altered when the weekly wind takes place. To some this

LACQUERED LONG-CASE CLOCK, ANON., EARLY EIGHTEENTH CENTURY

Case decorated with chinoiserie with a red ground and decorated with flowers, birds and scenes with figures. When lacquered cases first became popular after the restoration of Charles II in 1660 some were actually sent to China to be done, but the length of the trip involved soon proved to be unacceptable and the technique was developed in England. This was not, however, true lacquerwork, since this was done by applying many coats of the sap of the lac tree (*Rhus vernicifera*) and the basic material for this process was not available in Europe. The lacquer was polished and the final result has a high polish and is hard and durable. The substitute process developed in Europe was japanning. Here the coats applied are of shellac, gum-lac or seed-lac dissolved in spirits of wine. The gloss obtained can be good but the result is not so durable as true lacquer, being especially vulnerable to damp which can cause it to flake off. This is why it is relatively rare for japanning to have escaped restoration at some time or other.

Japanning is available in many colours including red, as in this case, blue, green, yellow and simulated tortoisehell. However the more commonly used was black. This ground was then decorated, usually with Oriental scenes in various shades of gold, the main details being built up with whiting paste so as to give relief. Strangely enough this raised decoration, usually confined to the trunk, tends to survive better than the purely flat decoration. The original qualities of japanned work varies enormously and so does the restoration work done, some of which is appalling and some so good as to be indistinguishable from fine early work.

Height 7 ft (213.4 cm).

would be considered perfection. In a way of course it is, since the behaviour of such a clock is entirely predictable. A wise clockmaker then will find out what perfect timekeeping means to the person who utters such a provocative statement and then decide on a course of action. A wise owner will resist the temptation to talk about perfect timekeeping and be pleased if, when the clock comes back, it has changed its performance, any change inevitably being for the worse but nevertheless indicating that the job has been done.

6 Repairing Your Own Clock

Many owners would like to look after their own clocks if they could and there is no reason why a man of a practical bent should not tackle routine maintenance as a beginning. The attributes one needs to make a success of repairing and restoring horological items are patience, mechanical aptitude and good eyesight. To augment these attributes one needs a decent place to work, good light, some tools, which must be good even if few, and knowledge.

First and foremost one needs a bench (see *fig. 18*). It need not be very large but should at least be solid. It needs to be about 3 ft (100 cm) in height and to do the different jobs that need to be done one needs both a stool and a chair to sit on. One needs a different height to file, say, than when assembling. If space is at a premium a collapsible bench can be installed; this can be stored away neatly when not in use. The bench top should have a back and sides to prevent things from falling off, but nothing

Figure 18

GLOBE CLOCK WITH MOON WORK,
FRENCH, c. 1880

This is a special version of the French
Four Glass clock. Brass case gilded
and glazed all round with door at
front and back. On top is a globe
revolving once every 24 hours. An
equatorial ring surrounds it, and
degrees of latitude are marked on
the piece that supports the globe
arbor. This arbor is driven by gearing
in the mechanism. Enamelled dial
with Roman numerals and at its
centre the phases and age of the
moon. The hour and half-hour
striking movement with recoil
escapement and mock compensated
pendulum.
Height 1 ft 6 in (45.7 cm).

along the front, as useful as this might appear to be. Instead one should have an apron such as jewellers use or alternatively a carpenter's apron that is fixed to the bench on either side and that will thus catch any part or tool that may fall.

Your Workshop

LIGHTING

Close work requires both good general lighting – north daylight if possible and a fluorescent light – and an individual light that can be moved at will. A light of the Anglepoise type is ideal, if available, but if a light is being purchased a low-voltage lamp is better. This is because less heat is generated with a resulting greater comfort. It might be thought that the amount of heat generated is unimportant but if the light is to be positioned to the best advantage it often comes very close to the head.

TOOLS

The following is a list of the tools that form a minimum requirement.

1 pair of flat-nosed pliers
Set of large screwdrivers with blades from about $\frac{1}{8}$ in to $\frac{3}{8}$ in wide (3–9 cm)
Set of watchmaker's screwdrivers with blades 0.60 to 2.50 mm wide
Tweezers (Dumont preferably), nos 00, 1 and 3
Set of oilers, fine and medium; and a clock oil pot with five depressions for different oils
Hand-removing levers, large and small
Sharp knife
Brushes, fine, coarse and medium

CONSUMABLE MATERIALS REQUIRED

Rags (lint-free)	Chamois leather
Pegwood	Emery sticks
Pith	Alcohol (not methylated spirit)
Rodico	Boxwood dust
	Goddard's Silver Foam

Moebius clock oils as follows:
8141 (heavy)
8040 (lighter)
8300 (for winding work and mainsprings)

Repairing an 8-Day English Clock

In general the smaller the timekeeper the more difficult it is to repair. Therefore start with a large clock such as the 8-day

English clock, typical of which is the grandfather or, as it is more correctly called, the long-case clock. Since fewer and fewer professionals will repair these clocks nowadays there are many around that require attention.

Removing the clock from its case should be done as follows. Remove the pendulum. This is supported by a delicate suspension spring which is easily damaged, and in fact may be broken or bent already. The pendulum passes through the crutch which gives it impulse and must first be moved up through this crutch sufficiently to enable the suspension spring chops to be freed from the back-cock. Once this is done, the pendulum can be carefully lowered guiding the suspension spring through the crutch to avoid damage.

Next the weights should be removed, noting which is the striking and which is the going weight. Then remove the screws that may be holding the movement which can then be lifted from the clock case and will come away complete with its seat-board. The whole is now ready to be taken to the bench.

Do not forget, though, to check the case. The clock is often standing on carpet and the case joints are loose. If rocking occurs, then the most perfect clock may stop. This is because the clock moves in sympathy with the pendulum and the energy to effect these movements is robbed from the energy that should go towards maintaining the pendulum. The best course is to fix the clock to the wall. A batten is usually required to space the clock away from the wall so that it clears the skirting-board. Measurements can be taken so that upon returning the movement to the case the necessary fixing can be carried out.

CLEANING THE MOVEMENT

It is usually necessary to clean the movement before much else can be done. The dirt present will often be thick enough to prevent one seeing the wear that may have occurred.

The first thing is to remove the seat-board. This is connected to the movement by two hooks. These are often useless for the purpose and can be replaced with studding. This can be purchased in various sizes. The threads should be hammered flat where the staple passes around the clock pillar and shaped so as to fit around the pillar. The seat-board should also be examined to see if the lines have been rubbing on the sides of the slots through which they pass. If this has been happening, the slots should be widened until they are clear of the line. It is also best that the seat-board be drilled so that it may be screwed to the case. If there are no holes, drill these whilst the seat-board is off. The underside of the seat-board will usually be marked so that the position of the bearers is known. If not, then this drilling must be left until the clock is back together again. This is because the dial must be aligned with the hood aperture.

CONTEMPORARY BRACKET CLOCK BY NEWCOMBE AND SON, CLERKENWELL

This figured walnut case houses a Clerkenwell-made striking movement with fusees. The firm also produces long-case clocks. Cases can be of solid mahogany or veneered in any desired wood. The dial can be hand-engraved or painted for long-case clocks; the hands are fretted out by hand and blued in the traditional manner.
Height 1 ft 6 in (45.7 cm).

Next disassemble the movement. The hands are removed by pushing out the collet pin and removing the collet, the minute and the hour hand. Sometimes the hour hand is retained by a small screw which should be placed in a box with the collet and collet pin. The seconds hand should then be removed. The dial is then ready to come off; it is usually retained by taper pins which should again be placed in the small box.

Upon removing the dial the motion work is revealed. Do not immediately remove it. First look to see if the teeth have been marked so as to facilitate the correct relative replacement of the hour and minute wheels. If the clock has datework the same comment applies. If no teeth have been marked, make a small pip on the tooth and tooth space of the gear meshing with it. Do not lay the clock on its back whilst doing this without first removing the crutch. This is retained by the back-cock which is held by two screws. This should be kept with the cock or put into a box which is marked 'back-cock screws'. Even when screws look the same they are seldom interchangeable.

The movement is now ready to be completely dismantled. All parts are first removed from the dial plate. A piece of stiff card is used to hold the parts such as pins, screws and posts as they are removed. They are pushed into it in the same relative positions that they occupy on the dial plate. Sketches of other parts may also be made on the card as a guide to assembly. The plates are then separated after removing the taper pins from the pillars. (Screws are sometimes used here.) Before going further,

ART NOUVEAU RAILWAY CLOCK AND BAROMETER BY ELKINGTON OF BIRMINGHAM, THE MECHANISM BY SWINDEN, ALSO OF BIRMINGHAM, 1906

This presentation piece comprises several elements: a clock, a barometer, two silver models of locomotives, small-scale sculpture and a case designed in the Art Nouveau style. The case is of bronze and silver. The bronzed copper is engraved (in the centre of the lower part) Elkington and Company London, and the silver elements are fully hall-marked Birmingham, 1906, with the maker's mark, Elkington and Company.

The lower part of the case with its projecting central feature has four bronze sculptural details in relief and two silver allegorical figures, probably denoting Industry and Communication – both executed in the round and measuring 9½ in (24 cm) high. The seated figure of Mercury (on the right) holds the caduceus in his hands and the seated

female figure (on the left) holds a wheel on her knee and in the other hand a large hammer. Between the two figures is placed the small silver model of an early form of locomotive bearing the name La Portena. It apparently represents the first locomotive used on the passenger-train service that commenced in Buenos Aires in 1857 on a six-mile-long line to one of the suburbs.

The large silver locomotive and tender, on top of the clock case, are thought to be a faithful model of one of the most up-to-date types being run on the Buenos Aires Railway in 1906, with movable pistons and brakes, made separately, and details, such as the cow-catcher and the external lamps on the driver's cab. This locomotive and tender are placed on a track of silver rails and sleepers and this flat surface extends beyond the vertical sides of the case; the under-side of the 'over-hang' has a silver frieze of foliate ornament and, on either side, a silver caryatid emerges from the fluid forms of the

silver corner elements. Between these caryatids are the two dials and a silver cartouche bearing the inscription *Al Senor Ingeniero Don David Simson Gerente 1897–1906*. Below the barometer dial is a silver panel bearing the inscription *From members of the staff of the 'Buenos Ayres Western Railway' who had the pleasure of serving under him*. The same inscription, written in Spanish, appears on the siver panel beneath the clock dial (on the left).

The clock mechanism has a dead-beat escapement, and maintaining power. Marked between the plates is *Swinden Birmingham* – a firm that had been in business in Birmingham since 1824; the movement is thus as much a local product as the case. After various changes of address, the firm of Swinden had premises in Temple Street, Birmingham, from 1866 and at the time when this clock mechanism was manufactured. Indeed the firm remained there until the business closed in 1954. The dial, its raised polished gilt Roman

numerals on a silvered background, is similar to those used on long-case clocks of the period.

At the time of its completion, this clock was published in *The Railway Magazine* for 1906 but presumably was sent to Buenos Aires for the presentation ceremony. David Simson died in 1916 at Ickleford Manor, Hitchin, and is said to have left the clock to his five sisters, the family home being a farm in Roxburghshire. The clock helps to illustrate the pioneering contribution made by Britain in the development of the railways in remote parts of the globe. The Buenos Aires Western Railway Company, to which David Simson belonged, was the oldest railway company in Argentina and was government owned until, in 1889, it was sold to a British concern. In 1890 there were only 5,848 miles of passenger track in Argentina but by 1909 the number of miles of track had tripled and the number of passengers a year exceeded 18

million. The clock summarises visually the transformation by contrasting *La Portena* with the latest locomotive on the top of the clock.

David Simson returned to Argentina in 1911 as Chairman of the Company but he was an engineer. Born in 1861, he was elected an associate member of the Institution of Civil Engineers in 1887, becoming a full member in 1897. His successful work in Argentina led to his promotion in 1906 and the commissioning of this presentation piece.

Length 3 ft 4 in (101.6 cm).
Height 2 ft 2 in (66 cm).
Depth 18 ft 2 in (35.6 cm).

MOVEMENT OF A GIANT REPEATING
CARRIAGE CLOCK BY M. F. DENT,
LONDON, c. 1865

Striking and chiming on eight bells.
The three train movement with chain

fusees. *Left* the striking work beneath
the dial; *below* the perpetual calendar
work mounted on the back of the
dial plate. The wheel on the extreme
left has two teeth broken, a
circumstance that might take some

time to come to light. The platform
has a detent escapement with a
chronometer type balance with a
helical spring.
Height 1 ft 6 in (45.7 cm).

make sure that the great wheels are visibly different in appearance so that it is evident which is which, or else that they are marked S and G (striking and going). There will seldom be any confusion between other wheels in the clock.

Most clocks are finely finished and do not require severe cleaning. Grease and tarnish can be removed with a mixture of washing-up fluid (neat) and Goddard's Silver Foam. Silver Foam is a harmless paste consisting mainly of rouge and has been analysed to make sure that it contains no chemicals that can attack metals. Metal polishes are in general to be avoided since they are not only abrasive but also contain chemicals that remove metal. Admittedly work with Silver Foam is slow, but then neither is any damage done. The parts need to be washed in warm water to remove the Foam and should then be dried in alcohol or in warm sawdust.

CLEANING HOLES

Small holes are cleaned with pegwood which has been sharpened with a long taper point. Start with the largest hole and work down for the most economical use of the pegwood. This should be sharpened and used as many times as is necessary to ensure that it comes out clean. Larger holes are cleaned with chamois strips. These are cut off so as to taper from end to end. The wide ends are sewn together so that all may be clamped in the vice. A suitable piece is then threaded through the hole to be cleaned and the part rubbed up and down the strip until clean.

Rusty parts – arbors or flat steel parts – can be restored with an emery buff or cloth on a piece of wood. If any pinion leaves appear to be rusty, polish them with fine emery powder mixed with oil and applied with a wedge-shaped piece of soft wood. Glass brushes are also very useful for removing rust, but should be used with a protective mask. Glass brushes are made by binding a multitude of fine glass filaments with tape or string. Before assembling the clock make sure that any parts that lie between the plates are free from defects: wheels may be loose on pinions, the crutch loose on the pallet arbor, etc. A escape-wheel tooth slightly bent can be very troublesome and in fact all teeth should be examined for damage. Lifting pins sometimes work loose; check the great wheel for freedom on its arbor and also see that the click works correctly in the ratchet wheel.

BUSHING

Although clocks seem to be delicate pieces of mechanism, easily broken and deranged, they nevertheless have heavily loaded bearings. Clocks, like aircraft, are designed near to the limit. As a result the pivots are near to the minimum practicable size. Making them larger to decrease the loadings and increase

CHIMING BRACKET CLOCK BY CRAIGHEAD AND WEBB, ROYAL EXCHANGE, LONDON, c.1850

Ogee-shaped walnut case moulded and carved with roses and other flowers with similar walnut bracket (not shown). Arched silvered dial with engraved spandrels and the inscription *Craighead and Webb, Royal Exchange, London*. In the arch two subsidiary dials; chime/not chime, slow/fast (regulation) dial. Blued steel moon hands. Three-chain fusee movement with maintaining power on the going side. Recoil escapement, pendulum lock and fine adjustment of the bob by rear screw and nut. Quarter-striking on eight bells, the hours on a gong. Back plate with repeat signature. Height 2 ft (61 cm), bracket 1 ft 6 in (45.7 cm).

145

the wear-life is to an extent self-defeating since more force is then required to overcome the frictional losses – which increase as pivot sizes increase. One thing that can be done at the design stage is to make the plates thicker. Since this involves an increase in the cost of the mechanism, thick plates in general indicate that one is dealing with a higher-quality mechanism. Making the plates thicker increases the bearing length which slows the rate of wear without any increase in frictional losses.

Wear usually starts once the lubricant has ceased to do its job properly. This happens inevitably with the passage of time. There is not much room at the bearings of clocks for a sizeable reservoir of oil. A proportionately large surface area (compared with the volume of oil present) encourages oxidation and contamination by dust particles, these being both organic and mineral in nature. Minute specks of metal are also shed by wheel teeth and the bearing surfaces, and these particles of metal enter the oil acting as catalysts in chemical changes. If surfaces are not suitably prepared, the oil can also literally run away spreading across the plates in all directions until it is no longer where it is needed.

The longest one can reasonably expect the oil in a clock to last is five years, and this only if a skilled man has cleaned the clock in the first place and then added the right amount of the correct oil. Some clocks do not seem to suffer much from being run after the day has arrived to clean and overhaul them. With others the results can be serious, and clocks with a black deposit in the pivot holes are usually suffering badly, and on dismantling the pivot will probably be ridged and scored. The pivot will have to be smoothed and repolished or, if the marks are too deep, replaced. This latter process is known as repivoting. It involves drilling up the hardened and tempered arbor and inserting a fresh piece of steel, which is then turned true and after bringing to size polished or burnished. Great care has to be taken during this operation to avoid any eccentricities in the finished gear. The pivot hole is then bushed, that is, it is opened and relined with a fresh bearing – again great care has to be taken to ensure that the new hole is in the correct position. Performing this operation on four or five holes in a clock is a lengthy business and is the price someone has to pay for the neglect from which the clock has suffered.

THE PENDULUM

The pendulum may have to be dismantled so that it can be cleaned up. If a grid-iron is dismantled, mark every part if it is not already marked, so that it can be reassembled exactly as it was. Do not use centre pop marks that are visible after assembly. They should need keen eyesight or an eyeglass to make them visible even if one or two have to be deepened

OBSERVATORY TABLE REGULATOR BY A. L. BREGUET, PARIS, FIRST SOLD 1803

Mahogany-cased observatory regulator with gilt-metal dial plate with glazed aperture for viewing the escapement, subsidiary enamel dial for hours and minutes and enamel centre seconds dial ring. Single large going barrel and grid-iron pendulum beating half-seconds. The pendulum is knife-edge suspended. Constant force escapement driven by falling platinum weight. The escapement single-beat chronometer type thus giving a seconds-beat to the hand. Provision for a bell to be struck each second for the convenience of the observer. M. de Prony's fine adjustment on top of the pendulum and showing within a small glazed dome. The weighted arm registers against a degree scale marked on a ring beneath the dome.

This clock, although it bears Breguet's name, was purchased from M. Lallot and entered in his records as no. 1064. It was then sold to M. de Prony who modified it to include his regulator after which Breguet repurchased it. It was finally sold to M. Meyer four years later in 1819. Height 1 ft 4¾ in (42.5 cm).

FREE STANDING WEIGHT-DRIVEN
YEAR-GOING REGULATOR BY BIGGS
OF MAIDENHEAD, MID-NINETEENTH
CENTURY

This individual piece with its
impressive weight has a most unusual
figured mahogany case. The
regulator-type dial has a heavily
engraved surround typical of the
work done in the second half of the
nineteenth century and the only clue
as to the date of this piece. The
escapement is the Graham dead-
beat and there is a temperature-
compensated half-second pendulum.

because they are disappearing in the cleaning process. Measure the position of the rating nut so that it can be replaced nearly correctly.

REASSEMBLY

Having seen to all these things the clock is now ready for reassembly. Before starting, however, oil the great wheel bearings with Moebius clock oil. It will not be easy to reach these bearings once the clock is assembled and it is essential that they be oiled. Also oil the click pivots and lightly grease the ratchet teeth. A drop of oil where the wheel crossings rub on the barrel is also desirable.

Now lay the pillar plate on a large chamois leather or Selvyt cloth. Large because it should be able to overlap the top plate so as to prevent finger marking as assembly continues. Then continue as follows:

1. Screw down hammer spring.
2. Put in centre wheel.
3. Put in great wheel.
4. Put in third wheel.
5. Put in hammer.
6. Put in pin wheel.
7. Put in gathering pallet wheel.
8. Put in warning wheel.
9. Put in fly wheel.
10. Put in escape wheel.

The hammer tail should be just free of a lifting pin so that the end has just dropped (see Appendix B) with the warning pin about half a turn away from the warning slot in the plate. Once the warning has occurred, the train must be able to run so as to obtain some speed before lifting of the hammer commences.

Now it is not always easy to check the striking when the top plate is not on and supporting the various parts in their proper positions. It is often worth while to put in the critical parts so that the striking action can be checked and, if there are no marks already, an appropriate wheel-tooth space marked where it matches with a marked pinion leaf. If the marks are permanent (such as a dot made with a drill), then assembly will be simplified for those craftsmen who will work on the clock in the future.

To return to the assembly sequence, the next step is to position the top plate carefully so that it passes over the various extended pivots (the winding squares, the centre pinion and the gathering pallet square). Start to guide the pivots nearest the barrel end into their holes until such time as the taper pins can be inserted in their holes in the pillars nearest to the barrels.

EXHIBITION BALSA-WOOD CLOCK
BY FONTEROY, END OF NINETEENTH
CENTURY

The balsa-wood case is in the form
of a temple spire surmounted by a
weather cock above a fretted faceted
section. Below this is the rectangular
central section which houses the
clock movement. Below the clock
is a base with bowed ends opposed
by outset porticoes enclosing a
revolving mirrored pillar. The whole
standing on a fretted base. The clock
mechanism chiming on five gongs
stamped *Fonteroy made in France
number 16/163 540.* The whole clock
contained in a glazed cabinet with
plush drapes and a chequered floor
and a stand with a parquetry-
veneered surface on turned legs
enclosing a double-sided cupboard.
Wired for electric lights and an
electric motor.
Height of whole 8 ft 3 in (251.5 cm).

Note that if the taper pins are short, so that they will not enter the holes, fresh pins should be used that have a full taper.

NEW PARTS

Many of the parts that one had to make oneself ten years ago are now available from specialists. Consult Appendix E to see whether someone can relieve you of work you do not really want to or cannot do yourself.

HANDS A large selection of hands is available today from Miles (see Appendix E), but these will need finishing and blueing. It takes a long time to make a hand when it is not your speciality and a long time to blue one. There appears to be no quick and easy answer to blueing. Burying the hand flush with filings never works since some parts still take up the heat first. However, it is a good way to start the job, as long as one quenches the hand as soon as any of it is a satisfactory blue. The rest must be done in the flame without haste and with a quench always near at hand. If things do not go well, it can take a whole morning to blue a pair of hands.

NEW WEIGHT LINES are sometimes a problem, not because they are not available but because there is such a choice. For weight-driven clocks, I prefer mono-filament nylon over and above gut

DOULTON FAIENCE CLOCK GARNITURE BY S. J. ROOD AND CO., BURLINGTON ARCADE, LATE NINETEENTH CENTURY

Each piece with Doulton mark and in the form of a decorative Islamic building picked out in bright colours and with gilding. The flanking 'tower' vases with onion-shaped roofs. Gilded French going barrel movement inscribed *S. J. Rood and Co, Burlington Arcade*, with going barrels striking the hours and the half-hours. Brocot regulator and pendulum.
Height of clock 1 ft 3¼ in (38.7 cm).

and plastic-covered steel lines to plain. Nylon lines are not much use in fusee clocks, however, because they stretch and upset the 'set-up'.

Cleaning a French Striking Clock

Perhaps the next clock to tackle is a late French clock with going barrels; it has sufficient problems to present a challenge, yet the difficulties which will be encountered are not overwhelming. Every clock that is spring-driven is a potential bomb and it is dangerous to separate the plates without understanding what has to be done beforehand. Ensure therefore that the operation of 'letting down the mainsprings' has been done before separating the plates. Failing to do this could result in costly damage and even injury.

Firstly remove the pendulum, if this is not already off. Usually it is just hooked on to the suspension spring and is easy to get off although the bell may have to be removed first. Then look to see what secures the movement to the case. Usually there are screws that pass through the rim of the door in the back of the case. Once these screws have been removed, the mechanism is liable to fall out of the case, so hold it securely. This is where one needs some way of ensuring that the location of each screw will be known when it comes to reassembly. To do this, get a piece of stiff card large enough to take a diagram of the front and back plate. Make holes small enough to hold the screws when they are pushed into the card. When it comes to the screws, studs, etc. in the main plates, push them into the card in the same position they occupy on the plates. This procedure can save a lot of time and avoid possible damage upon reassembly.

Next get three boxes about half the size of a shoe box. One is for the plates and dial, one for the going train, one for the striking train. Now all is ready for removing the hands. Do not put levers beneath the hour hand and try to lift both hands; first remove the minute hand, which is usually kept on by a pin. When removing the pin, ensure that it is pushed in the right direction, for it is tapered. Then take the movement out of its case. This often can be accomplished without first removing the gong, should there be one. If it must be removed, simply undo the nut that clamps it to the bottom of the case. Put the nut back on to the rod so that it will not be lost.

DISMANTLING AND REASSEMBLY

There are not many fundamental differences between the English clock and the French clock from the point of view of dismantling, cleaning and reassembling, except where the

SEDAN CARRIAGE CLOCK BY LAWSON AND SON, c. 1900

The Sedan case cast and gilded with a fleur-de-lis finial above, a solid back and glazed sides. The lower part of the case has cast-in cartouches. Engraved gilt dial with Roman numerals and Breguet hands inscribed *Lawson & Son*. The French movement with strike is wound and set from the back and has a lever platform escapement. Height 11 in (28 cm).

striking work and its arrangements are concerned.

In French clocks there is no tail on the gathering pallet and the locking arrangement is consequently different. This is made clear in Appendix B, where it will be seen that to put the work back correctly there must be a specific relationship between the position of the pallet wheel pinion and the pin wheel. Often one leaf of the pinion is filed to mark it and there is a dot against one of the tooth spaces in the pin wheel; this enables one to get the positions right on reassembly. In addition, when the pallet wheel is locked, the warning-wheel pin must be half a turn from the warning lever stop block. There is often another dot in the rim of the warning wheel which should be put against the fly pinion. Even when put together with the marks correctly set, it may be found that all is not well. At the worst the plates will have to be separated sufficiently to put matters right, but with many French clocks it will be found that there is a small cock that can be removed to put things right. Of course, none of this should be done with the power on. The train can be urged round by hand for testing purposes. Even after this the first few winds should be done with caution, just to establish that nothing untoward has happened.

Most snails in French clocks have no steps but are a smooth curve. This makes it more difficult to see whether or not the rack tail is falling correctly. Once again the motion work will be found to bear dots which when aligned should lead to correct results. To test it, the clock is caused to strike at both 12 and 1 o'clock, first to see that the rack tail clears the face at the long step and secondly to see that it falls safely on the high part of the snail.

When one of these clocks is found stopped with the rack tail jammed, it may indicate that the striking work has been set incorrectly or that the striking has failed to operate at all. If this happens, the rack tail rests on the snail after it has fallen, just running around its edge until it jams against the step face. Just not winding the strike side is sufficient to cause this trouble, although there can be many other reasons. These might be:

1. Mainspring breakage.
2. Bent pivot or tooth.
3. Bad depths, often due to wear in the pivot holes.
4. Dry or rusty warning pin.
5. Hammer on the rise.
6. Gathering pallet catching on the points of the rack teeth.
7. A fly 'out of poise' meaning that it is heavy one side causing extra resistance to starting.

Fault 6 can be cured by moving the hour wheel a tooth in the minute pinion, thus letting the rack fall not quite so far or a little further, as the case may be. If the clock strikes the hour at

QUARTER-STRIKING CARRIAGE CLOCK BY J. R. LUND, LONDON, c. 1870

Although it has no carrying handle I take the liberty of calling this a carriage clock because it is nearest to this family of clocks in character. Rectangular case of gilt metal with door back and front and with engraved base, pilasters and ball finials, the sides each with a putto. Instead of a handle a glazed compass set into a shallow gadrooned vase standing on first a square plinth and then an engraved and shaped pad. Both the dial of the compass and the main dial silvered, the latter engraved with leafy scrolls. Blued steel fleur-de-lis hands. Twin chain-fusee movement with lever escapement with plain balance, the back plate inscribed J. R. Lund (late W. and I. Baird) 4 Hatton Garden, London. Striking on a gong. Complete with travelling case. Height 5 in (12.7 cm).

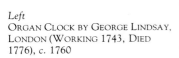

Left
ORGAN CLOCK BY GEORGE LINDSAY, LONDON (WORKING 1743, DIED 1776), c. 1760

Case mahogany veneered with numerous fretted panels to allow the sound of the organ pipes to be heard. The pediment designed as a model of an organ. Chased scroll foliage feet. Arched dial also with fretted surround and silvered centre to main chapter ring and with chased silver spandrels. Five subsidiary dials, at the top centre in the arch the tune selector (eight tunes, all dances); on the left the 'going or stopped' control for the going train and on the right the regulator dial.

Below the main dial on the left the strike/silent dial for the striking and play/not play for the organ. Above the false pendulum aperture the inscription *Geo Lindsay Servant to the Prince of Wales*. This was previously covered with a plaque with *Geo Lindsay Watchmaker to His Majesty*. Eight-day movement which strikes the hours and at every third hour (3, 6, 9 and 12 o'clock) plays one of the eight tunes selected three times. Rise-and-fall regulation. Verge escapement.
Height 3 ft (91.4 cm).

Above
'SHEEPSHEAD' LANTERN TIMEPIECE BY ROBERT EVENS, HALSTED, c. 1720

Spring-driven fusee movement with anchor escapement and bob pendulum. 'One-at-the-hour' striking on the bell at the top. $7\frac{1}{2}$-in (19-cm) square dial plate engraved with scrolling foliage, silvered chapter ring inscribed *Robt Evens, Halsted*. This type of lantern clock with an over-large dial is known as a 'sheepshead', but the reason for this is obscure.
Height 1 ft 3 in (38 cm).

157

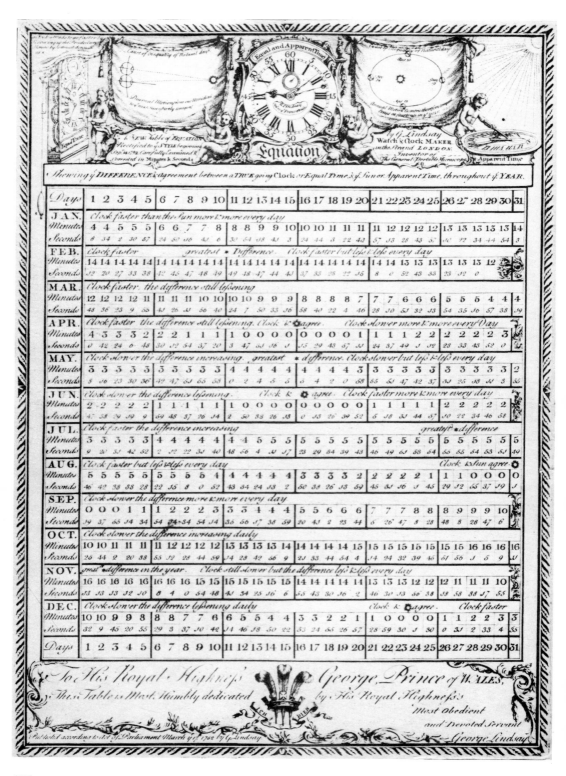

the half-hour as well as at the hour, the pin that operates the striking at the half-hour is lifting the arm too high; bending the pin inwards a little should cure this fault. If only one is struck regardless of the hour, then the other pin should be bent outwards a little to lift the arm higher.

Repairing Precision Clocks

The restoration of precision clocks involves similar techniques to those used in other branches of clockwork, but there are some special problems that need to be discussed. Firstly, perhaps, precision clocks should be defined. To me they are clocks that have certain features as follows: 1. temperature compensation, probably adjusted for the individual clock, but not necessarily; 2. a 'precision' escapement, which itself needs defining; 3. constant power supply and/or a constant force device in the train or escapement. Precision clocks, by the above definition, began with Harrison and Graham soon after the beginning of the eighteenth century. George Graham developed the dead-beat escapement, John Harrison, the grasshopper escapement; Graham invented the mercurial pendulum and Harrison the grid-iron pendulum.

The dead-beat escapement is that most likely to be met with in precision clocks and restorers will find this escapement has special difficulties. One is bent wheel teeth, since the wheel is more delicate than that of a recoil escape wheel. The teeth can usually be straightened if care is exercised. A good eye is needed for this job but causing the escapement to work will soon reveal any residual inaccuracies. One way of damaging these teeth is to give the pendulum a good swing to start the clock. To avoid this possibility, the pendulum should be given small pushes until such time as the clock begins to operate. Also the clock should not be allowed to run down as, with the power off and the pendulum still swinging, damage can result.

If there is a danger of the clock running down during the owner's absence, it should be stopped and restarted upon his return.

The better the clock the less locking there is (see Appendix B); it can be as little as $\frac{1}{2}$ degree, which can be quickly lost if the pallets, wheel teeth and holes are worn. Extensive repair work can lead to an alteration in the geometry of the teeth and wheel which can lead to malfunctioning. Often this can be overcome by putting the wheel and pallets into the depth tool (see p. 163), when it may well be found that a new centre distance combined with some judicious manipulation of the pallet arms puts matters to right (pallet arms should be soft – only the nibs should be hardened). Regulator pallets are often jewelled and the same remarks apply, except that the pallets will have to be

TABLE OF THE EQUATION OF TIME
BY GEORGE LINDSAY, 1752

Before the time of telegraph or wireless time signals one could check one's clock by use of a sundial if one knew the equation of time. Here it is set out for each day of the year. At the top of the chart are illustrated the reasons for the difference between mean solar time and sun time, or apparent solar time, as it should be called. In the centre is a clock displaying both types of time. Since the difference stands at four minutes we can tell that the date is 11 May or 13 September (the clock time being slower than sun time). These charts were often stuck inside the door of a long-case clock.

attacked with diamond paste if grooving has to be removed. Copper polishers are effective for carrying the paste.

Slop in the pivot holes must be kept to a minimum and endshakes at the escapement should also be tighter than in non-precision clocks. This is because any lack of perfect squareness across the pallet face can, as the endshake is taken up one way or another, lead to changes in geometry and thus in rate. However, at no time should any pinion or arbor be so tight that it will not fall under its own weight as the clock is turned, first on its back and then on its front.

Oiling should be carried out with care, for too much at the pallets does not help. However, do not under-oil the pivots; their reservoirs (the oilsinks) should take all they can without overflow or running. How much this is, is unfortunately a matter of experience.

Another type of regulator escapement, much favoured on the Continent, is the pin wheel. This is not, however, as good, owing to the greater difficulty of keeping oil at the escapement. For this reason such clocks may need overhauling more frequently. A good variant of the dead-beat escapement is the Vulliamy – the type with inserted pallets. This type of escapement is used on Vienna regulators, and the inserted pallets, which run in concentric grooves, are a gift to the restorer since they are often first reversible and then can be dressed and moved around in their grooves to bring them back into the correct position. These pallets in English practice often had cast brass bodies. The Vienna regulator is discussed separately (see p. 164).

The pendulum of a Vienna regulator provides an example of another type of compensated pendulum, the 'wood rod-lead bob' combination. If the pendulum is to be satisfactory, the wood must not suffer because of changes in humidity and to this end must be varnished. The grid-iron pendulum is normally not adjustable as few makers after Harrison have really understood the need for the adjuster that he used. It is, of course, possible to alter the level of the mercury in a mercurial pendulum; only do so, however, on the bases of actual trials, since a calculation of the height of mercury required is difficult owing to the complication of the expansion of the vessel that contains the mercury. If the mercury is dirty, it can be cleaned by running it through a paper cone.

Regulator suspension springs require to be carefully chosen and fitted. Many regulators have little supplementary arc, this being the arc over and above the minimum required to allow the escapement to act. Fitting too stiff a suspension spring can reduce this arc to a point when the clock will no longer work. The width of the spring should also be as great as the chops allow, since this is important for preventing any tendency of the

A WATER NIGHT CLOCK BY ARNOLD
FINCHETT, LONDON, 1735

The water is in the sealed drum
which has pierced partitions and
is about half full of water. As
the water trickles from one
compartment to the next the drum
descends. As it descends the hour
hand is turned by the thread that
attaches its pulley to the arbor of
the drum. The dial is pierced to
allow the light of an oil lamp to
show through the numerals. The
excrescence at the top of the clock
is the chimney. The case is of
japanned iron.
Height 11 in (28 cm).
Drum: diameter 5 in (12.7 cm);
width $2\frac{3}{8}$ in (6 cm).

JAPANESE 'STICK' CLOCK, FIRST HALF
OF THE NINETEENTH CENTURY

This was the last and most
sophisticated way of telling the time
using unequal hours developed by
the Japanese. The hours of dark and
daylight were divided into an equal
number of hours, daylight being
taken as including twilight. The
results are graphed out for the year
on a plate over which passes a cursor.
By checking the date at the top of the
plate the time can be read off. The
cursor is in fact fixed to the weight
of this weight-driven clock which
takes 24 hours to descend. The
mechanism with its fancy pierced-
out plate is visible through the glazed
top portion. It has a verge escapement
and a balance with spring.
Height 2 ft (61 cm).

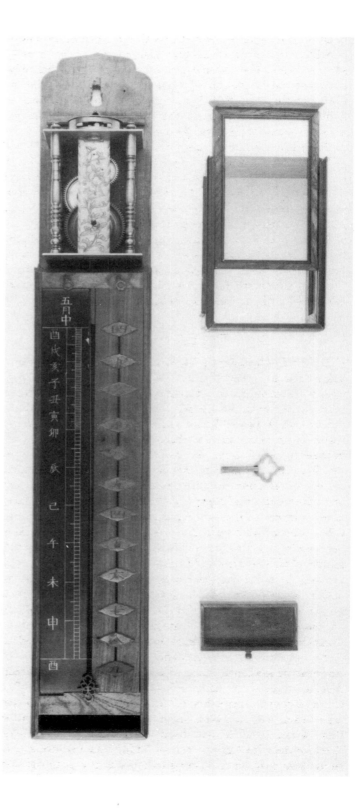

pendulum to wobble. Sometimes the top pendulum chop is provided with a rod which then rests in two vee-grooves in a support piece. The rod may also be clamped in its vees. Make sure that the pendulum is allowed to hang free in the final positions that the clock is to take up before the clamps are tightened. If this is not done, the weight of the pendulum may actually buckle the spring because it is being restrained.

Don't forget to oil the crutch where it works with the rod.

The gearing in a regulator is in some ways likely to be less fussy than that in a cheaper clock since the number of leaves in the pinions will be greater than normal. However, since we are expecting much more from the regulator, it should still be as good as we can get it. In general, wear is likely to be less rapid with precision clocks, even if they are neglected, because they have smaller driving weights and have good thick plates. Nevertheless, holes can wear and eventually have to be rebushed. To assist in this process one needs a depth tool in which pairs of gears can be mounted and checked.

THE DEPTH TOOL

Using the depth tool properly is not as easy as it might seem. A description of its use follows. The tool is held in the left hand with the adjusting screw to the right. After ensuring that the pivots or points of the pinions are true, carefully place them in the tool which should be sufficiently opened to avoid damage. Close the runners so that there is no shake of the pinions between them. Meanwhile close the tool rotating the wheel slowly to ensure that the teeth of the wheel and pinion engage safely. Some lateral adjustment of the runners may be necessary to position the wheel correctly lengthwise in the pinion. As the depth is increased the running together of the wheel and pinion will become smoother. This can be felt only when some restraint is put on the pinion by pressing a finger-nail against the pinion shaft (near one of the runners to avoid bending the pinion). As the engagement continues to deepen, the gearing will eventually run rough again. The narrow band of engagement that gives smooth running is an indication of what tolerances are allowable in the gearing. For an individually made clock the centre distance chosen should be in the middle of the smooth engagement band. If the gearing will not run smoothly at any centre distance, then the gears are not correctly matched and it will usually be found that a check on the DPs or the modules will verify this. Alternatively, the form of the gears may be incorrect and visual examination should again confirm this. When satisfied that the depth is correct, mark it off. Remove the wheel and pinion and adjust the positions of the runners so that when scribing with the tool it is upright and square with the plate surface. A fair amount of skill is required to do this but it will be of assistance if the plate is roughly polished until a reflection of the tool can be seen in the surface. Adjust the runners so that the reflections appear in one continuous straight line from all angles and thus ensure uprightness. Usually two centres need to be established to determine the pivot point which will then be at the intersection of the two circles scribed by the points of the runners. Scribing should be done on the inside surfaces and if done neatly is traditionally left showing in all but the finest work. In any case it should be left until the pivot hole is in and checked to appear correct with both scribed lines.

There can, of course, be errors in a depth tool; and it should be checked. Runners must have true centres or sinks and can be corrected if not true in the lathe.

The Care of Vienna Regulators

The Vienna regulators mostly found are clocks produced in large quantities by such firms as Lenzkirch of Lenzkirch in Baden, Germany. This firm produced particularly fine models, nearest in fact to the superb originals made in Vienna on which all these German clocks were based. As clocks go, Vienna regulators are particularly delicate and fragile.

The plates are usually of rectangular or trapezoidal shape and are of hard, well-finished and polished brass. The wheels are small and as light as possible to cut down the power required to drive the clock. The pinions are of properly hardened and tempered steel, the pivots being as small as they can safely be. Great care must be taken during assembly to avoid breaking a pivot. The pinions being well hardened are difficult to drill if repivoting is attempted, and the small arbor diameters make the job even more difficult. In some three-train clocks and miniature weight-driven regulators the wheel work is not much larger than in a good-sized pocket-watch.

All the pivots must be well polished and the depths correct, especially that of the escapement. When holes are worn they must be rebushed with special care. The acting faces of the pallets must be free from grooving and highly polished and, although locking must be safe, it must not be excessive. There is virtually no spare power in these clocks to overcome losses in power owing to bad depths or escapement faults. The general requirements for suspension springs are of even more importance too; there must be no bends, cracks or distortion, and the spring must not be too thick or the clock will fail to go at all.

The crutch pin must also be square to the pendulum slot and with no excess shake. In the best Lenzkirch regulators there is even an adjustment for the play of the crutch pin in the slot.

Almost every Vienna regulator has a beat adjustment device and it is most important that the beat is correct. A finer line than normal is required for these clocks, which have finely grooved barrels and slim pulleys that simply will not take a gut line that is too thick. The effort required to keep these clocks in good order is well rewarded since they can be most reliable. Because they have compensated pendulums (the wood rod-lead bob type), they can often perform to better than a minute a month with some even running six months with an error of less than a minute. A Vienna regulator is most odd in that the seconds hand does not always revolve once a minute (see p.115)!

Repairing Cases

Although many readers may not feel like tackling the repair of the mechanisms of their clocks, they may well feel quite differently about repairing the cases. With this in mind I shall start first with the repair of wooden cases which can often be in a very poor state indeed. Important clock cases should be given to an expert to deal with. This man will not usually be a

THE HOROLOGICAL STUDENTS' ROOM IN THE BRITISH MUSEUM (see p. 197).

clockmaker, although a good clockmaker will have recourse to a furniture restorer and could thus mastermind the restoration of the whole clock. For run-of-the-mill clocks, however, some work can be tackled successfully by a practical man.

VENEERS

Veneers are a common source of trouble with cases; pieces may be missing or there may be bubbling or lifting. Bubbling may be dealt with first by slitting across the blister with a razor blade, then inserting glue beneath the loose veneer with a fine spatula. Pressure should then be applied, a matching piece of wood being required if the surface is curved. A piece of oiled paper should be put beneath the pressure pad to prevent it from sticking to the surplus glue that must be extruded from between the veneer and the case carcase. This process will not succeed if dirt has got beneath loose veneer – if this has happened, the loose piece must be removed and the surfaces to be glued cleaned thoroughly.

Sometimes the veneer is lifting because of trouble with the carcase; this is especially so with trunk doors, which are so often constructed on unsound principles. This is the type of problem that should be left to a specialist.

Eighteenth-century veneers are thick; having been produced by sawing, they are usually a minimum of $\frac{1}{16}$ in (1.6 mm) and cannot be matched with modern veneers. Restorers hoard every piece of veneer that comes their way – soaking off veneers from all furniture that is not economically repairable. Otherwise veneers are still obtainable from specialist suppliers, although finely patterned pieces are very expensive.

The case should be polished regularly with furniture polish, as if it were a table, and will repay this attention by obtaining a beautiful glossy finish – as it would have had originally.

SLATE AND MARBLE CASES

These, if damaged, can be made good with resin, which must, however, be coloured appropriately before starting the job. The overwhelming majority will be black, and the appropriate black can be obtained from a materials dealer (see Appendix D).

Appendix A:
Glossary of Clock-Case Terms

ABACUS The topmost member of a column capital.

ACANTHUS Because of the elegance of its leaves this has been since classical times the most favoured foliage represented in decoration.

ACORNS Used extensively as a motif for FINIALS.

ACROTERIUM A pedestal for a figure.

APPLIQUÉ Decorative brass or silver work applied to the top and other parts of clock cases.

APRON A decorative drop-piece. May be between the feet of a case or the piece attached to the pallet cock of some verge clocks.

ARABESQUE Decoration in low relief or inlay with fanciful intertwining of leaves, scrollwork, etc.

ARABIC NUMERALS The numerals in normal use, i.e. not Roman.

ARCH Referring only to the shape as in arch-top case or arch-top dial.

ARCHITECTURAL STYLE has a curiously specific meaning when clock cases are spoken of as really being in classical architectural style with a triangular-shaped superstructure usually supported or appearing to be supported by columns.

ATROPOS The last of the Three Fates. Clotho spins the thread of life, Lachesis distributes men's lots and Atropos cuts the thread.

BALL FOOT A foot of ball shape.

BANDING A strip or band of VENEER in a panel or around a door. The grain of the wood may be across or in line with the banding.

BARLEY TWIST The shape similar to that of barley sugar from which the name is derived. Used of pillars.

BASKET TOP The pierced metal top to a case. If there are two tiers it is called a 'double basket top'. Usually applied to a bell top and often surmounted by a handle.

BAS-RELIEF Where the carving or casting is in relief as opposed to being incised.

BEAD A small half-round moulding.

BELL TOP Presenting a profile similar to the section of a bell.

BLIND-FRET A decorative carved effect where the base material appears to be covered in FRETwork.

BLOCK FOOT A square section foot of cube proportions or longer.

BLOCK FRONT Where a door or panel projects rather than being let in flush or recessed.

BOB PENDULUM Where the pendulum of a clock is fixed directly to the pallet arbor instead of there being an intermediate crutch.

BOLECTION Refers collectively to all the projecting parts of mouldings.

BOLT AND SHUTTER A form of maintaining power. The shutters obscure the winding squares and when moved aside operate the bolt which takes over the driving of the train by pushing on the centre wheel. Some form of alternative drive has to take over as the weight is being raised if the clock is not to stop.

BOMBÉ A design that bulges as in the plinth of many Dutch long-case clocks.

BOSS A rounded projecting ornament similar in appearance to the boss of a shield.

BOULLEWORK Inlay work usually of brass in tortoiseshell but can be of various combinations. Named after André Charles Boulle. Both base and inlay are cut together so that a perfect fit is achieved.

BOULLE, COUNTER The reverse of the above technique accomplished by making use of what would otherwise be discarded when doing BOULLEWORK, i.e. if the boullework was brass in tortoiseshell then the counter boulle would be tortoiseshell in brass.

BOW FRONT A gently curved front, similar in shape to the unstressed bow.

BRACKET FOOT A foot which has the appearance of a small bracket.

BRACTS A decoration in the form of a leaf that bears a flower in its axil.

BREAK ARCH An arch which terminates at each side in a right-angled piece. There are break-arch cases and break-arch dials.

BREAK FRONT Where the front is not an unbroken line, being interrupted by a projection or recess.

BROKEN PEDIMENT When the pediment is broken at the top.

BUN FOOT A flattened ball foot.

BURR As in burr-walnut.

CABOCHON A rounded protrusion.

CABRIOLE The curved leg like a shallow S.

CALENDAR APERTURE The opening in a dial through which the date may be seen.

CALYX A decoration resembling the outer case of a bud.

CANTED CORNERS Sloping corners.

CAPITAL The top part of a column. It may be carved or moulded.

CARCASE The underlying frame of a clock, often oak in the past. VENEERS and mouldings are applied to the carcase to make it into a finished case.

CARTOUCHE An applied or engraved piece that resembles a tablet or a scroll unrolled.

CARYATID Sculptured female figures used instead of columns.

CAVETTO A hollow moulding.

CERTOSINA A type of PARQUETRY employing small pieces of inlay to give a geometrical design.

CHAPTER RING The hour circle on the dial.

CHASING Similar to REPOUSSÉ work but hammering is from the front instead of the back. Often used to 'crisp up' castings and can be done in conjunction with engraving.

CHEQUER Alternate squares of light and dark wood to give a chequer-board effect.

CHEEKS The upright supports in the case on which the seat-board rests.

CHEESE FOOT Another term for BUN FOOT.

CHINOISERIE Chinese ornamentation.

CLAW AND BALL A foot formed so as to resemble a claw holding a ball.

CONSOLE An especially long CORBEL BRACKET.

CORBEL BRACKET A bracket that is or has the appearance of being built into the wall.

CORINTHIAN COLUMN A Grecian column with bell-shaped capital with rows of acanthus leaves.

CORNER PIECES Another name for SPANDRELS.

CORNICE The topmost member of a structure, usually a moulding in a clock case – the uppermost member of an ENTABLATURE.

COUNTER BOULLE See BOULLE.

CRESTING The carved addition above the CORNICE, mainly on early long-case clocks.

CROSS BANDING Where the grain of the veneer runs across the length of the wood.

CURL The natural figure in wood grain where a large branch meets the trunk of the tree.

CYMA RECTA An OGEE MOULDING.

DAMASCENING The inlaying of gold and silver in some other metal.

DENTILS or DENTICKS A tooth-like ornamentation consisting of small rectangular blocks with spaces between. Usually placed below a CORNICE.

DÉCOUPAGE Also known as *Lacca povera* (poor man's lacquer). Coloured prints prepared for the purpose are glued on to a painted surface and the whole varnished.

DIAL ARCH The arch formed in the case to accommodate an arched dial.

DIAL FRAME The frame that may surround the dial and be revealed once the door has been opened.

DOG TOOTH A repeating ornamentation of pyramid shapes in low relief.

DOLPHIN FRET A metal FRET containing or mainly composed of figures of dolphins usually found on the sides and the top of a lantern clock.

DROP HANDLE A ring hanging from a boss, which may be a LION'S MASK.

DUTCH FOOT A foot that terminates in a bulge.

EBONISING The process whereby a wood is made to resemble ebony by filling, staining and polishing. Many woods are used but close-grained ones, such as apple, cherry, pear, holly and sycamore, should be used for the best results.

EGGSHELL FINISH A matt finish.

ENCARPUS A festoon of fruit and flowers on a frieze.

ENCAUSTIC The art of burning in with heated wax so as to produce a pattern or picture.

ENDIVE SCROLL A scrolling foliage form.

ENRICHMENT The addition of ormulu, inlay, carving and so on.

ENTABLATURE The frieze moulding and CORNICE forming the part above the column and supported by it.

ESCUTCHEON The applied surround to a keyhole.

EXTRADOS The outside curve of an arch. See IN-TRADOS.

FAN A popular MARQUETRY motif.

FAUN Half man/half goat figure used as a decorative motif.

FAVAS A honeycomb effect.

FEATHER BANDING Another term for HERRINGBONE.

FESTOON Another term for SWAG, a decoration in a curved draped form.

FIDDLE-BACK A figured VENEER similar in appearance to a fiddle-back.

FIELDED When a panel is broken up into smaller panels.

FILIGREE Ornamental work made from wire with interstices.

FINIAL A projecting piece, often the termination to a column. Can be stylised pine cones, acorns, pineapples, balls, spires, tulips and so on.

FLAMEAU FINIAL A finial representing a flaming torch.

FLEMISH FOOT A scroll-type foot.

FLEUR-DE-LIS The French royal symbol. A representation of three iris-shaped parts tied with a narrow band.

FLUTING Grooving of a regular nature. A stopped flute does not run the full length of the surface it is decorating.

FOIL The space between the cusps or points in Gothic tracery. Three cusps: trefoil; four: quatrefoil, etc.

FOLIATED A term with two meanings: the first, when foils are used (see above); and the second, enriched with leaf forms.

FRET Wood or metal that is pierced, often to allow the sound of striking to be heard more clearly.

FRIEZE The middle member between the CORNICE and the supporting column.

GADROON A decoration resembling reeds or inverted flutes.

GALLERY A decorative wood or metal edge often pierced to resemble railings.

GESSO A mixture of parchment size and gilder's whiting which is built up on a groundwork, this often carved. The gesso itself can also be carved and often then gilded.

GILDING (See also MERCURIAL GILDING.) Gold leaf can be applied to almost any surface. The process may be known as water gilding since the gold leaf is laid with a mixture of clear water and parchment size. A much cheaper method of gilding employs gold size; this is known as 'oil gilding'.

GOTHIC The pointed-arch-style period, twelfth to sixteenth century. There was a revival of the Gothic style in the nineteenth century.

GRIFFIN A decorative motif composed of a lion's body with an eagle's head and wings.

GUILLOCHÉ Engine-turned. An ornamentation of curved and interlacing lines.

HERRINGBONE A VENEER cut obliquely into strips and placed in such a manner that the result resembles a herringbone.

HOOD The upper removable portion of the case that houses the mechanism and dial. May lift as in earlier clocks or pull forward.

HUSKS a form of decoration of the Sheraton period. It consists of a row of open seed pods each separated by a ball or seed.

IMPOST The part of the pillar upon which the arch rests.

INCISED ORNAMENT Cut in with a chisel or graver.

INLAYING A general term embracing all those techniques that rely on a ground having some other colour or type of material let down flush into it. See BANDING, INTARSIA, MARQUETRY, PARQUETRY.

INTARSIA Derived from the Latin *interserere*, to insert, intarsia means the inlaying of one wood into another by chiselling out and then filling.

INTRADOS The underside of an arch.

INVERTED BELL TOP Refers to the bell top where the curves are reversed, concave above, convex below.

JAPANNING An opaque varnished finish usually with gilt decoration in imitation of Chinese lacquer work.

KERF The cut made by a saw.

KETTLE FRONT Where the form takes the shape of the old-fashioned kettle.

KEY PATTERN A FRET pattern.

LACQUER True lacquer work is an Oriental technique but the term is often incorrectly applied to JAPANNING. Lacquer is also the name of a protective finish applied to metal to colour and/or protect it.

LAMBREQUIN Engraved drapery panel sometimes used on early dials to take the maker's signature.

LAMINATE To build up in layers of the same material as in plywood or different layers as in Formica.

LANCET Pointed arch of the thirteenth century or Gothic.

LATTICE Interlaced work resembling network in wood or metal.

LENTICLE A glazed aperture usually round or oval through which can be seen the pendulum bob.

LIGNUM VITAE A hard, dark, dense wood from the West Indies. Sometimes used in the seventeenth century in place of ebony for VENEER. Because of the waxiness it has self-lubricating properties, and John Harrison used it for pallets, bearings and as the trundles of his lantern pinions. Still used today as the upper bearing of the diamond lap.

LIMED OAK Oak treated with lime to give it a whitish-grey appearance.

LION'S MASK AND RING HANDLES A decorative handle formed of a lion's head with the ring clenched in its teeth.

LOTUS LEAF A decorative motif based on the lotus water-flower.

LOW RELIEF Shallow carving where the detail is raised up; see also BAS-RELIEF.

LOZENGE A diamond-shaped pattern.

MACHICOLATION A space between CORBEL BRACKETS which support a parapet.

MAHOGANY Although used in furniture from about 1730, mahogany was rarely used for clock cases until the middle of the eighteenth century. It was first imported from the West Indies and was very hard, straight-grained and dark in colour. Soon Cuban mahogany, which is finely figured, came into use, followed later in the century by Honduras mahogany. This is of more open grain, of a higher colour and not as well figured as Cuban mahogany. Country clocks, although appearing to be of mahogany, can often be of cherry or pear which can closely resemble it.

MARQUETRY A word of French origin coming from the word *marqueter*, to spot, to mark. It is applied to the technique where different sheets are cut simultaneously and then fitted one into the other.

MASK An impression of a face used as a form of decoration.

MATTING The finely punched centre of dials. The quality of seventeenth- and eighteenth-century matting has never been matched since.

MEDALLION A motif in the shape of a plaque or medal, may be of PARQUETRY, or figures or heads in LOW RELIEF.

MERCURIAL GILDING Also known as fire gilding. Where an amalgam of gold and mercury is applied to the part to be gilded. After washing off the excess the article is heated to drive off the mercury, leaving a durable gilding whose colour varies according to that of the base metal, the finish and the gold used. This process is illegal in many places owing to the extreme danger from the mercury fumes.

MOCK PENDULUM A small disc fitted to an arm integral with the pendulum in verge clocks; the disc shows through an aperture in the dial and can be seen oscillating to and fro when the clock is going. It can also be pushed to start the pendulum moving.

MODILLIONS Projecting decorative brackets under the CORNICE of a column.

MOSAIC A pattern or picture formed of many minute pieces of marble, gems, etc., of various colours.

MUNTIN The central vertical member of a door, that part of a door which divides the panels.

NECKING The small band or moulding near the top of a column.

OBELISK An upright tapering column with a pyramidal top.

OGEE MOULDING A moulding of double curvature, concave below, convex above.

OIL FINISH A finish achieved by several applications of boiled linseed oil.

ORMULU Originally bronze fire-gilded, often used nowadays to describe any gilded metal piece.

OUTSET COLUMNS Projecting columns.

OYSTER A circular grain formation from cross-sections of small branches of wood, for example olive, to mention the most commonly used of the woods for this purpose.

PAD FOOT A form of foot usually associated with the CABRIOLE leg.

PARCEL GILT Gilt in part. Most common with silver articles, only part being gilt for contrast and decorative purposes.

PARQUETRY MARQUETRY formed into geometric as opposed to naturalistic shapes.

PATERA Round or oval flat decorative motifs carved or inlaid, often applied loosely to rosettes and other flat ornaments.

PATINA The finish resulting from long exposure to the elements or from countless polishings.

PEDIMENT Used loosely in horology to refer to the structure above the CORNICE.

PENDULUM APERTURE The aperture in the dial through which can be seen the MOCK PENDULUM.

PERPENDICULAR STYLE A style where the perpendicular lines are emphasised.

PIE-CRUST EDGING A decorative carved edging resembling that given to a pie crust.

PIETRA DURA Inlaying in marble.

PILASTER A pillar attached to a surface or corner, that is, not free-standing.

PLINTH That section of the case below the trunk.

POLLARD A tree that has had its boughs and trunk lopped, causing peculiar growths at the top, which yields a figured wood that can be cut as VENEERS.

PORTICO TOP Alternative name for the pediment of an architectural-style case.

PRINCES WOOD An alternative name for kingwood used in the seventeenth century.

PULVINATED FRIEZE Frieze which is cushion-like; pillowy; bulging.

PUTTO A cherub. When associated with decoration it means a representation of a cherub; the plural is putti.

QUATREFOILS See FOIL.

QUIRK An acute sharp-edged groove at the side of a bead or moulding.

REEDING Small parallel rounded elements resembling reeds used on columns or as mouldings.

REPOUSSÉ Ornamental metalwork hammered into relief from the reverse side.

RESERVE Space on an engraved or matted surface left plain to accommodate an inscription.

RIBBON DECORATION A form of decoration resembling ribbon.

RIBBON STICK A form of decoration resembling ribbon wound around a stick.

ROCOCO A style of decoration based on C scrolls with flowing foliage, rocks and shells. A term also used to define an over-abundance of ornament, a frivolous development of the Baroque.

ROE A type of figure in wood of a spotty appearance not unlike SHAGREEN.

ROUNDEL The bull's-eye glass or bottle glass used in the doors of long-case clocks.

RUN OUT When a moulding runs out to a point – as happened before mitres were used.

SATIN FINISH A dull finish to French polish and a fine straight-grain finish to metalwork.

SCALLOP or SCOLLOP A representation of an escallop shell in carving or MARQUETRY.

SCOTIA A hollow moulding.

SCROLL FOOT See FLEMISH FOOT.

SCROLL ORNAMENT A form of ornamentation resembling a roll of parchment.

SEAWEED MARQUETRY A late type of MARQUETRY with fine scrolling foliage giving a dense pattern.

SERPENTINE When the lines of a vertical surface are, in plan, curved in and out, that is, of serpentine shape.

SHERATON Many inlaid mahogany pieces are loosely called Sheraton. Thomas Sheraton (1751–1806) was a well-known furniture designer who published books of designs. His clock-case designs were fanciful.

SHAGREEN The skin of a shark which has a granular appearance but when polished a series of irregular rings shows up. Usually dyed green.

SKIRTING Board fixed round bottom of clock case.

SPADE FOOT Another name for BLOCK FOOT.

SPANDREL The space left between a circle and a surrounding square. This space may be decorated by engraving (engraved spandrels), or fitted with applied decorative pieces, in which case these are also called spandrels.

SPOON FITTING A fitting resembling a spoon used to lock the HOOD in seventeenth-century long-case clocks.

SPRUNG MOULDING Referring to a moulding which is sprung to force it to take up the shape of a curve.

STRAP HINGES A hinge which has one side lengthened giving it the appearance of a strap which shows on the inside of the doors of long-case clocks.

STRAPWORK A style of decoration resembling straps which are curved, interlaced, etc. May be engraved, inlaid or fretted.

STRINGING Thin inlay running in lines of a wood of contrasting colour to the ground wood.

SUNK PANEL Where a panel is beneath the level of what surrounds it.

SWAG A hanging form of decoration such as a drapery or festoons of flowers.

TERM A bust in continuity with its pedestal.

TERMINAL The finishing piece to a post or standard.

TERN FOOT A foot with a three-scroll pattern.

THERM A trunk pillar or pedestal small at the base and larger at the top – a sort of inverted obelisk.

TINTING Tinting and staining of woods began in

Florence in the fifteenth century with liquors and tints boiled with penetrating oil to produce light and shadow effect in MARQUETRY.

TORCHILUS An alternative name for a SCOTIA.

TORTOISESHELL The shell of the hawksbill turtle, now an endangered species.

TORUS A large bead, one of the classical mouldings.

TRACERY FRETwork in stone, wood or metal.

TREFOIL See FOIL.

TREILLAGE Trelliswork.

TRUNK The body or main part of the case of the long-case clock. The case has three main parts: TRUNK, HOOD and PLINTH.

TURKISH NUMERALS Islamic numerals.

TWIST PILLAR Another name for the BARLEY-TWIST pillar.

TYMPANUM The triangular space forming the field of an architectural pediment.

URN FINIAL FINIAL in the shape of an urn.

VENEERS The sheets of wood used to cover another wood, usually finely figured. Early veneers are a minimum of $\frac{1}{16}$ in thick (1.5 mm) as they could only be produced by sawing. Veneers are now produced on a machine using a long skiving blade.

VIGNETTE An ornamentation resembling vine leaves and tendrils.

WAX POLISH Before the introduction of French polishing in the early eighteenth century, wax polishing – using a polish of beeswax and turpentine – was the only form of polishing.

Appendix B:
Technical Information

ANCHOR ESCAPEMENT This recoil escapement invented about 1670 is the one most generally used in ordinary clocks. When well made it gives good results, but the pallets are often incorrectly formed, although no escapement is easier to set out correctly. This escapement requires a greater variation of the driving power to alter the arc of the pendulum than the dead-beat escapement. It is inexpensive to make but it is unquestionably inferior to the dead-beat for precision clocks. Fig. 19 illustrates a common form of the English anchor escapement. The pallets have no locking faces so

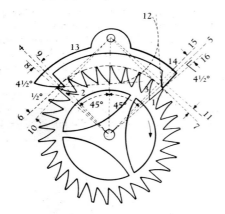

Figure 19

the wheel teeth fall upon the impulse faces and recoil until the momentum of the pendulum is exhausted, whereupon the wheel resumes its former forward motion and in so doing delivers the impulse.

The anchor is connected with the pendulum by the crutch (not shown), which is a short rod fixed to the pallet arbor terminating in a fork or pin which engages with the pendulum rod, thus communicating the impulse received by the pallets to the pendulum at one time and the motion of the pendulum to the pallets which causes the recoil at another.

English clocks usually have escape wheels of 30 teeth, the teeth being curved on the front and radial at the back. Some French makers varied the numbers of the escape-wheel teeth according to the length of pendulum. English makers as a rule varied the gear train, but seldom departed from a standard length of pendulum, usually one second for a long case, and half a second for bracket and dial clocks. The wheel normally moves in the direction of the arrow; tooth 1 has just completed its impulse on the pendulum, which owing to its momentum continues its movement to the right, with the result that it reverses the forward movement of the wheel until the momentum of the pendulum is exhausted by the combined resistance of the pull of gravity and the forward pressure of the wheel tooth. Thereupon the wheel resumes its forward motion and, in so doing, tooth 2 gives its impulse to 13, on completion of which tooth 3 falls on 14 and, in its turn, is forced back; the pendulum continues its leftward swing at the end of which 14 receives another impulse, and so on. Since the wheel does no work during the drop of the teeth from the corner of one pallet to their interception by the other, and since excessive drop increases pitting, it is important to limit this wasteful movement as much as possible by reducing the drop to no more than is necessary to ensure that the exit corners of the pallets do not catch the backs of the wheel teeth. Very little drop is necessary for this purpose, and it should be equal on each pallet and the same all round the wheel. If the drop varies from one side of the wheel to the other, the wheel either is not true or else is unequally divided; also the pivots may be out of line or the arbor bent.

There is no particular shape prescribed for the curves of the faces; a convenient one is an arc of the same radius as the wheel. The centre is found by intersecting arcs of that radius, struck from both ends of the two impulse planes. The object of curving the pallets is to lessen pitting. There will, however, be very little pitting if the wheels are light, but, bearing in mind that very thin wheels tend to pit pallets more quickly than do thicker ones, a compromise must be reached, and 1/32 in (1 mm approx.) may be taken as a minimum thickness. The backs of the pallets should point to the centre of the wheel when the tooth is at the beginning of its impulse; the shape of the anchor can be the designer's decision. One advantage of making the backs of the wheel teeth radial and the fronts curved is that, if for any reason the anchor is swung excessively, the pallets butt against the roots of the teeth and the points of the teeth will not be spoilt. *Fig. 20* shows an anchor escapement for a long-case clock.

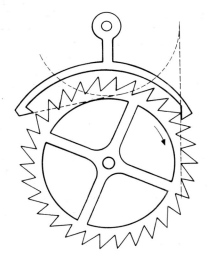

Figure 20

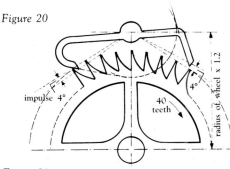

Figure 21

Makers of mass-produced English clocks did not confine themselves to this particular form of the recoil escapement. Some English makers adopted the strip pallet characteristic of cheap American and German clocks but have retained the span of $7\frac{1}{2}$ spaces and the impulse of 4 degrees (*fig. 21*). The strip pallet is simply a strip of steel bent to the same angles as the solid pallets and hardened. Provided it is mounted so that the staff is at the intersection of the two tangents, and that the impulse planes are at the correct angles, the action is quite satisfactory.

In many escapements, the pallets were not planted at the intersection of the tangents. If the difference is not great, these clocks go fairly well, especially if the workmanship is good, but, for the best results with the minimum of friction and wear on the pivots and holes, the tangent principle should be adhered to. In new work it should always be adopted, and in repair work, when new pallets have to be made, they should if possible be planted in conformity with the tangent rule.

Although the action of French recoil escapements is the same as that of the English ones, they differ from them in some particulars. The wheels have more teeth, usually 36 or 40, and the pallets span fewer teeth generally, but not less than $5\frac{1}{2}$ spaces, as anything less than this would bring the pallet staff too near to the wheel teeth and risk fouling them, the clearance of the wheel teeth and the belly of the pallets being too small. The impulse varies between 5 and 10 degrees; 6 degrees may be taken as an average. The faces are flat, not curved as in the case of the English anchor (*fig. 22*). The body of the anchor is usually gable-shaped and is fitted on a tapering squared part of the pallet arbor. One pivot of the pallet staff runs in an eccentric bush or

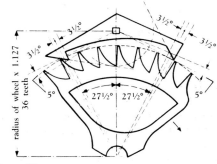

Figure 22

plug which is fitted friction-tight in the plate and is slit like a screwhead. This device renders the adjustment of the wheel and pallet depth a simple matter of turning the plug round with a screw-driver. Any alteration of the distance apart from the wheel and pallets does not affect the equality of the drops so much as it does with pallets of a wider span. In order to prevent any damage to the wheel teeth, the arc of the pendulum is limited by two banking pins planted in the plate on either side of the pendulum.

BAROMETRIC ERROR One of the frictioned restraints that balances and pendulums are subjected to is due to displacement of air in which they are immersed. If however the density of the air changes, the amount of frictional restraint will also be affected. The error is appreciable with precision clocks; it will be different for different clocks, but as a guide it might be as much as $\frac{1}{3}$ sec per day per 25-mm change in the air pressure. Experiments show that if a magnet is fixed vertically to a pendulum just above the pole of another magnet attached to the clock case, the rate of the clock is easily altered by the magnets receding from or approaching each other. The attractive power of dissimilar poles causes it to gain, the amount of the gain lessening as they move further apart.

There was therefore devised a barometric compensation (fig. 23), first fitted to one of the standard sidereal clocks at Greenwich. Two bar magnets about 6 in (15·2 cm) long were attached to the pendulum bob, one behind and one in front, 1, with their dissimilar poles towards a horseshoe magnet, 2, carried by a lever resting at 3, on knife

edges; so the horseshoe is always attracting the pendulum and increasing the acceleration due to gravity. The poles of the horseshoe are exactly under the bar magnets and about $3\frac{3}{4}$ in (9·5 cm) below. At the other extremity of the lever, a rod, 4, carries a float, 5, which rests on the mercury in the short leg of a barometer; the area of the cistern part of the short leg is four times the area of the upper part of the barometer tube, so a variation of 1 in (2·5 cm) in the barometric pressure would affect the height of the mercury in the cistern $\frac{1}{4}$ in (6 mm). As the clock loses with rising pressure, the bar magnet over the south pole of the horseshoe magnet is placed with its north pole downwards, and the bar magnet over the north pole with its south pole down, so there is attraction between bar magnets and horseshoe magnet. The bracket supporting the knife edges can be shifted to increase or diminish the action of the magnet, and the lever is balanced by placing weights in the pan, 6. The last of the precision pendulum clocks used in observatories were run under a low and constant pressure. Compensation can also be made by using aneroid drums.

BARREL and MAINSPRING The need for portable timepieces meant an alternative had to be found to the weight as the motive power. The energy stored in a coiled spring was at first a poor substitute because the power falls off as the coils unwind; how much it falls off depends on a number of factors, but much work has been done to try to make the mainspring as good a source of power as the falling weight, and with more success than its pioneers would have believed possible. The first attempt limited the turns of winding by stopwork, which prevents the very high torque that occurs when the spring is fully wound around its arbor. Early stopwork consisted of a pinion mounted on the barrel arbor that meshed with a wheel with a tooth space missing; and relative positions of pinion and missing tooth space brought the pinion to a stop when the mainspring was nearly wound.

Stackfreed In conjunction with the stopwork, another device called the stackfreed was used in German clocks and watches, and the earliest form appeared c.1540. A strong steel spring carries a roller which acts against the cam mounted on the stopwork wheel. Because of the geometry of the cam, when wound the spring carrying the roller robs the mainspring of power, but adds parts of its own strength to the mainspring as this unwinds.

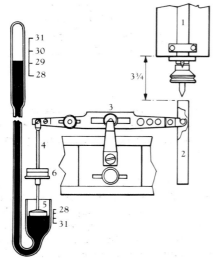

Figure 23

The stackfreed had a limited life with the fusee as a competitor.

Fusee The principle of the fusee *(fig. 24)* was known and illustrated in 1407 and it is still used. Combined with mainspring and barrel, it is usual to find it in portable timepieces from the first introduction of the mainspring in about the middle of the fifteenth century. The mainspring barrel was connected to the fusee by gut until around 1630, but after this it was often replaced by chain in high-

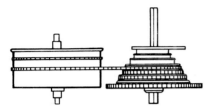

Figure 24

quality timepieces. Early fusee chains had long links; the techniques of manufacture improved until by the middle of the seventeenth century chains were made small enough to be used in watches.

Reversed Fusee, or Left-handed Fusee Where the pull of the chain is on the same side of the centre of the fusee as the force is communicated to the centre pinion, friction on the fusee pivots is reduced. The hooking in of the mainspring is reversed and the chain pulled off the fusee the opposite way round.

Going Barrel Eventually largely superseded the fusee, following improvements in the rest of the mechanism. The going barrel is usually mounted on an arbor that is turned during winding; it rotates and drives the train through gearing cut on its periphery. The arbor can be turned one way only by virtue of a ratchet wheel mounted on it which works with a click. The barrel still experiences the pull of the spring during winding so no maintaining power is necessary. Careful design of the clickwork can reduce the excessive maximum torque that occurs when the spring is fully wound.

Tensator Mainspring A stainless or carbon steel spring stressed by reverse bending and heat treatment so that it can be deflected from a small radius of curvature to the completely straightened condition and then curved in the opposite direction

without permanent deformation. The torque output, even with a spring pre-set throughout its length to a uniform radius of curvature, will not vary more than 5 per cent if it is deformed to thirty times its pre-set diameter. As an example of what may be achieved, *fig. 25* shows a tensator motor-powered clock. Here the spring is wound off the storage bobbin on to the torque output drum and thus the radius of curvature is reversed. It is the effort the spring makes to coil back around the

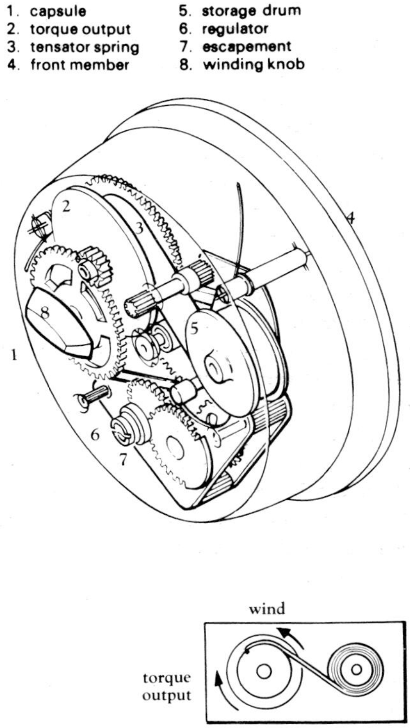

1. capsule
2. torque output
3. tensator spring
4. front member
5. storage drum
6. regulator
7. escapement
8. winding knob

Figure 25

storage bobbin that drives the clock. The working torque is produced purely by the bending that occurs during the transfer and there is no friction between the coils.

BELLS (TUNING) Bells only very slightly out of tune offend a musical ear, and may be easily corrected to the extent of half a tone. To sharpen the note the bell is made shorter by turning away its edge; to flatten the tone, the back, basin-shaped part of the bell is thinned by turning some of the metal off the outside.

177

BEVEL GEARS Gears used to connect shafts not in the same plane (*fig. 26*). They are cut on the sides of truncated cones whose apexes meet at the point of

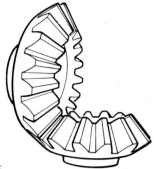

Figure 26

intersection of the shaft centres. Used in keyless work of English watches, the motion work of turret clocks, and in astronomical clocks.

BOB The main mass of a pendulum situated at its lower end.

False Bob A small disc which hangs from the pallet arbor of a verge escapement and shows through a slot in the dial. This enables the clock to be stopped and started from the front and also shows whether or not the clock is going. When a verge clock is converted to an anchor escapement, the disc is usually removed and the slot filled with an engraved plate; but if the slot is kept, the small travel of the false bob discloses the fact of the conversion.

BOB PENDULUM A special term for a type of pendulum directly fixed to the pallet arbor. The bob usually screws on to the rod. It is associated with antique verge and tic-tac clocks. A faceted bob may be furnished with a number of flat faces which are sometimes numbered, by which the amount they are turned can be gauged (*fig. 27*).

BOLT AND SHUTTER A maintaining power device used in antique clocks. The winding holes in the dial are covered by shutters which must be moved aside by operating a lever before winding can commence. The act of moving the shutters aside brings a sprung or weighted lever into mesh with the going train. Thus the clock is kept going while winding. This is necessary because the motive force is not operative during winding.

BREGUET KEY A key with a ratchet arrangement

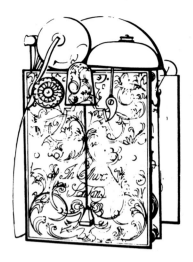

Figure 27

permitting winding in one direction only, invented by A. L. Breguet. Used both for watches and marine chronometers. Also known as a tipsy key.

BROCOT ESCAPEMENT A clock escapement invented by Achille Brocot of Paris (1817-78) and in French clocks often placed as a feature in front of the dial. The pins may be of steel or of jewel; they are half round in section, and the faces of the teeth are normally radial, so that the escapement is nearly dead beat. Drop occurs with the tooth safely tangential to the pin, and impulse as the tooth tip slides down the circumference of the pin, until it escapes (*fig. 28*). The angle of impulse bears a direct

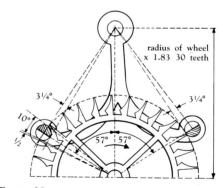

Figure 28

relationship to the number of teeth embraced; $10\frac{1}{2}$ is the usual number. English clockmakers objected to this escapement because of the difficulty of keeping oil at the pallets; if the pins are steel this trouble is more serious.

BROCOT SUSPENSION A form of pendulum suspension, named after its inventor, which allows regulation from the front of the clock by moving chops up and down the suspension spring. The chops fit the spring closely, and therefore the effective length of spring, and hence the pendulum, can be altered.

BUTTERFLY A winged nut; sometimes used for regulating a pendulum and placed above the pendulum suspension. This is a speciality of clocks made by Joseph Knibb.

BUTTING The condition when gears mesh incorrectly, for whatever reason, and the tips of the teeth butt on entering.

CALENDAR Division of time based on the revolutions of the earth, moon and sun into years, months and days. No system has achieved complete accuracy but that of the Mayan priests of the Incas accrued only one day's error in 10,000 years; the modern system of correction is a compromise between accuracy and ease of application. The Julian calendar accrued one day's error every 128 years until 1582 when it was amended by Pope Gregory XIII. The Gregorian calendar was adopted in most European countries from 1582 to 1587, and in others more gradually from 1700 to 1923; it was adopted in Great Britain in 1752. In the Gregorian calendar a normal year is 365 days, and every fourth year 366 days. One out of four century years is a leap year and there are 97 leap years in 400 years. The discrepancy is 26·5 sec per year, about 3 days in 10,000 years.

CALENDAR APERTURE A small aperture provided in a dial to show the date.

CALENDAR WORK One of the simple additions to a clock is a calendar showing the day of the month. This was a practical aid before 1785 when there were no daily newspapers and of course no radio to keep constant track of the date. The date is usually shown through an aperture in the dial, behind which lies a disc with the numbers 1 to 31, which is indexed by a day wheel rotating once every 24 hours; this has a pin or finger which engages with the teeth on the edge of the date disc. A jumper locates the date wheel correctly. For a month of less than 31 days the date disc is pushed on by hand; this cannot be done when the day-wheel pin

or finger is in mesh with the date ring, so for convenience the date change should be arranged to index in the early hours of the day. In some cases it is possible to reach behind the dial to index the date ring; in others there are small holes in the ring to enable it to be led around with a pin. In an alternative arrangement a hand moves around a small dial numbered 1 to 31.

Annual Calendar. Found on clocks from an early date. Every day of every month is marked around the outside of the dial, so the calendar is always correct except in leap years. In some clocks a subsidiary dial rotates once a year, attached to a disc with 365 teeth.

Day and Date and Month Work. A simple arrangement is shown in *fig. 29*. Gearing with the hour wheel is a wheel with twice the number of teeth, therefore turning once in 24 hours. A three-armed lever is planted just above this wheel; the lower arm

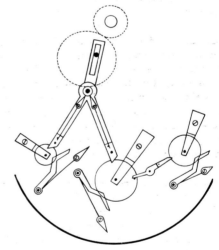

Figure 29

is slotted, and the wheel carries a pin which works in this slot so that the lever moves to and fro once every 24 hours. The three upper circles represent star wheels. The wheel on the right has 7 teeth for the days of the week; the centre one 31 teeth for the days of the month; and the one on the left 12 teeth for the months. Every time the upper arms of the lever move to the left they move forward the day-of-the-week and day-of-the-month wheels by one tooth. The extremities of the levers are jointed to yield on the return stroke and are brought back

179

into position again by a weak spring. A pin in the day-of-the-month wheel actuates a lever once every revolution and this moves the month-of-the-year wheel.

Perpetual Calendar Work Brocot's arrangement of calendar, lunation and equation work is shown in *figs 30, 31, 32*. The parts are on a circular plate of which the inner side (*fig. 30*) contains pieces for indicating the days of the week and days of the month. The outer side (*fig. 31*) has the mechanism for phases of the moon and equation of time; the dial (*fig.32*) is attached to this side. The calendar is actuated by a pin, 5, fixed to a wheel of the movement turning once in 24 hours (*fig. 30*). Two clicks, 6, 9, are pivoted to the lever, 8; 6 is kept in contact with a ratchet wheel of 31 teeth, and 9 with a ratchet wheel of 7 teeth. The parts of these clicks and wheels that are obscured are shown separately in *fig. 30*. When lever 8 is moved by pin 5, the clicks, 6 and 9, slip under the teeth, their beaks pass on to the following tooth, and the lever, not leaning on pin 5, falls quickly by its own weight and makes each click leap a tooth of the wheels of 7 and 31 teeth, respectively. The arbors of these wheels pass through the dial and carry a hand. This motion indicates the day of the week, and would be sufficient for days of the month if the index were shifted by hand at the end of the short months. To provide for the 30-day months, and for the 28-day

February for three years, and 29 days in leap year, the arbor, 15, of the month wheel goes through the circular plate; in the other side is a pinion of 10 teeth (*fig. 31*). This pinion, by means of the intermediate wheel 16, works another wheel centred at 17, with 120 teeth, which thus turns once in a year. The arbor of the last wheel bears a hand indicating the month. The arbor, 17, goes through the plate, and at its other end (*fig. 31*) is a wheel gearing with another with four times as many teeth, at 13. This wheel is partly concealed in *fig. 30* by disc 18, which is fixed to it and also thus makes a

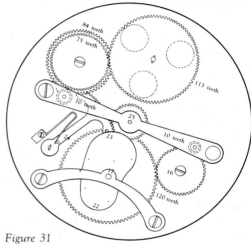

Figure 31

turn in four years. On this disc are 20 notches; the 16 shallowest correspond to the 30-day months; a deeper notch to 29 February; and the 3 deepest to the Februarys with 28 days. The uncut portions of the disc correspond to the 31-day months. The wheel of 31 has pin 14 placed before the tooth

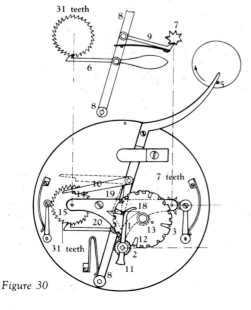

Figure 30

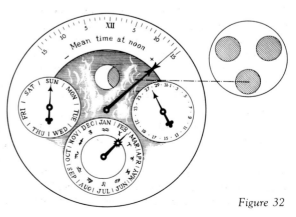

Figure 32

which corresponds to the 28th of the month; on lever 8 is pivoted freely a bell-crank lever, 10, with, at the extremity of the arm 19, a pin, 20, which rests on the edge of disc 18 or in one of the notches, according to the position of the month. The arm, 10, is therefore higher or lower according to the position of pin 20 on the disc. When pin 20 rests on the outside of the disc, the arm, 10, of the bell-crank lever is as high as possible (dotted in the figure), and the 31 teeth of the month wheel will leap successively one division by the action of click 6. But when pin 20 is in one of the shallow notches for a 30-day month, the arm, 10, of the bell-crank lever will take a lower position, and the forward movement of the lever, 8, will bring on the pin, 14, into contact with the bottom of the notch, just as the lever has accomplished $\frac{2}{3}$ of its movement, so the last third will make the 31 wheel advance one tooth; as a result the hand marks the 31st, the quick return of the lever putting the hand to the 1st. When pin 20 is in the shallowest of the four deep notches, for 29 February, the end of arm 10 will take a position lower still, and on the 29th the pin, 14, will be met by the bottom of the notch, just as the lever has made $\frac{1}{3}$ of its course; so the other $\frac{2}{3}$ will make 2 teeth of the 31 wheel jump, the hand will indicate 31, the ordinary quick return of the detent putting it to the 1st. When pin 20 is in one of the three deepest notches, for 28 February years, it will be in the bottom of the notch on the 28th just at the moment the lever begins its movement, and 3 teeth will pass before the return of the lever makes the hand leap from the 31st to the 1st. Pin 20 easily gets out of the shallow notches which are sloped away to facilitate this; a weighted finger, 12, on the arbor of the annual wheel helps it out of the deeper notches.

Phases of the Moon A pinion of 10 teeth on the arbor, 7, gears with a wheel of 84 teeth fixed on another wheel of 75 which gears with a wheel of 113, making one revolution in three lunations. There is an error of only 0·0008 day per lunation. On the wheel of 113 is fixed a plate, 21, on which are 3 discs coloured blue with a distance between them equal to their diameter (*fig. 32*); these, slipping behind a circular aperture in the dial, simulate the successive phases of the moon.

Equation of time In *fig. 31*, on the arbor of the annual wheel is fixed a brass cam or kidney piece, 22, on the edge of which rests the pin, 23, fixed to a

sector, 24. This rack gears with the central wheel, 25, which carries the hand giving the equation of time, i.e. the difference between solar and mean time.

Manner of Adjusting the Calendar First, the return of the lever, 8, must be made at the moment of midnight. To adjust the hand of the days of the week, look at an almanac to see when there was a full or new moon. If it was new moon on Thursday, say, use the small button fixed at the back on the axis of the hand of the week to make as many returns as requisite to obtain a new moon, this hand pointing to a Thursday; then bring back the hand to the correct date, passing the number of divisions corresponding to the days elapsed since the new moon. To adjust the hand of the month, see if pin 20 is in the proper notch. For the leap year, in the month of February it is in the shallowest of the four deep notches; for the same month of the first year after leap year, the pin should of course be in the notch, 1, and so on.

CHRONOMETER ESCAPEMENT Unlike the lever escapement this escapement gives impulse when the balance is moving in one direction but not in the other (*fig. 33*). In the drawing the moving balance is just about to pass the detent without unlocking the

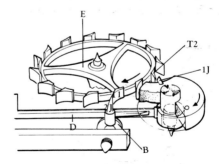

Figure 33

escape wheel. When the balance comes back in the other direction, the detent, D, is moved aside until the jewel, 2J, clears the tooth, T1, of the escape wheel. Tooth T2 then gives impulse to the balance via the jewel, 1J. B is the banking screw which prevents the detent going too far into the escape wheel.

CONSTANT FORCE ESCAPEMENT This is a special type of

escapement having a subsidiary spring or weight that provides the motive force to the escapement. This spring or weight is wound or lifted by the main train at frequent intervals. Thus the force at the escapement is made virtually independent of the fluctuations due to inaccuracies in gears and variation in the main motive force. One such is the gravity escapement, which although interesting in its action often tends to be noisy, and the purchase of a clock containing such an escapement should be considered carefully if intended for use in a living room. It was originally invented by Thomas Mudge, although no clock bearing his name survives with his escapement. The earliest examples are in clocks by Henry Ward of Blandford, who was making clocks during the late eighteenth and early nineteenth centuries. The best known type of gravity escapement is the double three-legged gravity as fitted in Big Ben.

DEAD-BEAT ESCAPEMENT First used successfully by George Graham in 1715, but designed originally by Thomas Tompion. Its distinguishing feature is the elimination of recoil in the escape wheel, accomplished by making the locking faces of the pallets circumferential with the pallet pivots. Thus the only restraint on the pendulum, once impulse has been given, is caused by frictional losses between the locking face and the escape-wheel tooth. To reduce this further, the supplementary arc is kept to a minimum consistent with sureness of action, and the acting part of the pallets may be made of jewel. The only defect inherent in it is that the thickening of oil on the pallets affects the rate. The pallets of the Graham escapement can embrace

many or few teeth. The one in *fig. 34* embraces only 8; for larger clocks of less precision 10 teeth embraced is a good compromise. In B. L. Vulliamy's version of the Graham escapement (*fig. 34*), the pallets are annular pieces of steel accurately turned to size inside and out to provide the dead-locking faces, the impulse planes being faced to the same angle as those in *fig. 35*; the pieces are closely fitted in circular grooves and secured by cover plates screwed on the pallet limbs. The wheel is hard-hammered brass, and for regulators is usually made $1\frac{1}{2}$–2 in (3·8–5 cm) in diameter, and very light. Many clockmakers put two banking pins in the plate, one on each side of the crutch, to prevent the pallets from being jammed into the wheel by careless handling.

Although the dead-beat escapement in a weight-driven clock with a seconds pendulum has proved an excellent timekeeper for regulators and astronomical clocks, it seems not so suitable for smaller clocks with shorter pendulums, or where the clock is spring- not weight-driven. It is difficult to make the escapement with sufficient accuracy on a smaller scale. There is a combination of the dead-beat and the recoil escapement called the half dead-beat escapement; the locking faces are not concentric with the pallet axis, but are struck with a larger radius to give a slight recoil of the wheel. The wheel teeth are either radial or slightly undercut. This was an escapement much used by Vulliamy.

FOLIOT The cross bar that carries a weight at either end and acts as the controlling member in clocks made before the pendulum or the balance and spring were introduced. It is fixed to the top end of

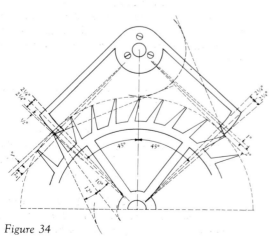

Figure 34

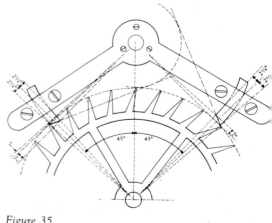

Figure 35

the verge (*fig. 36*). Moving the weights in and out alters the timekeeping. Moving them towards the centre causes the timepiece to gain.

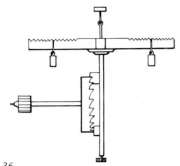

Figure 36

GRASSHOPPER ESCAPEMENT This escapement was probably designed by James Harrison, brother of John, but is usually attributed to John Harrison. It is similar to the chronometer escapement inasmuch as it requires no lubrication at the pallets, which are pulled and pushed by the escapement teeth without any sliding occurring. The earliest known example is in a turret clock made in 1726 by James Harrison. In *fig. 37* the right-hand pallet, the exit, is being pulled by the escape-wheel tooth.

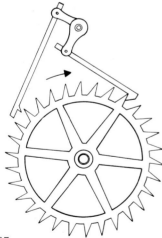

Figure 37

Eventually the pallet on the left side will be picked up by an escape-wheel tooth and the wheel will be recoiled. This will release the exit pallet, which will flick out of engagement against a resilient stop under the influence of a light spring. The same will happen when the pendulum moves back in the

other direction. This escapement was first used with a large arc of swing of the pendulum with an amplitude of $12\frac{1}{2}$ degrees. To achieve any sort of accuracy in such a clock, the pendulum has to swing between cycloidal cheeks; Harrison's cycloidal cheeks were far in advance of Huyghens's, and adjustable for angle and form. He achieved correct results by constant experimentation and made a final claim that his clocks with grasshopper escapements and cycloidal cheeks would keep time to a second in three months; there is no reason to doubt this. Because his regulators worked without oil and did not wear, once his adjustments were completed, the results were permanent.

GUT A strong cord made from the cured intestinal muscle of sheep or oxen.

GUT PALLETS To render the verge and the anchor (recoil) escapement silent, the metal of the acting part of the pallet can be replaced with a tightly stretched length of gut.

GYMBALS or GIMBALS Universal joints enabling a chronometer to remain horizontal in conditions where motion occurs, e.g. at sea when the flat surface on which its outer box rests is constantly shifted by the roll and pitch of the ship. Invented by Girolamo Cardano (1501–76) to suspend ships' lamps safely, this device was first used for a marine timepiece by Huyghens.

HOOP WHEEL A wheel associated with some types of locking-plate striking clocks. It has a rim attached to its face, which is cut away for a small portion of its circumference. A locking arm falls into this gap when the correct number of blows have been struck as dictated by the locking plate.(See STRIKING WORK).

HOROLOGY The art, science and practice of time measurement.

HORSE A wooden stand for supporting clock movements during testing. There are many different types, some for small movements and some for supporting long-case movements (*fig. 38*).

HUYGHENS (HUYGENS), CHRISTIAN Born 1629, died 1695. A Dutch mathematician, author of *Horologium Oscillatorium* (Paris, 1673). To him is due the credit of first successfully applying the pendulum to clocks.

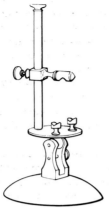

Figure 38

Huyghens's clock is shown in *fig. 39*. The upper part of the pendulum hangs on a double cord hanging between two cycloidal cheeks to give a cycloidal path to the bob. *Fig. 40* gives a better idea of this device, which was no doubt of advantage with the long arcs required by the verge escapement. Another feature of Huyghens's clock

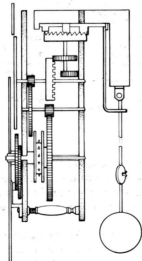

Figure 39

is his endless cord maintaining power. In *fig. 41*, 5 (right) is the driving weight, supported by an endless cord passing over the pulley, 1, attached to the great wheel, and also over the pulley, 3, which is provided with ratchet teeth. The cord, 4, is pulled down to wind the clock, and the ratchet wheel, 3,

then runs under its click. So that while winding, as in going, one half of 5 (right) minus one half of 5 (left) is driving the clock. The pulleys, 1 and 3, are spiked to prevent slipping of the cord or to locate the links of a chain.

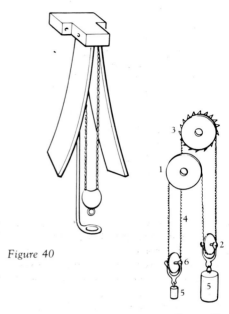

Figure 40

Figure 41

When this ingenious maintaining power is applied to a clock with a striking train, the pulley with the ratchet is attached to the great wheel of the striking train, one weight thus serving to drive both trains. A chain is preferable to a cord, owing to the dust which accumulates in the clock through the wearing of the latter.

LACQUERS Three well-known proprietary lacquers are Ercalene, Frigilene and Velvoid. Ercalene is a good quality general purpose air-drying lacquer, for metalwork, and it dries in a few minutes to give a hard and durable film. It may be applied by spray, brush or swab, and is available colourless and in 'old gold'. Frigilene is for use when a matt or satin finish, or a very highly polished finish, is to be protected without altering the surface characteristics. Velvoid is a matt black lacquer.

LANTERN PINION A pinion formed of two shrouds or sides connected by cylindrical rods or trundles. Lantern pinions are suitable as followers, but not for driving. For good performance, the spaces between the trundles should of course be equal. (See *fig. 42*).

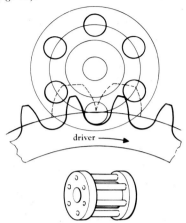

Figure 42

LATCH, or LATCHED PLATES High-quality clocks in the seventeenth century often had a front plate secured to the pillars by means of latches. The dial plate might also be attached to the front plate in the same way. The latch is dropped into a notch in the side of the pillar, the latch end being tapered in such a way that it pulls the plate down on to the pillar shoulder. *Fig. 43* shows a latch.

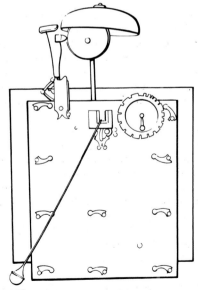

Figure 43

LEPAUTE'S ESCAPEMENT A pin-wheel type of dead-beat escapement for clocks. Invented by Amant, *maître*

horloger (Paris, 1749) and improved by J. A. Lepaute (Paris, 1709–89) *c.* 1753, it is analogous in its action to the Graham. The impulse is given by nearly half-round pins standing out from the face of the escape wheel. One advantage over the Graham is that the pressure on the pallets is always downwards, so that the pallet pivots do not tend to jump about in their pivot holes. With this shape of pin there is effectively divided impulse, part of the lift being given by the curved part of the pin and part from the impulse face of the pallets.

MOTION WORK *Fig.* 44 shows the motion work of a typical English clock. It comprises four gears which turn the once-an-hour revolution of the centre arbor into the once-in-12-hours (sometimes 24

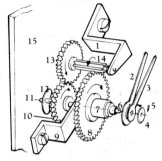

1. minute cock	9. bridge
2. hour hand	10. cannon wheel
3. minute hand	20 teeth
4. hand collet	11. centre arbor
5. retaining pin	12. minute spring
6. pipe squared for	13. minute wheel
minute hand	20 teeth
7. hour wheel pipe	14. minute pinion 6 leaves
8. hour wheel 72 teeth	15. plate

Figure 44

hours) revolution of the hour wheel. It also allows the setting of the hands to be done; the cannon wheel, 10, is held friction-tight on the centre arbor via the oval spring which lies between them.

PLATFORM ESCAPEMENT A separate assembly of escape wheel, pallets and balance mounted on a platform. The sample shown (*fig. 45*) is modern, having a club-tooth lever escapement and a plain balance with a self-compensating balance spring. A self-compensating balance spring corrects for changes in temperature without the need for a compensation balance in ordinary-grade work.

REMONTOIRE A device interposed between the mainspring and the escapement whereby the force

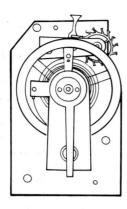

Figure 45

delivered to the escapement is made more constant. The mainspring merely serves to rewind the device at regular intervals. When the device is incorporated into the escapement, it is more explicit to describe it as a constant force escapement, even though it still comes under the general heading of remontoires.

SKELETON DIAL A pierced-out dial of a clock designed to show the movement or to be in keeping with a skeleton clock.

SINGLE-BEAT ESCAPEMENT An escapement in which the escape wheel moves only at every alternate beat of the balance or pendulum. The chronometer and

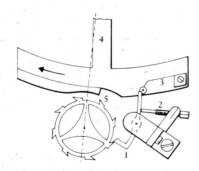

Figure 46

the duplex are examples of single-beat escapements. *Fig. 46* shows a single-beat chronometer escapement applied to a pendulum clock.

STRIKING JACK Figures on clocks which may be human, holding hammers, clubs, etc. for striking

bells that sound the hours, etc. Jacks were sometimes used to indicate the time of day to the public before dials were introduced. Although jacks are mostly fitted to public and church clocks, some can be found on domestic clocks.

STRIKING WORK *Fig. 47* shows the front plate of an English striking clock with rack striking, invented by Edward Barlow (1636–1716). The going train occupies the right and centre, and the striking train the left-hand side. The wheels of the striking train are shown by dotted circles. The connection between the going train and the striking work is by the gathering pallet, and also by the warning piece, which projects from the boss of the lifting piece. This warning piece goes through a slotted hole in the plate, and during the interval between warning and striking lies in the path of a pin in the last wheel of the striking train, called the warning wheel. The motion wheel on the centre arbor, turning once in an hour, gears with the minute wheel, which has an equal number of teeth. There is, projecting from the face of the minute wheel, a pin which, in passing, raises the lifting piece every hour. Except for a few minutes before the clock strikes, the striking train is kept from running by the tail of the gathering pallet resting on a pin in the rack. Just before the hour, as the boss of the lifting piece lifts the rack hook, the rack, impelled by a spring at its tail, falls back until the pin in the lower arm of the rack is stopped by the snail. This occurs before the lifting piece is released by the pin in the minute wheel, and in this position the warning piece stops the train. Exactly at the hour the pin in the minute wheel gets past the lifting piece, which then falls, and the train is free. For every hour struck, the gathering pallet, which is really a one-toothed pinion, gathers up one tooth of the rack. After it has gathered up the last tooth, its tail is caught up by the pin in the rack and the striking ceases.

In the drawing (*fig. 48*) the gathering pallet is just about to gather up the last tooth of the rack. This operation will bring the locking pin, which projects from the face of the rack, into the path of the longer end of the gathering pallet and stop its motion. It is essential that the moment the rack hook is lifted the rack should be free to fall, and that the form of gathering-pallet tail, where it rests on the pin in the rack, should be such as to accelerate rather than retard the movement of the rack. Within reasonable limits the position of the resting pin is unimportant, provided the surface of the tail where it rests, the pin, and the centre of motion of the rack form an angle of less than 90 degrees, so that the tail passes the pin with a sort of wedge-like action. And with the half-round termination of the gathering-pallet tail this condition is secured. To insist that the end of the tail should then be filed to form a

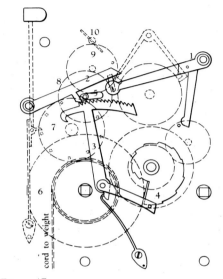

Figure 47

slanting plane is quite unnecessary and would spoil the symmetry of the tail.

The steps of the snail are arranged so that at 1 o'clock it permits only sufficient motion of the rack for one tooth to be gathered up, and at every succeeding hour additional motion equal to one extra tooth. The centre of motion of the rack hook, the point of its tooth, and the centre of motion of the rack form a right-angle; but in planting the work it is better to put the centre of the rack hook higher on the plate rather than lower, for, if it is lower, the pressure of the rack teeth may cause the hook to jump out occasionally, a very tiresome fault. The extreme point of the lower arm of the lifting piece should point to the centre of the motion wheel which carries the pin lifting it, or more to the centre of the plate than the other way, to avoid the possibility of engaging friction in their action.

When reassembling the striking train, see that the pin in the wheel, 9, is about in the position shown, to allow little run to the projecting catch of the lifting piece, and that a pin in the pin wheel is not close to the hammer tail, but placed so that the hammer tail drops off just before the train is locked. The allows all the run possible on to the pin.

The lower arm of the rack and the lower arm of the lifting piece can be made of brass, and thin, so as to yield when the hands of the clock are turned back; the lower extremity of the lifting piece should be a little wider, and bent to a slight angle with the plane of the arm, so as not to butt as it comes into contact with the pin when this is being done. If the clock is required to repeat, the snail, instead of being placed upon the centre arbor, may, with advantage, be mounted on a stud with a star wheel, as shown in *fig. 48*. Indeed, many good clockmakers always mount it so, because the position of the snail is then more accurate, owing to the backlash of the motion wheels.

Half-hour Striking The usual way to make a clock strike one at the half-hour is to place the first tooth of the rack lower than the rest, and the second pin in the minute wheel a little nearer the centre than the hour pin, so that the rack hook is lifted free of the first tooth only at the half-hour. This adjustment is rather delicate, and the action is liable occasionally to fail altogether or to strike the full hour, from the pin getting bent or from uneven wear of the parts. The arrangement shown in *fig. 48*

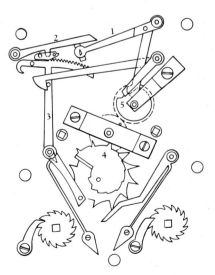

Figure 48

is safer. One arm of a bell-crank lever rests on a cam fixed to the minute wheel. The cam is shaped so that just before the half-hour the other extremity of the bell-crank lever catches a pin placed in the rack and permits it to move the distance of one tooth only. This is the position shown in the figure. After the half-hour has struck, the cam carries the catch free of the pin.

Quarters The quarter-hours may also be sounded on the short-toothed rack principle without a special train. In this case there are three extra teeth in the rack, all lower than the hour teeth, and arranged in steps, the outermost tooth being the lowest of all. There are then three lifting pins in the motion wheel besides the one for the hour, and they are placed at such a distance from the centre of the wheel that the first one after the hour lifts the rack sufficiently to allow the lowest tooth only to escape when one stroke is given on the bell. The half-hour pin, being a little further from the centre, allows two teeth to escape, and so two blows are given. The third pin after the hour is still a little further from the centre, and allows the three short teeth to pass, so that of course three blows are given. This arrangement works well if the graduations in the height of the teeth are sufficiently pronounced to ensure uniform action and the pins in the wheel are of adequate size so that they do not get bent. Using but one bell is, of course, apt to cause uncertainty as to the meaning of the sounds between the hours of one and three. By providing a second bell, Ting-Tang quarters can be struck. Pins to lift the second hammer are placed on the other side of the pin wheel, and that hammer arbor is slid longitudinally out of the way as the hour approaches and allowed to move back to its normal position when the hour is struck.

The snail is mounted on a star wheel placed so that a pin in the motion wheel on the centre arbor moves it one tooth for each revolution of the motion wheel. The pin, in moving the star wheel, presses back the click or jumper, which not only keeps the star wheel steady, but also completes its forward motion after the pin has pushed the tooth past the projecting centre of the click.

Division of the Hour Snail The length of the lower arm of the rack, from the centre of the stud hole to the centre of the pin, should be equal to the distance between the centre of the stud hole and the centre of the snail. The difference between the

radius of the top and the radius of the bottom step of the snail may be obtained by multiplying the distance of twelve teeth of the rack by the length of the lower arm, and dividing the product by the length of the upper arm. Divide the circumference of a circular brass blank into twelve parts, and draw

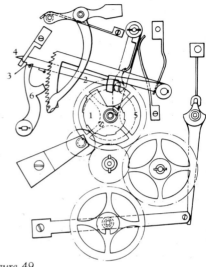

Figure 49

radial lines (*fig.* 49). Each of these spaces is devoted to a step of the snail. Draw circles representing the top and bottom step. Divide the distance between these two circles into eleven equal parts, and at each division draw a circle which will represent a step of the snail. The rise from one step to another should be sloped as shown, to throw off the pin in the rack arm if the striking train has been allowed to run down, and it should happen to be resting on the snail when turning the hands back. The rise from the bottom to the top step is bevelled off, as shown by the double line, so as to push the pin in the rack arm to one side, and allow it to ride over the snail if it is in the way when the clock is going. Clockmakers generally mark off the snail on the clock itself after the rest of the striking work is planted. A steel pointer is fixed in the hole of the lower rack arm, and the star wheel jumped forward twelve teeth by means of the pin in the motion wheel. After each jump, a line is marked on the blank snail with the pointer in the rack arm by moving the rack arm. The motion wheel is then turned sufficiently to carry the pin in it free of the star wheel, and the star wheel click fastened back, leaving the star wheel and blank snail quite free on their stud. The rack hook is placed in the first tooth of the rack, and, while the pointer in the rack is pressed on the blank snail, the latter is rotated a little, so that a curve is traced on it. The rack hook is then placed in the second tooth, and afterwards in the succeeding teeth consecutively, and the operation is repeated till the twelve curves are marked. There is one advantage in marking off the snail in this way for, should there be any inaccuracy in the division of the teeth of the rack, the steps of the snail will be made to match.

Clocks Striking One at the Hour These have the hammer tail lifted by a snail on the minute wheel. Although a snail of this kind is not divided into steps, the contour of the snail is a curve cutting through the intersection of the circles with the radial lines. If formed in this manner, it is evident that the hammer tail will be lifted uniformly throughout the revolution of the minute wheel. Sometimes these snails are wrongly made so that nearly the whole of the lifting occurs as the hour approaches, and the extra strain of the minute wheel can stop the clock, or cause the motion wheel to slip on the centre arbor.

Carriage-Clock Striking Work Fig. 49 shows an example of hour and half-hour striking work for small clocks. Though the principle is the same as in *figs* 47 and 48, the parts are differently arranged. The snail, 1, is mounted on the hour wheel, and the arm, 2, which takes the place of the lifting piece, is pivoted to a lever which is biased by a weak spring. In the cannon pinion are two pins, one placed nearer the centre than the other. At the half-hour, the pin nearest the centre has pushed back the lever till the first notch, 3, in the arm, 2, has fallen over the pin in the rack hook, 6; the pin then releases the end of the lever, and the rack hook is pushed far enough to allow one to be struck, though not far enough to allow the rack to fall. At the hour, the notch, 4, engages the pin, and pushes the hook clear of the rack. The striking is kept locked by an upright arm on the arbor of 6, which engages a pin in the last wheel of the striking train. Note that there is no tail to the gathering pallet; consequently, the striking is let off at once, and there is no preliminary warning. The horizontal lever at the top of the frame and the curved arm coming down in front of the rack are for pushing out the hook to repeat the striking of the previous hour. The small wheel below the hour wheel is connected with the

cannon pinion through the intermediate wheel on the left, and is for setting hands at the back.

Alarm The wheel at the bottom of the plate in *fig.* 49 is connected with the hour wheel by the intermediate wheel on the right, and is for letting off the alarm. The notched collar is fixed to the arbor, which can be turned round till the notch corresponds to the hour required. The wheel rides loose on the arbor and is pressed forward by the spring at the back. There is a projection on the boss of the wheel facing the collar, and when this projection comes opposite to the notch, it enters, and the spring is thereby allowed to come forward sufficiently to disengage itself from the vertical lever on the extreme right of the figure. To the axis of this lever on the right side of the plate is fixed a pair of pallets, and a hammer to strike the bell. On the arbor of the wheel, which engages with the pallets, is a small mainspring barrel, so that, if the mainspring is released, the hammer vibrates rapidly, striking the bell or gong. The short end of the lever carries a banking pin, which works between a spring fork as shown. One side of the notch in the collar is sloped off at the back, so that, as the wheel continues its rotation, the projection is pushed out of the notch and the spring again locks the alarm lever. With this type of alarm work the hands should not be turned backwards.

Three-train Quarter-chime Clock Fig 50 shows the mechanism of a quarter-chiming clock. The going

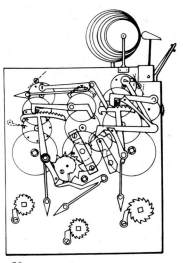

Figure 50

train occupies the centre of the plate; the striking train is planted on the left, and the chiming on the right hand. As the gathering pallet makes one complete revolution for every blow struck, the pin wheel must contain as many times more teeth than the pinion on the gathering pallet arbor as there are pins in the pin wheel. The number of teeth in the pallet wheel must also be a multiple of the teeth in the pinion on the warning-wheel arbor.

There are four pins in the minute wheel for raising the quarter lifting piece, and therefore the quarter-rack hook, every quarter of an hour. One, two, three, or four quarters are chimed according to the position of the quarter snail, which turns with the minute wheel. At the hour when the quarter rack is allowed to fall its greatest distance, it falls against the bent arm of the hour-rack hook, and releases the hour rack. As the last tooth of the quarter rack is gathered, the pin in the rack pulls over the hour warning lever, and lets off the striking train. The position of the pieces in the figure is as they would be directly after the hour is struck.

Difficulties with quarter clocks sometimes arise from the method often adopted for knocking out the hour-rack hook, which, as just explained, is effected by the falling of the quarter rack, aided by a strong rack spring. Failure to strike the hour occasionally occurs through too weak a quarter-rack spring, or one that has been bent in cleaning. The clock is also liable to strike the hour at the third quarter, if the quarter-rack teeth are too fine: this allows the quarter rack to lift the hour-rack hook.

A suggested improvement is shown in fig. 51. If, instead of the dotted arm, 1, which, as in fig. 50, is attached to the hour-rack hook, an arm such as 2 is brought down behind the minute wheel that carries

the quarter snail, and a pin placed in the wheel to lift the hour-rack hook by pressing on the arm, 2, and drop it just before the hour, the difficulties mentioned above will be overcome. The lifting of the hour rack will not depend upon the fall of the quarter rack; consequently coarse teeth to the quarter rack, and the abnormally strong quarter-rack spring, will be unnecessary. The quarter rack must, of course, be made to fall before the hour-rack hook is lifted.

Figs 52 and 53 are front and back views of a three-train chiming and striking clock of modern design and construction.

Improvements in chiming and striking clocks have simplified the mechanism, made it self-

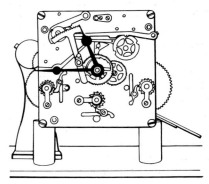

Figure 52

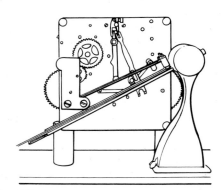

Figure 53

correcting, and made reassembling the clock after cleaning easier. One of these improvements is the substitution of the locking plate for the rack system in the chiming train, coupled with some device for automatically correcting any derangement of the sequence of the quarters. There are several of these devices, but the underlying principle is the same: it is to hold up or lock more

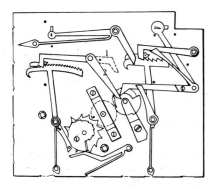

Figure 51

deeply the chiming train after the striking of the third quarter, and then, by means of a longer lifting spur on the quarter cam, to raise it clear of the lock at the striking of the hour. One of the simplest consists of a stepped catch pivoting on a screw in the locking plate of the quarter train and under the control of a spiral spring which exerts a clockwise pull on it. The actual lock is performed by a pin so fixed in the warning detent as to intercept the stepped catch at the conclusion of the chiming of the third quarter; it will then rock the catch slightly, but not enough to allow the pin to fall into the step. If the chimes are in order, the next release of the train (for striking the hours) will be by the long spur of the lifting cam, which will raise the pin free of the catch, and this, actuated by the spring, will then be pulled clear of the detent. Should the chimes be incorrect, the next lifting operation will be effected by one of the short spurs provided for letting off the quarters. This will only raise it high enough to allow the pin on the warning detent to fall into the step; thus the train will be locked, and remain so until the long spur of the hour comes round and lifts the detent and its pin clear, so restoring the correct sequence.

There are several devices for preventing damage occurring through turning the hands backwards. One of the simplest consists of a shaped piece like a bell-crank lever interposed between the lifting pin or quarter cam and the warning detent. It is arranged so that during the movement of the hands forward it lifts the detent, but when the hands are reversed it is merely moved aside.

Grand Sonnerie Striking Work with Minute Repeating Beneath the Dial of a Carriage Clock This striking work is let off automatically by the clock each quarter of an hour, when it will strike the quarters and then the hour at the hour or, if desired, the quarters and hours at every quarter. When the repeat button at the top of the clock is depressed, the clock will strike the hour, the quarters past that hour *and* the minutes past that quarter. All driven by one barrel, this is the most sophisticated type of striking work ever developed. Really stemming from watchwork practice, this type of clock was made by one of the most eminent firms of Victorian watchmakers, Nicole Nielsen (*fig. 54*).

Tic-tac A type of recoil escapement where the pallets embrace just a few teeth of the escape wheel, from $1\frac{1}{2}$ to about $4\frac{1}{2}$. Tic-tac escapements are

mostly found in French drum clocks (*fig. 55*), but first appeared in clocks by Thomas Tompion and Joseph Knibb.

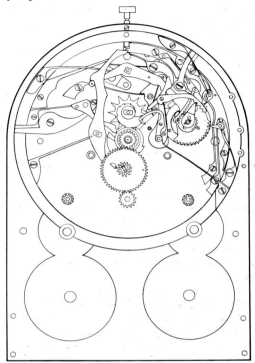

Figure 54

Figure 55

VERGE, or CROWN-WHEEL ESCAPEMENT A recoil escapement in which the pallet axis is set at right-angles to the axis of the escape wheel, the earliest of all the escapements (*fig. 56*). It can have no pretensions to accuracy, for the balance or foliot has no free arc, and its vibration is limited to about 110 degrees each way. The escape wheel, or crown wheel, usually has an odd number of teeth. The staff, or verge, is made as small as proper strength will allow, and planted close to the wheel so that the tips of the teeth just clear it. The pallets, which form part of the verge, are placed at an angle of 95 -

191

100 degrees with each other. The drawing shows a plan view of the escape wheel and verge. The width of the pallets apart, from centre to centre, is equal to the diameter of the wheel. A tooth of the escape wheel is just leaving the upper pallet, 3; as it drops

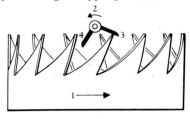

Figure 56

off, the under-tooth will reach the root of the lower pallet, 4, but the motion of the verge will not be at once reversed. The escape wheel will recoil until the impetus of the balance is exhausted. The teeth of the wheel are undercut to free the face of the pallet during the recoil. To ensure good performance, the body or arbor of the verge should be upright, and, when in the frame and viewed through the follower, the potence hole should be seen crossing the balance-wheel hole of the dovetail, viewed in a line with the arbor of the balance-wheel pinion when in the follower. The drops off the pallets should be equal, and the balance-wheel teeth true.

Appendix C:
Clocks Exhibited throughout the World

Museums with Clocks in the British Isles

ABERDEEN Provost Skene's House, Guestrow, City Centre.
—— Aberdeen Art Gallery and Industrial Museum, School Hill.
ABERGAVENNY Abergavenny and District Museum, Castle House.
ABERYSTWYTH The National Library of Wales.
ABINGDON Town Museum, County Hall.
ALTON The Curtis Museum, High Street.
ARBROATH Arbroath Art Gallery, Public Library, Hill Terrace.
ARMAGH Armagh County Museum, The Mall.
ASHBURTON 1 West Street.
AYLESBURY Bucks, County Museum, Church Street.
—— Waddesdon Manor, Waddesdon, near Aylesbury.
AYR Ayr Museum and Art Gallery, 12 Main Street.

BAMBURGH The Grace Darling Museum.
BANFF High Street.
BANGOR Bangor Borough Museum Town Hall, The Castle.
BARNARD CASTLE The Bowes Museum.
BARNET Barnet Museum, 31 Wood Street.
BARROW-IN-FURNESS Barrow-in-Furness Museum, Ramsden Square.
BASINGSTOKE The Willis Museum, New Street.
BATH American Museum, Claverton Manor.
—— The Holburne of Menstrie Museum of Art, Great Pulteney Street.
—— The Pump Room, Bath Roman Museum, Abbey Churchyard.
—— Victoria Art Gallery, Bridge Street.

BATLEY Bagshaw Museum, Wilton Park; and Oakwell Hall, Birstall.
BEDFORD Cecil Higgins Art Gallery, Castle Close.
—— Elstow Moot Hall – one mile south of Bedford.
BELFAST Ulster Museum, Stranmillis.
BIDEFORD Burton Art Gallery, Victoria Park, Kingsley Road.
BIGGAR Gladstone Court.
BIRKENHEAD Williamson Art Gallery and Museum, Slatey Road.
BIRMINGHAM Birmingham City Museum and Art Gallery, The Department of Science and Industry, Newhall Street.
—— University Medical School Museum, Hospitals Centre.
BLACKBURN Museum and Art Gallery, Library Street.
—— Turton Tower, Turton.
BLAIR ATHOLL Blair Castle and Atholl Museum – eight miles NW of Pitlochry on A9, Perthshire.
BOURNEMOUTH Rothesay Museum, 11 Bath Road.
—— Russell Cotes Art Gallery and Museum, East Cliff.
BRADFORD Bolling Hall Museum, Bowling Hall Road.
—— City Art Gallery and Museum, Cartwright Museum Hall.
BRIDLINGTON Bayle Gate Museum.
—— Bridlington Art Gallery, Sewerby Hall.
BRIDPORT Bridport Museum and Art Gallery, South Street.
BRIGHTON The Royal Pavilion.
—— Thomas-Stanford Museum, Preston Manor.
BRISTOL Blaise Castle Folk Museum, Henbury.
—— Bristol City Museum, Queen's Road.
—— Georgian House, Great George Street.
—— Red Lodge, Park Row.

BRIXHAM Brixham Museum, Higher Street (overlooking harbour).

BROADWAY Snowshill Manor.

BROMSGROVE The Norton Collection, 28 Birmingham Road.

BURNLEY Towneley Hall Art Gallery and Museum, Towneley Hall.

BURTON-UPON-TRENT Burton-upon-Trent Museum and Art Gallery, Guild Street.

BURWASH Batesman's (Rudyard Kipling's home).

BURY Bury Art Gallery and Museum, Moss Street.

BURY ST EDMUNDS The Gershom-Parkington Memorial Collection of Clocks and Watches, 8 Angel Hill.

CAMBRIDGE Fitzwilliam Museum, Trumpington Street.
—— Whipple Museum of the History of Science, Free School Lane.

CANTERBURY Canterbury Royal Museum, Beaney Institute, High Street.

CARLISLE Museum and Art Gallery, Tullie House, Castle Street.

CASTLEFORD Castleford Public Library and Museum, Carlton Street.

CASTLETOWN Nautical Museum, Bridge Street.

CHELMSFORD Chelmsford and Essex Museum, Oaklands Park.

CHELTENHAM Cheltenham Art Gallery and Museum, Clarence Street.

CHERTSEY The Cedars, Windsor Street.

CHESTER Grosvenor Museum, Grosvenor Street.

CHESTERFIELD Chesterfield Public Library.

CHICHESTER Chichester City Museum, 29 Little London.

CHRISTCHURCH Red House Museum and Art Gallery, Quay Road.

COLNE The Colne Museum, Public Library.

COVENTRY Herbert Art Gallery and Museum, Jordan Well.

DARLINGTON Darlington Museum, Tubwell Row.

DARTFORD Dartford Borough Museum, Market Street.

DEVIZES Devizes Museum, Long Street.

DOUGLAS The Manx Museum.

DOVER Dover Corporation Museum, Ladywell.

DOWNE Darwin Museum, Downe House.

DUMFRIES Dumfries Burgh Museum, The Observatory, Corberry Hill.

DUNBLANE Dunblane Cathedral Museum, The Cross.

DUNDEE Dundee Central Museum and Art Galleries, Albert Square.

DUNFERMLINE Viewfield.

EASTBOURNE The Towner Art Gallery, Manor House, 9 Borough Lane.

EAST COWES Osborne House.

EDINBURGH Canongate Tolbooth, Canongate.
—— Huntly House, Canongate.
—— Lady Stair's House, Lady Stair's Close, Lawnmarket.
—— Lauriston Castle, Cramond Road South.
—— Museum of Childhood, Hyndford's Close, 34 High Street.
—— Royal Scottish Museum, Chamber's Street.
—— Scottish National Portrait Gallery, Queen Street.
—— Scottish United Services Museum, Crown Square, Edinburgh Castle.

EXETER Royal Albert Memorial Museum, Queen Street.

GLASGOW Art Gallery and Museum, Kelving Grove.
—— The Hunterian Museum, Glasgow University.

GLENESK (ANGUS) The Retreat.

GLOUCESTER Gloucester City Museum, Brunswick Road.

GODALMING Godalming Borough Museum, Old Town Hall.

HALIFAX Bankfield Museum and Art Gallery, Ackroyd Park.

HARROGATE Corporation Art Gallery, Library Building, Victoria Avenue.

HASTINGS Public Museum and Art Gallery, John's Place, Cambridge Road.

HAWORTH Brontë Parsonage Museum.

HEREFORD Hereford City Museum and Art Gallery, Broad Street.

HERTFORD Hertford Museum, 18 Bull Plain.

HITCHIN Museum and Art Gallery, Paynes Park.

HONITON Honiton and Allhallows Museum, High Street.

HOVE Hove Museum of Art, New Church Road.

HULL   Hull Museums:
   Georgian Houses, 23–4 High Street (Museum
      Headquarters).
   Maritime Museum, Hessle Road.
   Wilberforce House, 25 High Street.

ILFRACOMBE   Ilfracombe Museum, Wilder Road.
IPSWICH   Ipswich Museums and Art Galleries, High
   Street.
—— Ipswich Museums and Art Galleries, Christ-
   church Mansion.
ISLE OF WIGHT   The Museum of Clocks, Alum Bay,
   near Freshwater.

JERSEY   St Helier, 9 Pier Road.

KEIGHLEY   Keighley Art Gallery and Museum,
   Cliffe Castle.
KENDAL   Abbot Hall Art Gallery.
KIDDERMINSTER   Kidderminster Public Library.
KILMARNOCK   Dick Institute Museum and Art
   Gallery, Elmbank Avenue.
KING'S LYNN   27 King Street.
KINGSTON-UPON-THAMES   Kingston-upon-Thames
   Museum and Art Gallery, Fairfield West.

LEEDS   City Museum, Park Row; and Abbey House
   Museum, Kirkstall.
LEICESTER   Leicester Museum and Art Gallery, The
   New Walk; The Newarke Houses; and Belgrave
   Hall, Belgrave.
LEWES   Sussex Archaeological Society:
   Anne of Cleves House, High Street, Southover.
   Barbican House Museum, High Street.
   Michelham Priory, Hailsham.
   Priest House, West Hoathly.
LICHFIELD   Public Library.
LINCOLN   Lincoln City Museum, Broadgate.
—— Lincoln Cathedral.
—— Usher Art Gallery, Lindum Road.
LIVERPOOL   Liverpool City Museums, William
   Brown Street.
LONDON   The London Museums are listed separ-
   ately at the end of this list.
LUTON   Wardown Park.

MACCLESFIELD   West Park Museum and Art Gallery, Prestbury Road.

MAIDSTONE   Museum and Art Gallery, St Faith's
   Street.
MONTROSE   Montrose Natural History and Anti-
   quarian Society, Museum Street.

NEWARK-ON-TRENT   Newark-on-Trent Municipal Mu-
   seum, Appleton Gate.
NEWBURY   Newbury Borough Museum, Wharf
   Street.
NEWCASTLE-UNDER-LYME   Borough Museum and
   Hobbergate Art Gallery, Brampton Park.
NEWCASTLE-UPON-TYNE   Laing Art Gallery and Mu-
   seum, Higham Place.
—— Museum of Science and Engineering, Exhibi-
   tion Park, Great North Road.
NORTHAMPTON   Central Museum and Art Gallery,
   Guildhall Road.
NORWICH   Bridewell Museum of Local Industries
   and Rural Crafts, Bridewell Alley.
—— Castle Museum.
—— Strangers' Hall, Charing Cross.
NOTTINGHAM   Castle Museum.
   Midland Group, 24–32 Carlton Street (entrance
   Warser Gate).
NUNEATON   Nuneaton Museum and Art Gallery,
   Riversley Park.

OXFORD   Museum of the History of Science, Broad
   Street.
—— Ashmolean Museum of Art and Archaeol-
   ogy, Beaumont Street.

PERTH   Perth Art Gallery and Museum, George
   Street.
PORT SUNLIGHT   The Lady Lever Art Gallery.
PRESCOT   34 Church St, Prescot.
PRESTON   Harris Museum and Art Gallery, Market
   Square.

READING   Museum and Art Gallery, Blagrave
   Street.
ROCHDALE   Sparrow Hill.
ROCHESTER   Guildhall, High Street.
ROTHESAY   Buteshire Natural History Museum,
   Stuart Street.

ST ALBANS   City Museum, Hatfield Road.
ST FAGANS   Welsh Folk Museum.
SALFORD   City Art Gallery, The Crescent, Peel
   Park.

SALISBURY Salisbury and South Wilts. Museum, St Ann Street.

SHAFTESBURY Local History Museum, Gold Hill.

SHEFFIELD City Museum, Weston Park.

SHUGBOROUGH Staffordshire County Museum and Mansion House.

SKIPTON Craven Museum, Public Library and Museum, High Street.

SOUTHEND-ON-SEA Prittlewell Priory Museum, Priory Park

SOUTH MOLTON South Molton Museum, 1 East Street.

SOUTH QUEENSFERRY The Hopetoun House Museum, near South Queensferry.

SOUTHWOLD Southwold Museum, St Bartholomew's Green.

SPALDING Spalding Museum, Broad Street.

STIRLING Smith Art Gallery and Museum, Albert Place.

STOKE-ON-TRENT City Museum and Art Gallery, Broad Street, Hanley.

STRANRAER Wigtown County Museum, The County Library, London Road.

STRATFORD-UPON-AVON The Shakespeare Centre.

STROUD Stroud and District Museum, Lansdown.

SUDBURY Gainsborough's House.

SUNDERLAND Museum and Art Gallery, Borough Road.

SWANSEA Glynn Vivian Gallery and Museum, Alexander Road.

SWINDON Swindon Museum and Art Gallery, Bath Road.

TAUNTON Somerset County Museum, Taunton Castle.

TILBURY Thurrock Local History Museum, Civic Square.

TIVERTON St Andrew Street.

TORQUAY Torre Abbey Art Gallery, Abbey Gardens.

TOTNES The Elizabethan House, 70 Fore Street.

TRURO County Museum and Art Gallery, River Street.

TUNBRIDGE WELLS Royal Tunbridge Wells Museum and Art Gallery, Civic Centre.

WADDESDON Waddesdon manor, Waddesdon, near Aylesbury, Bucks.

WARRINGTON Municipal Museum and Art Gallery, Bold Street.

WEST BROMWICH Oak House Museum, Oak Road.

WIGAN Powell Museum, Station Road.

WINDSOR The Guildhall Exhibition, High Street.

YORK York Castle Museum, Tower Street.

—— The Yorkshire Museum, Museum Street.

MUSEUMS IN THE LONDON AREA

Bethnal Green Museum, Cambridge Heath Road, E2

British Museum, Great Russell Street, WC1

Broomfield Museum, Broomfield Park, N13

The Cuming Museum, Walworth Road, SE17

Department of the Environment, Lambeth Bridge House, SE1

Dr Johnson's House, 17 Gough Square, EC4

Geffrye Museum, Kingsland Road, E2

Goldsmiths Hall, Foster Lane, EC2

Gunnersbury Park Museum, W3

Hampton Court Palace, Hampton Court

The Jewish Museum, Woburn House, Upper Woburn Place, WC1

Lancaster House, Stable Yard Road, St James's, SW1

London Museum, London Wall, EC2

National Army Museum, Royal Hospital Road, SW3

National Maritime Museum, Old Royal Observatory, Greenwich Park, SE10

St John's Gate Library and Museum, St John's Square, Clerkenwell, EC1

Science Museum, Exhibition Road, SW7

Sir John Soane's Museum, 13 Lincoln's Inn Fields, WC2

Tower of London, Tower Hill, EC4

Victoria and Albert Museum, Exhibition Road, SW7

Wallace Collection, Hertford House, Manchester Square, W1

Wellington Museum, Apsley House, Hyde Park Corner, W1

Wesley's House and Museum, 47 City Road, EC1

Woolwich Local and Natural Museum, 232 Plumstead High Street, SE18

The Clocks and Watches of the British Museum and its Horological Students' Room

The British Museum moved on to its present site in Bloomsbury in the mid-seventeenth century, but for a while had no collection of clocks and watches of any great note. This state of affairs began to alter in 1874, however, when Lady Fellows left various items to the Museum. These were augmented by the Octavius Morgan bequest of 1888, when the total number of horological acquisitions stood at 46 clocks, 238 watches and 84 watch movements.

At this stage the collection, although important, could not have been called a major world collection, but an event in 1958 changed this and overnight the collection became one of the most important in the world. In that year the Trustees of the British Museum were extremely fortunate in acquiring the splendid collection of clocks, watches, and chronometers built up by the late Courtenay Adrian Ilbert, of Chelsea. The collection was acquired virtually in its entirety, the executors retaining only a few items for private use. Courtenay Ilbert, by profession a civil engineer – whose firm, amongst other things, looked after the machinery which operates Tower Bridge – collected steadily from his school days at Eton until his death in 1957. He bought with great knowledge and discrimination, concentrating on mechanisms and on details, however small, which added anything to the history of the development of time measurement. There were, inevitably, some sections – for example, Continental bracket clocks – where the collection was not strong, but it was generally agreed to be the finest concentration of material in existence for the systematic study of horology from a technical viewpoint.

The saving for the nation of the Ilbert Collection was made possible by one of the Museum's major benefactions of the century, owing to the generosity of the late Mr Gilbert Edgar, CBE. Mr Edgar was Chairman of the H. Samuel group of companies, and also in 1968 Master of the Worshipful Company of Clockmakers. He purchased, for £50,000, the whole of the collection of clocks and later made a further very substantial contribution of about £10,000 towards the acquisition of the watches. The funds for the purchase of the watch collection, which was to have been sold separately, were raised through a public appeal launched by Mr M. L. Bateman, one-time Chairman of Ingersoll's, at the time Master of the Worshipful Company of Clockmakers. It was Mr Bateman who first approached Mr Edgar in the matter of the collection, and to his initiative, drive and enthusiasm the Trustees are greatly indebted. The remainder of the purchase price, beyond what resulted from the public appeal, was provided from funds at the disposal of the Trustees of the British Museum.

To the collection then were added: 207 European clocks, 70 Japanese clocks, 38 chronometers, 968 watches (old), 62 relatively modern watches, 741 watch movements, 7 Japanese watches and a number of miscellaneous items. At this time the total numbers of clocks and watches in the collection were: 323 clocks, 1,275 watches and 825 watch movements.

There is also a collection of scientific instruments ranking about fourth in importance in the world, the catalogue of which was published in 1979 (see Further Reading). So rich is the collection that only a small portion of it, although admittedly some of the best, can be shown, the reserve collection being kept in the Students' Room. This room is probably unique among the museums of the world, being available for the study of the items in the collection.

THE STUDENTS' ROOM

It was in 1963 that the Students' Room was set up and opened, appropriately enough, by Mr Gilbert Edgar. The British Museum was particularly fortunate in having Philip Coole, who joined the staff in 1960, as the first of the Superintendents of the Students' Room, for he was to win himself a reputation that matched the excellence of the Museum's collection. Philip Coole worked with Malcolm Gardner after the war and then with Courtenay Ilbert, whose collection he maintained until Ilbert's death in 1957. After his untimely death in 1969 his place was taken by his colleague Beresford Hutchinson who in the course of his fourteen years with the Museum built himself an equally enviable reputation as a world expert. Richard Good took over from Beresford, who after a spell at the National Maritime Museum is now retired. Richard Good has himself now retired although he is still cataloguing for the British Museum.

The main services offered in the Students' Room at the British Museum are as follows:

1. Dealing with enquiries whether by telephone, letter or from visitors (about 500 people a year come in person). Amongst the visitors are experts from other museums, collectors, representatives from the auction houses, restorers and even art students who might have as a project the making of a clock model!

2. The authentification and identification of material, naturally an important aspect of the Museum's work.

3. Answering questions on restoration and methods and styles of construction.

4. Cataloguing the collection of watches. The first catalogue covering stackfreed watches is nearly completed and should be ready for publication this year. Volume VI, precision timekeepers and chronometers, was published in 1990. Volume V, lever watches, is nearing completion.

The Students' room also contains the workshop where two of the staff of four tackle the demanding task of keeping the collection in good condition. To do this they must possess an intimate knowledge of the mechanisms not only from a mechanical standpoint but also as historical pieces. Dealing with a sixteenth-century clock or watch is an entirely different matter from coping with a precision piece of the nineteenth century – so much so that it is unusual to find a specialist in both in the world outside that of the Museum. Although there is an extensive library in the Students' Room, this is for the use of the staff (with certain exceptions), being used for research and to help in answering enquiries. However, the public may, of course, use the British Library and can always get guidance as to the choice of appropriate works.

Eventually the whole of the collection will be photographed, the more important pieces from many different angles and with details of piece parts so that postal enquiries can be dealt with in the most efficient manner. Many such enquiries are dealt with each week. Some people require photographs for forthcoming books or articles, some for research or reference purposes. It is part of the duties of the staff to oversee the photography so as to protect the object and to obtain the correct views.

It must be said that few people are in fact aware of all the facilities offered in the Students' Room of the British Museum, although this is perhaps just as well since it is only part of the staff's duties to help the public; there must also be time set aside for fundamental research, for the preparation of papers and books and for the apparently never-ending task of cataloguing the vast collections.

Major Museums in Countries other than Great Britain

AUSTRIA
VIENNA Österreichisches Museum.

FRANCE
PARIS Louvre.
—— Musée des Arts Decoratifs.
—— Musée des Arts et Métiers.
TOULOUSE Musée Paul Dupuy.
—— Musée Saint Raymond.

GERMANY
AUGSBURG City Museum.
FURTWANGEN Clock Museum.
MUNICH Bavarian National Museum.
NUREMBERG Germanisches National Museum.
SCHWENNINGEN Collections of the Manthe and Kienzle Factories.
BADEN WÜRTTEMBERG Collection Landesgewerbeamt.

HOLLAND
AMSTERDAM Rijksmuseum.
ASTEN Dutch Carillon Museum.
GRONINGEN Groningen Museum.
LEIDEN Dutch Science Museum.
SCHOONHOVEN Netherlands Clock and Watch Museum.

SWEDEN
STOCKHOLM Nordliches Museum.
—— Stadsmuseum.

SWITZERLAND
BASLE Kirchgarten Museum.
GENEVA Musée d'Horlogerie.
LA CHAUX DE FONDS Musée d'Horlogerie.
LE LOCLE Musée d'Horlogerie.
NEUCHÂTEL Musée d'Horlogerie.

UNITED STATES of AMERICA

CALIFORNIA
San Francisco California Academy of Sciences, Golden Gate Park, San Francisco 94118.

COLORADO
Denver Hagans Clock Manor Museum, Bergen Park, Evergreen, Denver 80439.

CONNECTICUT
Bristol American Clock and Watch Museum Inc., 100 Maple St, Bristol 06010

ILLINOIS
Chicago Adler Planetarium and Astronomical Museum, 1300 South Lakeshore Drive, Chicago 60605.
—— Rockford Time Museum, Clock Tower Inn, 7801 East State Street, Rockford, Illinois 61125.
—— Springfield Illinois State Museum, Spring and Edwards Sts, Springfield 62706.

MASSACHUSETTS
Sturbridge Old Sturbridge Village, Sturbridge 01566.

NEW YORK
Metropolitan Museum of Art, 5th Avenue at 82nd St, 10028.
—— James Arthur Collection, New York University, Washington Square.

OHIO
Cincinnati Taft Museum, 316 Pitce St, 45202.

PENNSYLVANIA
Columbia National Association of Watch and Clock Collectors, 514 Poplar St, 17512.

VERMONT
Shelburne Shelburne Museum, Shelburne 05482.

WASHINGTON DC
Smithsonian Institution, 1000 Jefferson Drive SW, 20560.

Appendix D:
Dealers, Retailers and Suppliers

Dealers and Retailers

The Guide to the Antique Shops in Britain 1985, published by the Antique Collectors' Club, 1984, has a section on clocks and watches giving over 100 specialists in this field, or at least people who keep a sizeable stock of these items. Many of the dealers and retailers listed below also do restoration work.

AARON ANTIQUES
90 High Street,
Snodland,
Kent

TEL: 0634 241748

ALLEN AND WAINWRIGHT
33A Burnt Ash Hill,
Lee,
London SE12

TEL: 081 851 3749

ANDWELL ANTIQUES
The Row,
Hartley Wintney,
Hants.

TEL: 0252 842305

ASPREY
165-9 New Bond Street,
London W1Y 0AR

TEL: 071-493 6767

BANHAM, Keith
See Grimaldi

BEECH, J.
Nurses Cottage,
Ampney Crusis,
Glos.

TEL: 0285 851495

THE BENKENDORF COLLECTION
6 Baybrook Lane,
Oak Brook,
Illinois 60521
USA

TEL: (708) 323 0605

BROCKLEHURST, Aubrey
124 Cromwell Road,
London SW7

TEL: 071-373 0319

CAMPBELL, Gerard
Maple House,
Market Place,
Lechlade,
Glos.

TEL: 0367 252267

CAMERER CUSS AND CO.
17 Ryder Street,
London SW1Y 6PY

TEL: 071-930 1941

CAPON, Patric
350 Upper Street,
London N1 0PD

TEL: 081-467 5722

CARLTON SMITH, John
17 Ryder Street,
London SW1 6PY

TEL: 071-930 6622

CHELSEA CLOCKS
479 Fulham Road,
London SW6

TEL: 071-352 8646

THE CLOCK CLINIC LTD
85 Lower Richmond Road,
London SW15 1EU

TEL: 081-788 1407

THE CLOCK HOUSE
75 Pound Street,
Carshalton,
Surrey

TEL: 081-773 4844

THE CLOCK SHOP
64 Church Street,
Weybridge,
Surrey

TEL: 0932 855503

CLOCKS AND THINGS
The Piece Hall,
Halifax,
W. Yorks.

TEL: 0422 66571

COLLYER, R.
185 New Road,
Rubery,
Birmingham,
W. Midlands

TEL: 021-453 2332

CURIOSITY SHOP
127 Old Street,
Ludlow,
Shropshire

TEL: 0584 875 927

DAVIS, R. A.
19 Dorking Road,
Great Bookham,
Surrey

TEL: 0372 57655

DE HAVILLAND (ANTIQUES) LTD
48 Sloane Street,
London SW1

TEL: 071-235 3534

DOUGHERTY, Lawrence G.
2640 East Coast Highway,
Corona Del Mar,
California 92625,
USA

EVANS AND EVANS
40 West Street,
Alresford,
Hants.

TEL: 0962 73 2170

EXTENCE LEIGH, E.
2 Wellington Street,
Teignmouth,
Devon

TEL: 0626 773353

FELL, Peter
81 High Street,
Thame,
Oxon.

TEL: 084 421 4487

GARRARD
112 Regents Street,
London W1A 2JJ

TEL: 071-734 7020

GOOD HOPE ANTIQUES
2 Hogshill Street,
Beaminster,
Dorset

TEL: 0308 862119

GRANDFATHER CLOCK SHOP
2 Bondgate House,
West Street,
Shipston-on-Stour,
Worcs.

TEL: 0608 62144

GRAUS ANTIQUES
125 New Bond Street,
London W1

TEL: 071-629 6680

GRIMALDI
12 Royal Arcade,
Old Bond Street,
London W1

TEL: 071-493 3953

HADLOW ANTIQUES
No. 1 The Pantiles,
Tunbridge Wells,
Kent

TEL: 0892 29858

KEITH HARDING'S WORLD OF
MECHANICAL MUSIC
Northleach,
Nr Cheltenham,
Glos.

TEL: 0451 860181

HAWKINS, Andrew
74 High Street,
Billericay,
Essex

TEL: 027 74 56280

HILL, F. F.
The Gate House,
Lombard Street,
Shackleford,
Nr Godalming,
Surrey

TEL: 0483 810330

HOFFMAN
Owsley House,
Ashley,
Nr Market Harborough,
Leics.

TEL: 0858 83 315

HOLLANDER, E.
The Dutch House,
Horsham Road,
South Holmwood,
Dorking,
Surrey

TEL: 0306 888921

HOROLOGICAL WORKSHOPS
204 Worplesdon Road,
Guildford,
Surrey

TEL: 0483 576496

IT'S ABOUT TIME
ANTIQUE CLOCK SHOP
863 London Road,
Westcliffe on Sea,
Essex

TEL: 0702 72574

KATS, F.
Voorhaven 4,
Rotterdam,
Holland

TEL: (10) 476 4475

KENGEN, Charles
Rijksstraatweg 75,
Sassenheim,
Holland

KOWALSKI, J. A.
1- 3 Ashby Road,
Coalville,
Leics.

TEL: 0530 32373

LAURIE LEIGH ANTIQUES
36 High Street,
Oxford,
Oxon.

TEL: 0865 244197

LEE, Ronald A.
1-9 Bruton Place,
London W1X 7AD

TEL: 071-629 5600

MARSH, Gerald E.
32a The Square,
Winchester,
Hants.

TEL: 0962 84443

BAROMETER WORLD
Quicksilver Barn,
Merton,
Okehampton,
Devon

TEL: 08053 443

MUSEUM OF CLOCKS
Alum Bay,
Isle of Wight

OLD CHARON
57 North Street,
Thame,
Oxon

TEL: 084 421 3007

OLD CLOCK SHOP
63 High Street,
West Malling,
Kent

TEL: 0732 843246

OXLEY, P. A.
The Old Rectory,
Cherhill,
Nr Calne,
Wilts.

TEL: 0249 816227

PAWSON, T. W.
31 High Street,
Somersham,
Cambs.

TEL: 0487 841537

PHILLIPS, S.
Buxton Mill,
Buxton,
Norwich,
Norfolk

TEL: 0603 278080

PLANK, Terence
7 Lower Mall,
359 Upper Street,
Camden Passage,
London N1

TEL: 071-226 2426

RAFFERTY LTD
34 Kensington Church Street,
London W8 4HA

TEL: 071-938 1100

REYNOLDS, C.
The Spindles,
M1 Junction 24,
Tonge,
Nr Castle Donnington,
E. Midlands

TEL: 03316 2609

ROBERTS, Derek
24 Shipbourne Road,
Tonbridge,
Kent

TEL: 0732 358986

ROCHEFORT, Jean Pierre
14 Rue Des Saints Peres,
75007 Paris,
France

ROSE, R. E.
731 Sidcup Road,
London SE9 3SA

TEL: 081-859 4754

ROSEMARY AND TIME
42 Park Street,
Thame,
Oxon.

TEL: 084 421 6923

SAM ORR AND
MAGNUS BROE CLOCKS
36 High Street,
Hurstpierpoint,
E. Sussex

TEL: 0273 832081

STENDER, E. F. J.
Nieuwstraat 1,
5271 AB St Michielsgestel,
Holland

STRIKE ONE (ISLINGTON) LTD
33 Balcombe Street,
London NW1 6HH

TEL: 071-226 9709

TIME ANTIQUES
Millbrook House,
An-Garrack,
Hayle,
Cornwall

TEL: 0736 754065

TOCIAPSKI, Igor,
39 Ledbury Road,
London W11 2AA

TEL: 071-229 8317

VICAI, Thomas
2 Place du Palais-Royal,
75001 Paris,
France

VITALE AND VITALE
315 Morris Avenue,
Spring Lake,
New Jersey 07762,
USA

TEL: (908) 449 3000

WEISS, Peter K.
18 Silver Vaults,
Chancery Lane Safe Deposits,
London WC2A 1QS

TEL: 071-242 8100

PHILIP WHYTE
32 Bury Street,
London SW1Y 6AU

TEL: 071-321 0353

WOODBURN, Anthony
Orchard House,
High Street,
Leigh,
Nr Tonbridge,
Kent

TEL: 0732 832258

ZEEMAN ANTIEKE UURWERKEN
Dude Sluis 5,
Nienwegein (Nr Utrecht),
Holland

Material Suppliers

BARTLETT, V. J., AND SONS LTD
14 Middle Street,
Southampton,
Hants.

TEL: 0703 333413

BEECH AND SONS LTD
Meridian House,
Swanley,
Kent

TEL: 0322 63211

CLOCKSPARES OF DEREHAM
The Yard,
East Dereham,
Norfolk

TEL: 0362 694165

COUSINS MATERIAL HOUSE
Unit J.,
Chesham Close,
Romford,
Essex

TEL: 0708 757 800

EDWARDS, ALEXANDER, LTD
Coventry Time Works
17 Spon Street,
Coventry,
W. Midlands

TEL: 0203 25631

FINDLEY MEEKS AND CO
22 Warstone Lane,
Birmingham,
W. Midlands

TEL: 021-236 9058

FROST, C. R. AND SON
60-62 Clerkenwell Road,
London EC1M 5PX

TEL: 071-253 0315

GARRETT, James A.
68a Upper North Street,
Brighton,
Sussex

TEL: 0273 29541

HART, N. A. S., AND CO. LTD
206 Kenton Road,
Kenton,
Middx.

TEL: 081-907 1119

HOROLOGICAL SOLVENTS
Proctor Street,
Bury,
Lancs.

TEL: 061-764 2741

JEVON AND STANLEY
19 Queen Street,
Wolverhampton,
W. Midlands

TEL: 0902 26309

MAHONEY ASSOCIATES
58 Stapleton Road,
Bristol,
Avon

TEL: 0272 556800

MEADOWS AND PASSMORE
Farningham Road,
Crowborough,
E. Sussex

TEL: 089 26 62255

NATHAN SHESTOPAL LTD
1 Grangeway,
London NW6

TEL: 071-328 3128

RICHARDS OF BURTON
WOODHOUSE CLOCK WORKS
Swadlincote Road,
Woodville,
Burton-on-Trent,
Staffs.

TEL: 0283 219155

ROBERTS, A. R.
61 Goldhawk Road,
Shepherd's Bush,
London W12

TEL: 081-743 1411

ROSE, R. E.
731 Sidcup Road,
London SE9 3SA

TEL: 081-859 4754

SOUTHERN WATCH AND
CLOCK SUPPLIES LTD
Precista House,
48-56 High Street,
Orpington,
Kent

TEL: 0689 824318/875206

SUMMERSONS
15 Carthouse Walk,
Hatton Country World,
Hatton,
Warwicks.

TEL: 0926 843443

TEMPLE, H. M., AND CO. LTD
93 Broughton Street,
Edinburgh,
Midlothian

THOMAS, A. G.
Tompion House,
Heaton Road,
Bradford,
W. Yorks.

TEL: 0274 497171

VANNER, E.
89 Shudehill,
Manchester

TEL: 061-832 2714

VIOLA (solid brass
ornamentation)
Aparisi y guijarro,
4y 9 Mislata,
Valencia,
Spain

TEL: 379 3242

WALSH, H. S., AND SONS LTD
243 Beckenham Road,
Beckenham,
Kent
also
12-16 Clerkenwell Road,
London EC1

TEL: 071-778 7061/9951

WARDLE, JOHN (Clockmakers)
Express Works,
Brailsford,
Ashbourne,
Derbys.

TEL: 0335 60475

WATCH GLASSES INTERNATIONAL
39 Churchgate,
Leicester

TEL: 0533 625698

WESTCLOX (UK) LTD
8 Heathcote Way,
Heathcote Ind. Estate,
Warwick

TEL: 0926 885400

WILD, J. MALCOLM
12 Norton Green Close,
Sheffield,
Yorks.

TEL: 0742 745693

WINGFIELD, F. F. LTD
Winchester House,
Firvale Road,
Bournemouth,
Hants.

TEL: 0202 27091
(mail order service)

WOODHOUSE CLOCK WORKS
See Richards of Burton

PETER WRIGHT ANTIQUES
36b High Street,
Great Missenden,
Bucks.

TEL: 0494 891330

Raw Materials

BOOTH, GEOFFREY (pinion steel)
Tower House,
Tower Hill,
Bere Regis,
Dorset

TEL: 0929 471586

REPTON CLOCKS (invar rod)
48 High Street,
Repton,
Derby

TEL: 0283 703657

SMITHS, J., AND SONS
42-56 Tottenham Road,
London N1 4BZ

TEL: 071-253 1277

Auctioneers

BEARNES
Rainbow
Avenue Road,
Torquay,
Devon

TEL: 0803 26277

BONHAMS
Montpelier Galleries,
Montpelier Street,
London SW7

TEL: 071-584 9161

CHRISTIE'S
8 King Street,
London SW1

TEL: 071-839 9060

CHRISTIE'S (SWITZERLAND)
8 Place de la Taconnerie,
1204 Geneva,
Switzerland

CROTT, DR. H., AND
SCHMELZER, K.
Pontstrasse 21,
Postfach 146,
D-5100 Aachen,
Germany

GALERIE D'HORLOGERIE
ANCIENNE
Rue de la Corraterie 9,
CH 1204 Geneva,
Switzerland

INEICHEN PA
8001 Zurich,
Neumarkt 13,
Switzerland

KEGELMANN, PETER
Saalgasse 3 (Am Dom),
D-6 Frankfurt (Main) 1,
Germany

LAWRENCE — FINE ART
AUCTIONEERS LTD
South Street,
Crewkerne,
Somerset

TEL: 0460 73041

Fairs

BARNES AND DUNGATE TIME FAIRS
PO Box 273,
Uxbridge

TEL: 0895 834357

ESSEX CLOCK AND WATCH FAIR
Enquire Unit 1,
R/O Bosworth House,
Thorpe le Soken,
Essex

TEL: 0255 861913

LONDON INTERNATIONAL CLOCK
AND WATCH FAIR

TEL: 0202 672475

TOM TOM FAIRS
PO Box 629,
Stoke-on-Trent,
Staffs.

TEL: 0782 312670

Street Markets in London and Greater London

G GENERAL MARKET
A ANTIQUES
C KNOWN ESPECIALLY FOR
CLOCKS

BATTERSEA HIGH STREET, SW11
Mon-Sat (Wed am only). G
BELL LANE, E1,
Sun am only. G
BELL STREET, NW1,
Mon-Sat. G
BERESFORD SQUARE, SE18,
Mon-Sat (Thurs am only). G

BERMONDSEY STREET, SE1,
Fri only. G
BERMONDSEY SQUARE, SE1,
Fri only. AC
BERWICK STREET, W1,
Mon-Sat. G
BETHNAL GREEN ROAD, E2,
Mon-Sat. G
BRICK LANE, E1,
Sun am only. GC
BRIXTON STATION ROAD, SW9,
Mon-Sat (Wed am only). G
BROADWAY, E8,
Mon-Sat. G
BURDETT ROAD, E3,
Mon-Sat. G

CAMDEN PASSAGE, N1,
Mon-Sat (Wed until 8pm).
AC
CATFORD BROADWAY, SE6,
Sat. G
CHAPEL MARKET, N1,
Tues-Sun am (Thurs am only).
G
CHATSWORTH ROAD, E5,
Mon-Sat. G
CHESHIRE STREET, E2,
Sun am only. G
CHOUMERT ROAD, SE15,
Mon-Sat (Thur am only). G
CHURCH STREET, NW8,
Mon-Sat. G
COBB STREET, E1,
Sun am only. G
COLOMB STREET, SE10,
Mon-Sat. G
CROWN STREET, W3
Thur only. G
CYGNET STREET, E1,
Sun am only. G

DAWES STREET, SE17,
Sun only. G
DEPTFORD HIGH STREET, SE8,
Sat only. G
DEVONS ROAD, E3,
Mon-Sat. G
DOUGLAS WAY, SE8,
Fri and Sat. G

EARLHAM STREET, WC2,
Mon-Sat. G
EARLSWOOD STREET, SE10,
Mon-Sat. G
EAST STREET, SE17,
Tues-Sun am (Thur am only). G

EXMOUTH STREET, EC1,
Mon-Sat (Thur am only). G

FAIRFIELD WEST, Kingston, Surrey,
Mon am only. G

GOLBORNE ROAD, W10,
Mon-Thur am only). G
GOULSTON STREET, E1,
Mon-Fri and Sun am. G

HIGH STREET, Epsom,
Sat only. G
HIGH STREET, E17,
Mon-Sat. G
HILDRETH STREET, SW12,
Mon-Sat (Wed am only). G
HOLLOWAY ROAD, N7,
Mon-Sat (Thur am only). G
HOXTON STREET, N1,
Mon-Sat. G

INVERNESS STREET, NW1,
Mon-Sat. G

JUBILEE MARKET, Covent Garden,
WC2, Mon-Fri. G

KINGSLAND ROAD, E8,
Sat only. G

LEATHER LANE, EC1,
Mon—Sat lunchtimes. G
LEWISHAM MARKET, SE13,
Mon—Sat. G
LEYDEN STREET, E1,
Sun am only. G
LOWER MARSH, SE1,
Mon—Sat (Thur am only). G

MARKET PLACE, Kingston, Surrey,
Mon—Sat. G
MARKET PLACE, Romford, Essex,
Wed, Fri and Sat. G
MARKET SQUARE, Woking, Surrey,
Tue, Fri and Sat. G
MIDDLESEX STREET (Petticoat
Lane), E1, Sun am only. GC
MILE END ROAD, E1,
Mon—Sat. G

NEW GOULSTON STREET, E1,
Sun am only. G
NORTHCOTE ROAD, SW11,
Mon—Sat (Wed am only). G
NORTH END ROAD, W14,
Mon—Sat. G

NORTH STREET, Guildford, Surrey,
Fri and Sat. G

OLD CASTLE STREET, E1,
Sun am only. G

PETTICOAT LANE see Middlesex Street
PLUMSTEAD ROAD, SE18,
Mon—Sat. G
PORTOBELLO ROAD, W10,
Mon—Fri (Thur am only). G.
Sat mainly AC

QUEEN'S CRESCENT, NW5,
Mon—Sat. G

RIDLEY ROAD, E8,
Mon—Sat. G
ROMAN ROAD, E3,
Mon—Sat. G

SALMON LANE, E14,
Mon—Sat. G
SCLATER STREET, E1,
Sun am only. G
SLYFIELD GREEN, Guildford, Surrey,
Wed, and Bank Hols. G
STAMFORD ROAD, Dagenham, Essex,
Mon—Sat. G
STRUTTON GROUND, SW1,
Mon—Fri and Sat am. G
STRYPE STREET, E1,
Sun am only. G
SURREY STREET, Croydon, Surrey,
Mon—Sat. G

TACHBROOK STREET, SW1,
Mon—Sat. G
TOWER BRIDGE ROAD, SE1,
Mon—Sat (Thur am only). G
TONYBEE STREET, E1,
Mon—Fri and Sun am only. G
TYLER STREET, SE10,
Mon-Sat. G

WATNEY STREET, E1,
Mon—Sat. G
WELL STREET, E9,
Mon—Sat. G
WENTWORTH STREET, E1,
Mon—Fri and Sun am only. G
WESTMORELAND ROAD, SE17,
Daily (Thur and Sun am only). G
WHITECHAPEL ROAD, E1,
Mon—Sat. G
WHITECROSS STREET, EC1,
Mon—Sat (Thur am only). G

Appendix: E Services

Repairers and Restorers

The following lists are of those who advertise in the trade and learned journals. Only a few of these people are known to the author personally so there can be no guarantee as to their performance. Another source of information is the British Horological Institute. A letter to the Secretary will lead him to consult the branch in your area who will then recommend the best member of the Institute to contact. However, if you are in a hurry, it would be best to use the following lists as a source of information.

It should be noted that most clockmakers specialise and will not handle all types of clock, even though the quality of what they are offered may be good. The best craftsmen are selective and can afford to concentrate on the type of clock they like best. Some do not repair above carriage-clock size, others prefer larger clocks. Similarly, some specialise in early work, others in precision clocks.

ARNOLD, L. J.
6 The Square Aynho,
Banbury,
Oxon.

TEL: 0869 810730

BARNES, B. P.
23 High Street,
Lewes,
E. Sussex

TEL: 0273 474400

BENNETT, Alan
The Old Farriers Workshop
Ten Gallop,
Welbeck,
Nr Worksop,
Notts.

BRIGHTON CLOCKWORKS
19 Cleremont Road,
Brighton,
E. Sussex

TEL: 0273 553581

BROCKLEHURST, Aubrey
124 Cromwell Road,
London, SW7

TEL: 071-373 0319

BROOKS, T. P.
Sycamores,
School Lane,
Lodsworth,
Petworth,
W. Sussex

TEL: 07985 248

CHURCHILL, David
21 Lodge Hill Road,
Farnham,
Surrey'

TEL: 0252 715527

CLARK, T. P.
6 London Road,
Henfield,
W. Sussex

TEL: 0273 492568

CLARKE, John
1 Redwood Close,
Wing,
Leighton Buzzard,
Beds.

TEL: 052 53 78554

THE CLOCK CLINIC LTD
85 Lower Richmond Road,
London SW15 1EU

TEL: 081-788 1407

THE CLOCK SHOP
161 Victoria Street,
St Albans,
Herts.

TEL: 0727 856633

THE CLOCK WORKSHOP
17 Prospect Street,
Caversham,
Reading,
Surrey

TEL: 0734 470741

COOME CLOCKS
Roborough Mill,
Winkleigh,
N. Devon

TEL: 08053 386

FRYATT, R. L.
10 Amberley Court,
Lowestoft,
Suffolk

TEL: 0502 560869

GIBBARD, Julian
1803 Pacific Avenue,
Forest Grove,
Oregon 97116,
USA

GOOD, R.
36 Blatchington Hill,
Seaford,
Sussex

TEL: 0323 895484

HATT, John
(Chronometers)

TEL: 071-249 8017

HOLLANDER, E.
The Dutch House,
Horsham Road,
South Holmwood,
Dorking,
Surrey

TEL: 0306 888921

INNES, John
255 King's Road,
London SW3

TEL: 071-352 3529

NEWELL, D.
55 Shelton Street,
London WC2H 9HE

TEL: 071-836 1000

PATTEN, F.
107 Western Road,
Hove,
E. Sussex

TEL: 0273 733745

PEGLER, Martin
87 Homestead Road,
Hatfield,
Herts.

PETERSON CLOCKS
RRI Selkirk,
Ontario NOA 1PO,
Canada

TEL: 416 7761223

PRICE-THOMAS, R.

TEL: 0603 665552

REDFERN, John
The Clockhouse,
Craignish,
Lochgilphead,
Argyll

TEL: 0546 238

REPTON CLOCKS
48 High Street,
Repton
Derby

TEL: 0283 703657

SOUTH EAST TIME SERVICE
12 Stirling Road,
St Leonards-on-Sea,
Hastings,
E. Sussex

TEL: 0424 52309

THOMPSON
8 St Catherines Grove,
Lincoln,
Lincs.

TEL: 0522 527322

TYRELL TIMEKEEPERS LTD
(Andrew L. King)
Burnhill Road,
Beckenham,
Kent

TEL: 0909 530190

VAN DE GEER LTD
Odstock,
Salisbury,
Wilts.

TEL: 0722 329737

CASES (INCLUDING MANUFACTURERS)

COBB, Clive and Lesley
(lacquered case restoration
and dials)
Newhouse Farm,
Bratton Fleming,
Barnstaple,
Devon

TEL: 0598 710465

MOSS, Christopher
Old Lilly Hall,
Ledbury,
Herefords.

TEL: 0531 633888

NEWCOMBE AND SON
89 Maple Road,
Penge,
London SE20

TEL: 081-0778 0816

SPICE, H. W.
8-12 Harold Mews,
St Leonards-on-Sea,
E. Sussex

TEL: 0424 440630

MATERIALS

HOUSE OF HANBRU
Unit 3,
Cuba Ind. Estate,
Bolton Road,
Norwest Stubbings,
Rambottom,
Lancs.

TEL: 0706 827719

WEAVES AND WAXES
65c Church Street,
Bloxham,
Banbury,
Oxon.

Dials

Carter, J. P.
17 North Main Street,
Wigtown, Scotland

Tel: 098 84 3215

Cobb, Clive and Lesley
Newhouse Farm,
Bratton Fleming,
Barnstaple,
Devon

Tel: 0598 710465

Village Time
43 The Village,
Charlton,
London SE7

Tel: 081-858 2514

Faulkner, Terry
(porcelain and enamel dials)
Proctor Street,
Bury,
Lancs.

Tel: 061-764 2741

Lynton Dials
(for enamelled dials)
22 Norwich Street,
Fakenham,
Norfolk

Tel: 0328 863666

Pearson, John
Church Cottage,
Birstwith,
Harrogate,
N. Yorks.

Tel: 0423 770828

Stow Antiques
The Square,
Stow-on-the-Wold,
Glos.

Tennant, D. A.
The Stone House,
Rossett,
Clwyd

Tel: 0244 5070405

Wilby, G. H.
32 West Beach,
Whitstable,
Kent.

Tel: 0227 274736

New Dials

Southern Watch and Clock
Supplies Ltd
Precista House,
48-56 High Street,
Orpington,
Kent
(deal with the *Selva* range of
dials and hands)

Security Device for Long Case Clocks

Bowie, Robin
52a Burry Road,
St Leonards-on-Sea,
E. Sussex

Tel: 0424 422438

Other Technical Specialists

Balance Staffs and Cylinders

Perry, R.
16 Dallington Close,
Bexhill-on-Sea,
E. Sussex

Tel: 0424 212768

Brass Castings

Devon Metal Crafts Ltd
2 Victoria Way,
Exmouth,
Devon

Tel: 039 5272846

Ceramic, Glass and Porcelain Repairs

The Conservation Studio
Unit 21,
Pennybank Chambers,
33-35 St John's Square,
London EC1M 49S

Tel: 071-251 6853

Engine Turning

Elton, Christopher
Evans Bros. (Engravers) Ltd
20 Clerkenwell Green,
London EC1R 0DP

Tel: 071-253 5773

Pledge and Aldworth
Unit 157,
31 Clerkenwell Close,
London EC1R 0AT

Tel: 071-251 0555

Engraving

Elton, Christopher Evans Bros.
(Engravers) Ltd
20 Clerkenwell Green,
London EC1R 0DP

Tel: 071-253 5773

Goodacre Engraving
Lodge House,
Wyvern Industrial Estate,
Long Eaton,
Notts.

Tel: 0602 734387

Peters, John E.
3 Arthur Road,
Rainham,
Kent

Tel: 0634 363468

FRETS, RESTORED AND COPIED

MAC AND ME
19 Mill Lane,
Welwyn,
Herts.

TEL: 043-871 4710

GEARS

TOOLS FOR CUTTING GEARS
(INCLUDING CUTTERS)

COLIN WALTON CLOCKS
Tunbeck Cottage,
Alburgh,
Harleston,
Norfolk

J. M. W. (CLOCKS)
12 Norton Green Close,
Sheffield,
S. Yorks.

TEL: 0742 745693

P. P. THORNTON (SUCCESSORS)
LTD
The Old Bakehouse,
Upper Tysoe,
War.

TEL: 0295 680454

WHEEL AND PINION
CUTTING

ALEXANDER, John
11 Prince Street,
Urangan,
Queensland 4658,
Australia

BOOTH, Geoffrey,
Tower House,
Tower Hill,
Bere Regis,
Dorset

TEL: 0929 471586
(also supplies steel for
pinions)

THE CLOCKMAKER
131 Brockhurst Road,
Gosport,
Hants.

TEL: 0705 525665

COLLINS, A. H.
99 Venables Avenue,
Colne,
Lancs.

TEL: 0282 865274

J. M. W. (CLOCKS)
12 Norton Green Close,
Sheffield,
S. Yorks.

TEL: 0742 745693

JONES AND CHAMBAULT
Gronfa,
Station Road,
Clynderwen,
Dyfed

TEL: 0437 563579

WOODHOUSE CLOCK WORKS
Swadlincote Road,
Woodville,
Burton-on-Trent,
Staffs.

TEL: 0283 219155

GILDING AND LACQUERING

PAIRPOINT AND SONS LTD
10 Shacklewell Road,
London N16

TEL: 071-254 6362

PRESTON, J.
52A Tor Hill Road,
Torquay,
Devon

TEL: 0803 293274

STRONG AND WOODHATCH
12 Hornsey Street,
London N7 8HR

TEL: 071-700 2404

GLASS DOMES

REYNOLDS, M. P.
PB 16 28,
D2110 Buchholz,
Germany

TEL: (4181) 5582

HAND PIERCING, SKELETON DIALS AND FRETS

MILES, Thos.
36-42 Clerkenwell Road,
London EC1

HOROLOGICAL ILLUSTRATION

PENNY, David
49a Langdon Park Road,
London N6 5PT

Tel: 081-341 0529

ORNAMENTATION FOR CLOCK CASES

BEARDMORE
3, 5, Percy Street,
London W1

TEL: 071-637 7041

TOOLS (INCLUDING LATHES)

CHRONOS
95 Victoria Street,
St Albans,
Herts.

TEL: 0727 32793

HEGNER UK LTD
Unit 8,
North Crescent,
Diplocks Way,
Hailsham,
E. Sussex BN27 3JF

TEL: 0702 617298

J. M. W. (CLOCKS)
12 Norton Green Close,
Sheffield,
S. Yorks.

TEL: 0742 745693

PEATON MACHINE TOOLS
19 Knightlow Road,
Alarbourne,
Birmingham,
W. Midlands

STEVENS MACHINE TOOL CO.
Blue Gates,
Willow Bank,
Denham,
Uxbridge,
Middx.

WALKER ELECTRONICS LTD
(cleaning and timing machines)
Collingham,
Newark,
Notts.

TEL: 0636 892410

Societies

ASSOCIATION FRANÇAISE DES
AMATEURS D'HORLOGERIE
ANCIENNE
Palais Granvelle,
BP33 25012,
Besançon,
France

ASSOCIATION NATIONALE DES
COLLECTIONNEURS ET AMATEURS
D'HORLOGERIE ANCIENNE
107 Rue de Rivoli,
75001 Paris,
France

ASSOCIATION SUISSE POUR
L'HISTOIRE DE LA MESURE DU
TEMPS
CH 2301 La Chaux de Fonds,
Postfach 331,
Switzerland

ANTIQUARIAN HOROLOGICAL
SOCIETY
New House,
High Street,
Ticehurst,
Wadhurst,
E. Sussex

TEL: 0580 200155

BRITISH HOROLOGICAL INSTITUTE
Upton Hall,
Upton,
Nr Newark,
Notts.

TEL: 0636 813795

NATIONAL ASSOCIATION OF
WATCH AND CLOCK COLLECTORS
INCORPORATED
PO Box 33,
Columbia,
PA. 17512,
USA

Courses

BRITISH HOROLOGICAL INSTITUTE
Upton Hall,
Upton,
Newark,
Notts.

TEL: 0636 813795

CENTRAL MANCHESTER COLLEGE
Openshaw Centre,
Manchester

TEL: 061-223 8282 (ext. 64)

HACKNEY COLLEGE
Keltan House,
Mare Street,
London E8

TEL: 081-985 8484

MARYLEBONE AND PADDINGTON
INSTITUTE
Quintin Kynaston School,
Finchley Road,
London NW8

PENMAN, Laurie
61 High Street,
Totnes,
Devon

TEL: 0803 866344

WEST DEAN COLLEGE
West Dean,
Nr Chichester,
W. Sussex

TEL: 024 363 301

Overleaf BIRDCAGE CLOCK, *see p. 81*

213

Further Reading

ALLIX, Charles, *Carriage Clocks*, London, 1974

BAILLIE G. H., *Clocks and Watches: an historical bibliography*, London, 1951

BAILLIE, G. H. *Watchmakers and Clockmakers of the World*, 3rd edn, London, 1951 (vol. 2, *see* Loomes)

BASSERMAN-JORDAN, Ernst von (rev. by Hans von Bertele), *The Book of Old Clocks and Watches*, London, 1964

BIRD, Anthony, *English House Clocks, 1600–1850*, Newton Abbot, 1973

BRITTEN, F. J., *Horological Hints and Helps*, London, 1934

BRITTEN, F. J., *The Watch and Clock Maker's Handbook, Dictionary and Guide* (ed. Richard Good), 16th edn, London, 1976

BRITTEN, F. J., *Old Clocks and Watches and their Makers*, 9th edn (rev. and enlarged by Cecil Clutton), London, 1982

BRUTON, Eric, *The Longcase Clock*, New York and Washington, 1968

BRUTON, Eric, *Antique Clocks and Clock Collecting*, London, 1974

de CARLE, Donald, *Watch and Clock Encyclopedia*, London, 1959

de CARLE, Donald, *Clocks and their Value*, London, 1968

de CARLE, Donald, *Practical Clock Repairing*, London, 1968

CESCINSKY, Herbert, *The Old English Master Clockmakers and their Clocks: 1670–1820*, London, 1938

CESCINSKY, H., and WEBSTER, M. R., *English Domestic Clocks*, London, 1913 (reprinted 1976, facsimile)

CHAMBERLAIN, Paul M., *It's About Time*, New York, 1941 (reprinted London, 1964)

CIPOLLA, Carlo, *Clocks and Culture: 1300–1700*, London, 1967

CLUTTON, Cecil, and DANIELS, George, *Clocks and Watches in the Collection of the Worshipful Company of Clockmakers*, London, 1975

COOLE, P. G. (under pseudonym CUMHAILL, P. W.), *Investing in Clocks and Watches*, London, 1967

CURTIS, Tony, *Antiques and Their Values – Clocks and Watches*, Galashiels (Scotland), 1976

DANIELS, George, *The Art of Breguet*, London, 1975

GAZELEY, W. J., *Clock and Watch Escapements*, London, 1956 (reprinted 1977)

GAZELEY, W. J., *Watch and Clock Making and Repairing*, London, 1958 (reprinted 1976)

GOULD, Rupert T., *The Marine Chronometer: its history and development*, London, 1923 (reprinted 1971)

HOBSON, Charles, *English Bracket Clock Repeating Work*, Sevenoaks, 1982

HASWELL, J. Eric, *Horology: the science of time measurement and the construction of clocks, watches and chronometers*, London, 1928 (reprinted 1975)

JAGGER, Cedric, *The World's Great Clocks and Watches*, London, 1977

JOY, Edward T., *The Country Life Book of Clocks*, London, 1967

KELLY, Alison, 'A Clockmaker's Taste for Ceramics', *Country Life*, 15 June 1967

LLOYD, H. Alan, *The English Domestic Clock – its Evolution and History*, London, 1938

LLOYD, H. Alan, *The Collector's Dictionary of Clocks*, London, 1964

LOOMES, Brian, *Watchmakers and Clockmakers of the World*, vol. 2, London, 1976 (*see* Baillie)

NICHOLLS, Andrew, *Clocks in Colour*, Dorset, 1975

RAWLINGS, A. L., *The Science of Clocks and Watches*, Wakefield, reprint of 2nd edn 1974

ROBERTSON, J. Drummond, *The Evolution of Clockwork*, with a special section on the clocks of Japan and a comprehensive bibliography of horology,

London, 1931 (reprinted Wakefield, 1972)

ROYER-COLLARD, F. B., *Skeleton Clocks*, London, 1969

SELLINK, J. L., *Dutch Antique Domestic Clocks*, Leiden, 1973

SHENTON, A., and SHENTON, R. *The Price Guide to Clocks, 1840–1940*, Woodbridge, 1977

SMITH, Alan, *Clocks and Watches*, London, 1975

SMITH, Alan (ed.) *The International Dictionary of Clocks*, London, 1979

SMITH, Eric P., *Repairing Antique Clocks: a guide for amateurs*, Newton Abbot, 1975

SMITH, Eric P., *Clocks: their working and maintenance*, Newton Abbot, 1977

TAIT, Hugh, *Clocks and Watches in the British Museum*, London, 1983

TARDY, H. Lengelle, *Dictionnaire des horlogers Français*, Paris, 1972

TARDY, H. Lengelle, *La Pendule Française*, 3 vols, Paris, 1948–50 (various reprintings), 1 'De l'horloge Gothique à la Pendule Louis XV'; 2 'Du Louis XVI à nos jours'; 3 'Provinces et Étrangers'

ULLYETT, Kenneth, *In Quest of Clocks*, London, 1950

WARD, F. A. B., *A Catalogue of European Scientific Instruments in the Department of Medieval and Later Antiquities of the British Museum*, London, 1981

WRIGHT, Lawrence, *Clockwork Man*, London, 1968

Journals

(other than those issued by societies)

Clocks
Dept. A, Wolsey House,
Wolsey Road,
Hemel Hempstead,
Herts.

TEL: 0442 41221

Polso
S. Fruttuoso 10,
20052 Mouza,
Italy

TEL: (039) 731 952

Uhren
Callwey Verlag,
Munich,
Germany

Periodicals

Antiques Bulletin
HP Publishing,
2 Hampton Court Road,
Harborne,
Birmingham

Antiques Trade Gazette
17 Whitcomb Street,
London WC2

Apollo
3 St James Place,
London SW1

TEL: 071-629 3061

Horological Book Specialists

CLOCK BOOKS
Argus House,
Boundary Way,
Hemel Hempstead

HADFIELD, G.K.
Blackbrooke Hill House,
Tickow Lane,
Shepshed,
Loughborough,
Leics.

TEL: 0509 503014

ROGERS TURNER BOOKS LTD
22 Nelson Road,
London SE10

TEL: 081-853 5271

and

24 Rue du Buisson Richard,
78600 Le Mesnil-le-Roi,
France

TEL: (1) 39121191

SHENTON, Rita
148 Percy Road,
Twickenham,
Middx.

TEL: 081-894 6888

SKAFTE, K.E.
D.K. 4800 Nykobing Falster 1,
Denmark

Photographic Acknowledgements

The author and publishers would like to thank the following for permission to reproduce photographs:

Bonham and Sons Ltd 52, 85, 97 (both); British Museum 10, 11, 12, 34, 35 (both), 40, 41, 48, 51, 58, 59, 60, 64, 65, 66, 71, 75, 109, 110, 117, 126, 127, 128, 141, 142, 143, 147, 156, 158, 161, 162, 165, 218; Christie Manson and Woods Ltd 17, 36, 99, 120, 121, 132; Ronald Lee 13, 18, 38, 72, 148; Newcombe and Son 138; Derek Roberts 20, 21, 42, 82, 83, 90; Science Museum 118; Sotheby Parke Bernet and Co. 14, 24, 30, 31, 32, 44 (both), 45, 47, 54, 76, 89, 92, 95, 100, 101, 102, 112, 113, 136, 144, 150, 151, 153, 154, 157; Surrey Herald Newspapers 125.

The author retains the copyright in photographs on pages 26, 103, 104 and 106.

Index

References in italic type are to illustrations.

Act of Parliament clock 78
alarm clock 30, 51, 54, 78, 117, 118
Allen and Hayes (Calcutta) 53
Amant, Louis 109, 185
Andevalt, Pasquale 96
annual calendar ring 52, 53
Antiquarian Horological Society 119
Arabic numerals 14, 90, 91
arch top 20, 58, 76
astronomical clock 46, 79, 129
Atmos clock 80, 98

Bagshaw, D. (1861–75) 102
Baker, Henry 76
balance and spring 75; without spring 24
ball-driven clock 81
barometer 141
barometric compensation 176
barrel and mainspring 176, 177
Barwise 13
beat regulation 20
beat scale 60
Beauvais, Paul 54
bells (tuning) 177
Benson, James William (1849–1973) 100
Berthoud, Ferdinand (1729–1807) 109
Biggs (Maidenhead) 148
binnacle clock 81
birdcage clock 81
blind frets 36, 85, 121
Boy (London) 32
bracket clock 31, 81, 95, 138
bracket feet 31, 35
break-arch hood 90
Breguet, Abraham Louis (1747–1823) 25, 122, 146
Breguet & Neveau & Companie 113
Bridges, Henry 129

British Horological Institute 119
British Museum 119
Horological Students Room 165, 197
Brocot, Achille 178
Brocot regulator or suspension 53, 179
Burgi, Jost 94
bushing 145
butterfly regulator 179

calendar 179
calendar aperture 31, 179
calendar work 179; perpetual 180
candle clock 81
carillon 85
carriage clock 13, 81, 92, 99, 142, 152, 154
cartel clock 81
cases
    burr walnut 44; corniche 99; damascened 117; drum 89; ebonised 94; ebony veneered 11; gorgé 99; lacquered 74, 132; mahogany 156; marquetry 64, 120; slate and marble 166
case repairs 165; repairers and manufacturers 211
case terms 167–73
centre seconds 40, 58, 82, 110
Ceulen, van (Amsterdam) 46
chapter ring 68
chiming 188, 189, 190
chiming clock 32, 84, 91, 95, 144
chinoiserie 36, 133
chops, plastic 55
chronometer escapement 99, 181; for pendulum 34
cleaning 139
Cole, A. F. 122
column clock 84
compensation 'sandwich' 58–60

comté clock see comtoise clock
comtoise clock 84
Condliff, James (1818–36) 101
conical pendulum clock 84
constant force 35, 104, 147, 181–2
controller 77
courses 213
Cox, James 96
Craighead and Webb, London (1847–61) 145
crown wheel 16
crucifix clock 85
cuckoo clock 85
cuckoo quail clock 86
cycloidal checks 30

dealers 201
decimal clock 86
Dent, Frederick (1853–60) 99
Dent, M. F. (1856–75) 143
depth tool 163
dials 68
    annual 41; arch top 85; break arch 36, 95; double 52; drop 97; glass 100, 101; moon 48; restoration of 211; skeleton 186; 24-hour 118
digital clock 87
Doulton 151

East, Edward 64, 121
Elkington and Co. (Birmingham) 141
Elton, Christopher 104
English dial clock 97
equation clock 40, 87
equation of time 40, 52
    table 158
epicyclic gearing 102
escapements 73
    anchor 85, 174–6, 174, 175; Brocot 53, 178; chronometer 99, 181; clock 146; constant

218